CENTRAL EUROPE

CENTRAL EUROPE

A translation by Christabel M. Meredith
from the original German of

MITTEL-EUROPA
By
Friedrich Naumann
Member of the Reichstag

GREENWOOD PRESS, PUBLISHERS
WESTPORT, CONNECTICUT

Originally published in 1917
by Alfred A. Knopf, New York

Reprinted from an original copy in the collections
of the University of Illinois Library

First Greenwood Reprinting 1971

Library of Congress Catalogue Card Number 75-109805

SBN 8371-4296-2

Printed in the United States of America

CONTENTS

	PAGE

I. PARTNERSHIP IN THE WAR AND ITS RESULTS   9

We must know in the midst of the war with what mutual relations Germany and Austria-Hungary intend to emerge from it : Each of the two Empires is too small by itself : The formation of new military boundaries between unallied States : The lack of programme at the outbreak of war : The test of Mid-Europe by history. Necessary reflections : Considerations of foreign-speaking partners in the union : The differences between the two allied Empires : Dissimilarities in the history of the countries, in their stages of capitalist development and in their rhythm of life : Currents in the German Empire setting against the Central European alliance : Opposing currents in Austria and Hungary : The political independence of the two Empires can only be maintained by the union : Whether or no Austria-Hungary must separate into its component parts? : Optimism : Criticism of the existing conditions of alliance : Whether or no a programme can be drawn up for Mid-Europe? : A single nation of brothers!

II. OF THE PREVIOUS HISTORY OF CENTRAL EUROPE   42

A new historical consciousness is needed for the formation of a union of Central European States : The extinction of the disputes between Austria-Hungary and Prussia : The political task of historians : The historians of Bismarck's founding of the Empire : The Central Europe of the old German Emperors : The period of the two disputing Ostmarks and of the pressure from the West on the German Empire : The Napoleonic period — between East and West : The Vienna Congress and St. Paul's Church at Frankfurt —"Lesser Germany" and "Greater Germany" tendencies : Bismarck's fight against Austria : Bismarck as a Mid-European in 1866 : The deliverance of Central Europe from France : The liberation from Russia : Bismarck and Andrassy — the Dual Alliance : Bismarck's legacy.

III. CREEDS AND NATIONALITIES   69

Temper on the journey towards Mid-Europe : The Mid-European type has still to be formed : Ancient struggles between West Rome and East Rome in Central Europe : Reformation and counter-Reformation : Prussia as leading Protestant Power and Austria as Catholic State : Protestant apprehensions : Austro-Hungarian Catholicism is not a political unity : Church and school questions must never be the business of the union : The

v

Central European Jews: Nationality questions in all Great States: The treatment of national minorities in the German Empire up to the present: Prussian Polish policy: The German spirit in the old Austrian State: Metternich: The democracy of 1848: The awakening of the masses to a share in politics: The vanished energy of the earlier Germanising influence: The peculiar character of the Magyars: The Hungarian Nationality Law and its enforcement: Roumanians and Southern Slavs: Austrian nationality disputes: The Polish question: The greatest danger for the Dual Monarchy is past.

IV. THE ECONOMIC LIFE OF CENTRAL EUROPE — 115

Historical evolution of the character of work: Capitalism of the first and second stages: Why do other nations not like us? The organised German type: English and German methods of work: Militarism in work during war and peace: The German economic creed must become characteristic of Mid-Europe: Individual economic output in Austria-Hungary: The backward sections of the people: The difference in the productivity of labour: The common rhythm of work to be striven after in Mid-Europe: Popular reasons for opposition to the systematisation of work: What the Hungarians might make of their land!: The worker as economic force: Apprehensions concerning an economic union owing to differences in the possibilities of production: Objections to be expected: The entrance into Mid-European partnership in work as a heartfelt resolution: The artistic task for Vienna and Austria: The example of the South German union with North Germany. The gradual fusion of the bonds of union.

V. JOINT PROBLEMS IN WAR ECONOMICS — 148

Share in the world's economic system: Exclusion from international trade through the English war policy — self-contained commercial state: Our stores have saved us: The State Socialism of war economics: War finances: The further development of Socialism owing to the war: State syndicates with workers' guarantee: State storage system: The approaching transition to peace economics after the war system: The organised economic State: Is Austria-Hungary one economic State or two?: No joint war economic system exists: A military partnership combined with economic separation?: Association in syndicates in virtue of the war-storage system: The Austro-Hungarian exchange: The financial problems after the war: The Germans of the Empire must only wish to help if they are called upon.

VI. OUR POSITION IN THE WORLD'S ECONOMIC SYSTEM — 179

The development of Great States and world-group economic areas: Russian, English and North American types of supernational government: The previous history of the international idea: World-group provinces as preliminary stages of internationalism?: Possibilities of joining with Russia to England: Small and solitary?:

CONTENTS

Our ability to understand her other Central European nations : The neighbouring States and their colonies : The area of the economic world-groups : The population of the economic world-groups : Are the world-group areas statistically comparable? : Greater Britain : The United States : Russia : Mid-European possibilities : The value of the world's economic system for the smaller folk.

VII. TARIFF PROBLEMS   216

A customs partnership without a further economic partnership is not practicable : The dangers of a mere reduction of tariff for Hungary, Austria, Germany : Why the customs partnership is more discussed than the other forms of economic partnership : Friedrich List and the Minister Bruck as the forerunners of the customs partnership : The Prusso-German Customs Union : Personal confessions about the tariff question : Formation of a uniform tariff : Imports and exports between Germany and Austria-Hungary : Partnership in demand, supplementary partnership, competition : Tariff rates : The opposition of interests in the Balkan States : Joint regulation of foreign markets : Customs union, preferential treatment, intermediate duties on the basis of a joint tariff classification : Storage treaties, syndicates' treaties, and commercial treaty : Financial results of the customs approximation.

VIII. CONSTITUTIONAL PROBLEMS   248

Who will undertake the foundation of Mid-Europe? : Demarcation of the political activities not touched by Mid-European centralisation : Mid-Europe can be no Federal State : Questions relating to religious creeds and to languages are and remain the business of the individual States : State treaties as the foundation of the union : Mid-European central administration for defined special activities : Law as regards the conclusion of treaties in the German Empire and in Austria-Hungary : The Austro-Hungarian Ausgleich as a permanent situation : The separation of the military and economic State from the nationality States : The danger to the parliamentary system through the foundation of Mid-Europe? : How the central administration may appear in ten years' time? : Military conventions : Joint foreign policy : Conclusion.

IX. STATISTICAL AND HISTORICAL   284

X. BIBLIOGRAPHY   324

INDEX   343

CENTRAL EUROPE

CHAPTER I

PARTNERSHIP IN THE WAR AND ITS RESULTS

AS I write this fighting is going on in the East and in the West. I write of set purpose in the midst of it all, for it is only in war time that our mood enables us to entertain broadly transforming thoughts of reconstruction. Once the war is over our everyday spirit will quickly take possession of us, and in the everyday spirit Mid-Europe can never be fashioned. Bismarck founded the German Empire during and not after the war of 1870, and our statesmen must lay the foundations of this new structure during this war, in the midst of bloodshed and the upheaval of the nations. Later it might, and it would, be too late.

The subject I wish to discuss is the growing unity of those nations which belong neither to the Anglo-French western alliance nor to the Russian Empire. But more particularly my subject is the welding together of the German Empire and the Austro-Hungarian Dual Monarchy, for all further schemes for a union of the Central European nations depend on whether or no, in the first instance, the binding together of the two Central Powers themselves is successful.

When war broke out many of us, myself included, thought that an understanding with France might still come about, since there is no enmity towards France either on the German or the Austrian and Hungarian side. Whenever the French are willing we shall be able to offer them the hand of friendship, but of course each additional month of war makes any mutual approach more difficult. France has chosen to link her fate with that of England and from henceforth will be made use of by England. She will no longer be willing to conclude an independent peace for herself, and will, unfortunately, for the immediate future, become a larger and more important Portugal at England's side. Hence, in what follows, we leave the French outside the discussion, whilst always hoping that in a more distant future they will rank themselves with Central Europe.

Nor can we speak of Italy except with reserve and caution. Italy, disregarding her old union by treaty, has, it is true, gone over into the camp of the enemy, yet she can hardly by this act have determined her political and economic alliances for all time. National humours and economic interests are indeed frequently inharmonious in Italy. Economically she belongs to Central Europe, but we recognise that her Latin nationality and the Adriatic-Alpine boundary problem have turned Italian thought into another direction. Now the armies on the Isonzo have the first word, and hence we shall discuss Mid-Europe without reference to Italy.

Of the Northern Powers, the Roumanians, Bulgarians, Serbians and Greeks, and also of Holland and Switzerland, we shall have something to say later on in our book. We shall not say very much however, for it would be a mistake to include these smaller Central European States in our scheme from the outset as fixed quantities, whilst actually they still have a breathing space before making their decision. They wish to see and they ought to see for themselves first whether the nucleus of Mid-Europe will form itself, whether the German Empire and Austria-Hungary will crystallise.

During the war we Germans, the Austrians and the Hungarians stand in friendly alliance with the Turks. In this alliance the Turks are fighting in their own interests. They are engaged in a brave fight for life for the remnant of a once powerful State, and for the political existence of the faith and being of Islam. A strange turn of history has brought us and the Turks together in that their enemies were our enemies. Their only hope of holding their own was an alliance with us, and hence also with the Austrians and Hungarians. We hail them, and hope that in the future too our paths may lie together, but Turkey is not in the first instance concerned in the formation of the Mid-European nucleus. It is not in direct contact with us geographically, and is a country of a very different type both nationally and economically; it is southern, oriental, antiquated and sparsely populated. In this case too the nucleus of crystallisation must first be in existence before the conditions of accession to the union can profitably be discussed.

Thus our attention must first be directed towards that portion of Central Europe which extends from the North and Baltic Seas to the Alps, the Adriatic Sea and the southern edge of the Danubian plain. Take a map and see what lies between the Vistula and the Vosges Mountains, and what extends from Galicia to Lake Constance! You must think of these stretches of country as a unity, as a brotherhood of many members, as a defensive alliance, as a single economic district! All the traditional separatism of these lands must be so effaced in the stress of the Great War as to make the idea of union tolerable. This is the demand of the hour, the task of these months. History speaks to us of it in the thunder of the guns, but it rests with us whether or no we listen.

. . . . . .

It may be questioned whether our partnership in this war is due to chance or to necessity. We maintain the latter. In old days indeed it was chance when, or if ever, Austria and Prussia combined. They united when they had some common task to complete such as the division of Poland or the conquest of Napoleon, but they fell apart again as soon as they had settled their own frontiers, or were attracted in diverse directions by other Powers. In the long years of the past there was much more fighting than harmony in Central Europe. Each section went its own way, and there were as yet no constraining reasons for a lasting unity. The States were merely territorial divisions, disputing sovereignties, and in no sense historically determinate political groups. They grew and fell apart like clouds. Even the partnership in the old German Empire involved no solidarity, for hardly ever, if at all, during the later centuries did this ancient Empire emerge as a complete political entity. It was broken in the Thirty Years' War, it crumbled in pieces in the Seven Years' War, it split in Napoleonic times and it was divided in the Civil War of 1866. We shall discuss the earlier history more in detail later on. For the present this statement is sufficient: there is more unity to-day than ever before in the old German Empire! To-day all the ancient States, large and small, in the stretch of country described above, have become a single united fighting entity, and victory and defeat are a like experience for all, from Heligoland to Orsova. This is no mere political intrigue, no patched-up defensive alliance. The war has come as a creator of the Mid-European soul, which is now coming into existence in advance of the external forms appropriate to it. It is this soul that we shall discuss, and its external embodiment that we shall examine.

All the allies in the Great War feel without argument that neither now nor in the future can small or even moderate-sized Powers play any large part in the world. Our conceptions of size have entirely changed. Only very big States have any significance on their own account, all the smaller ones must live by utilising the quarrels of the great, or must obtain leave if they wish to do anything unusual. Sovereignty, that is freedom to make decisions of wide historical importance, is now concentrated at a very few places on the globe. The day is still distant when there shall be "one fold and one shepherd," but the days are past when shepherds without number, lesser or greater, drove their flocks unrestrained over the pastures of Europe. The spirit of large-scale industry and of super-national organisation has seized politics. People think, as Cecil Rhodes once expressed it, "in Continents." The country which desires to be small and isolated will, in spite of this, become of its own accord dependent on the varying fortunes of the Great Powers. This is in conformity with an age of intercommunication and with centralised military technique. The country without alliances is isolated, and the isolated country is endangered. In this age of extending State federations and Great Powers, Prussia is too small, and Germany too small, and Austria too small, and Hungary too small. No single States of this kind can survive a world war. Suppose that we of the German Empire were fighting alone, or that Austria-Hungary had to offer a solitary defence. Such things are no longer possible. Their day is past. Hence to-day the Central European union is no chance but a necessity. People who do not feel enthusiastic about it must yet desire it, since the alternatives are even worse. The intelligent man is he who does of his own free will what he recognises as necessary.

. . . . . .

Nevertheless it will be very difficult to found Mid-Europe, and no one act or decision can be at all adequate to the task. It will occupy at least a generation. But for the moment it is for the Governments and the peoples to determine and say whether or no they desire Mid-Europe at all or not. For the representatives of the German Empire, equally with those of Austria and Hungary, will enter upon the coming peace negotiations in an entirely different spirit according to whether or no they mean to remain united in the future.

We have no intention of saying anything about the actual terms of peace, partly because at present publicity is still forbidden, partly because we ourselves think it a useless and doubtful policy to discuss something which is as yet subject to military successes or failures. But whether or no the frontiers of the two Central Empires of Mid-Europe be shifted somewhat more to the east or west as the result of military victories, this question will arise: Will the ambassadors from Berlin, Vienna and Budapest enter the hall of the International Peace Congress as declared and honest friends, or as secret opponents? We want them to return to their countrymen with the watchword: United for ever! Then they will indeed bring back something real for every one, a new creative work, a great hope, the beginning of a fresh epoch. Thus only shall we Central European nations appear finally justified for having shed our blood for one another. What was Serajewo to us Germans of the Empire? What were we seeking in the Carpathian passes? Why did the Hungarians or the Southern Slavs trouble themselves about Zeebrügge? Why should German Bohemians or Tzechs have defended the ridge of the Vosges? The entire history of the war with all its sufferings and heroic deeds becomes purposeless, meaningless, if the war ends with a misunderstanding between those who, throughout it, have been allied. But this misunderstanding is not so far off as many think, for even now the spirit of a unified Mid-Europe is no mere matter of course, and the approaching peace negotiations will supply to the full opportunities both small and great for friction and trouble. All coalition wars have, from of old, had difficult peace negotiations, for they end in gains and losses which must be equalised amongst the allies. But each allied Power can, and will, allow and make over advantages to its allies with a better grace, if it knows that they are certainly going to remain its allies. Both Powers will obtain much more from the Peace Congress if they negotiate throughout in common and do not enter into special settlements. These considerations ought to suffice, and will indeed be amply sufficient for those who remember the depressing history of the Vienna Congress in 1815. Then exactly that happened which now we must avoid. Temptations to break faith will creep in on both sides, since the future is assured to our opponents if they can succeed in dividing us. This weighs with them more than any other gain from the war. But for what then have we sacrificed our sons, and for what are we Germans, Austrians and Hungarians mutilated.

. . . . . .

It is occasionally said that the war will lead to a general slackening of the bonds between the Great Powers, and that every country must wish to emerge free and without obligations from this great tragedy of political alliances. There may be some truth in this in so far as the constraint of the State syndicates has been generally felt as such, but all the same, the outcome will be much what it is in the case of industrial syndicates: new ones are continually growing up when once the idea of combination has taken root. It is contrary to history to believe that in these days five or eight Great Powers will leave the precincts of the Peace Congress without having some fresh treaties in their pockets. What is called "freedom" is nothing but the already conceived desire to change one's alliance in the future.

It is not to be supposed that at the conclusion of the war the long jubilee years of an everlasting peace will begin! It is true, doubtless, that there will be a widespread inclination towards peace, for war sacrifices and war taxes speak an insistent language. Moreover, we shall be more careful than hitherto to suppress frivolous pretexts for war and to strive for understanding between nations. But, on the other hand, the war will leave behind it an immense number of unsolved problems, both new and old, and will lead to disillusionments which will express themselves in extensive armaments. All the War Ministers, General Staffs and Admiralties will ponder over the lessons of the past war, technical skill will contrive yet newer weapons, frontier fortifications will be made still wider and, above all, longer. Is it really credible that in such an atmosphere the isolated State can remain any longer in isolation?

As far as Germany and Austria-Hungary are concerned, they must either intrench their respective frontiers on the ridges of the Erzgebirge, the Riesengebirge and the Böhmerwald, or they must regard this line as, in essentials, only an inner administrative boundary in a territory looked upon by foreigners as one. This reasoning is as valid for Vienna as for Berlin. After the experiences of the present war no isolated country can remain unintrenched. For the primary and most important military inference from the war is that in future we shall fight only in long lines, and that the trench will become the essential form of defence for a country. The policy of trenches means that every country must consider what frontiers can and what cannot be defended by trenches. The argument is somewhat as follows: if France before 1914 had not applied its expenditure on defences to the erection of heavy fortresses, but instead had protected its whole frontier from Belfort to Dunkirk with trenches, probably the

German thrust into Northern France across Belgium would not have been possible. The same thing applies to our frontiers in East Prussia and to those in Austrian Galicia. After the war, frontier trenches will be made everywhere where there is any possibility of fighting. There will be a fresh system of Roman and Chinese walls made out of earth and barbed wire.

In consequence of this trench-making policy a country will be constrained to make certain, at the moment of planning out these military defences, with whom it proposes under all circumstances to live at peace. Europe will have two long ditches from north to south, one anyhow stretching from the Lower Rhine to the Alps, the other from Courland to either the right or left of Roumania. This will constitute the main and unavoidable triple division of the Continent. The problem for Central Europe to decide is whether or no another intermediate ditch, dividing Germany and Austria-Hungary, will be needed in between the two great north to south ditches. It will be needed if no unity or future policy can be guaranteed, but if it does become necessary it will be harmful and fateful in the highest degree to both parties.

The future trench-making policy will make it exceptionally difficult for small States to maintain their independence, for under this system military expenses will decrease as the size of the country to be defended increases in relation to its frontiers. A State like Roumania could hardly afford to maintain its own trench system on all sides. This means that it must choose from the outset which frontiers it will leave open. Higgling over neutrality will be rendered much more difficult by this coming trench policy. Possibly trench-making will be the most effective instrument of Providence in making war into a delusion by means of its own technique. But in the first instance the long trenches must be made and paid for and manned. And when this is done Mid-Europe will either be established, or she will be debarred from unity in any future that can be foreseen.

It is on these grounds that a decision must be based.

. . . .

During the war the responsible leaders of the combatant States

PARTNERSHIP IN THE WAR 17

are so pressed by their daily duties that in the midst of strenuous work they can hardly find time for historical reflections. They are not in the fortunate position of Bismarck in the winter of 1870–71, who knew from the outset approximately what he wanted, for this unprecedentedly serious war appeared, in the summer of 1914, undesired and diplomatically unprepared for. We purposely avoid entering into complicated discussions over the causes of the war, the time for this will come later, when all the documents have come to light. This much may, however, be stated with certainty: the two Central European Powers had no defined military aim because they were only prepared for defence. The war was not undertaken in order to secure this or that object. Hence it lacks any intrinsic unity of purpose, and the royal and ministerial proclamations calling the nations to arms lack a definite programme. There is no single watchword for all the combatants from Apenrade to Fiume. The war began purely as a war of defence, and hence from the point of view of Mid-Europe its ideals are essentially somewhat vague. This, in our opinion, is felt even more strongly in Austria and Hungary than in the German Empire. In the German Empire two ideas were always present in the minds of Government and people: that some time or other a break would occur with the Tsar, and that some time there must be a fight with England over the control of the sea. The only regret was that both things came about together with an overwhelming rush; the war with France, the war in the East and the naval war. Austria and Hungary, however, had no interest in either the French war or the Anglo-German naval war, but instead they had serious tension in the Balkans, among the Southern Slavs and in Italy. Thus at the outset they were evidently more concerned about their southern frontiers than about the risks in Galicia. It was only during the war itself that the nations in the Danube kingdom became fully conscious of and impressed by the Russian danger. The military objective shifted from Belgrade to Przemysl and the Carpathians, and then swung back again to Trieste and extended into Polish territory. A situation arose in which the two parties had a joint campaign in the east, whilst, in addition, the German Empire had its special international campaigns and the Austrians and Hungarians their special southern campaign. Obviously we were mutually helping one another in this way, but nevertheless the war was regarded, and is still regarded, rather differently in Vienna and Budapest than in Berlin. There was no controlling idea of joint statesmanship and like responsibility in all directions. This controlling idea, however, appeared during the war in peoples and Governments, in spite of many individual differences of opinion. Then for the first time the belief took root in the hearts of those concerned that this war is not merely a German war, and not merely a Danube war, but is the historical test of Mid-Europe. But this inspiring thought has not yet risen to general consciousness. It is yet far from certain that all utterances about the war are tuned to this note. It is our task to strengthen this consciousness, until even leading men in their official statements speak of the rapidly growing unity of Mid-Europe as a self-evident fact. The Germans of the Empire in their utterances concerning the war have not always kept in mind the effect that an insistence upon purely German aims must have on their Magyar and Slav allies. To talk, for instance, of a decisive struggle between German and Slav is a misconception, very natural indeed, but a serious departure from ideas proper to the alliance. Phrases of this sort necessarily sound very differently in the ears of Tzechs, or Poles or Slovenians than in ours. If we expect a hundred thousand Poles and other Slavs to join with us in driving out the Russian armies, we must never let these allies of ours slip out of our memories. This involves a certain sacrifice for us Germans of our accustomed national mode of thought, but we are faced ultimately by a definite alternative. Either this is a German war, in which case we have no right to complain if it is so regarded in Prague and Agram, or it is a Central European war, in which case we ought to, and must, speak of it as such and act accordingly.

The same thing applies to the preaching of " the German idea in the world." My friend Rohrbach has done us all a great

PARTNERSHIP IN THE WAR

service by becoming the prophet of this idea in his admirable and widely read book, and no patriotically minded Hungarian or Tzech will think evil of us patriotic Germans if we sing and dream and study and work for *Deutschland, Deutschland über alles.* We need this. It is our life's blood. Only, in doing so, we must not fail to remember that our non-German partners too have a life's blood, and want to realise for what they are prepared to die. In exalting our nationality we ought at the same time to exalt theirs.

Come what may we must not be petty. It is obvious that in a Germany at war all our old heroic traditions must be revived, and we must see around us the Prussian King Friedrich II., and Blücher, Moltke and Bismarck. We fight as Germans, but we fight with millions of non-Germans, who are prepared to go with us to battle and to death, so long as they have our respect and can believe that our victory will also be their victory.

On the Austrian and Hungarian side too a like mode of thought must be acquired more definitely than hitherto. The feelings of dislike and irritability often aroused now by any strong expression of German national feeling must vanish and be overcome in a common appreciation of the many-sided strength of our great and noble union. There are still in the Empire of the Danube some easily explicable remnants of the old temper of 1866, which are but ill-suited to the new Mid-Europe; anti-Prussian feelings which, when they are expressed, are just as unpalatable to the Northerners as the North German particularism, referred to above, is to the differently constituted South. Occasionally something appears which seems like envy, a grudging of the strength which yet is indispensable for us all as a body. To speak quite frankly: it sometimes happens that people accept help, and at the same time scold those who help them. The finer spirits in the Danubian Empire have always been sensible that this was unsuitable, but there, as here, there are people who have not such fine feelings. To such people on both sides the conception of comradeship in the joint war must be more openly preached than hitherto, and the leading men in both States must speak to their countrymen more frankly and decisively of the accomplished fact; that the past is forgotten, that we cancel all our earlier debits and credits, and from henceforward press onwards hand in hand like good and honest friends. The war unites.

. . . . . .

In the later sections of this book we shall have to discuss more in detail the difficulties in the way of the union, and even here we must briefly point out how different the two Empires are, so that we may face the whole complicated problem from the outset.

Austria-Hungary is a unit of long standing with strong disintegrating tendencies; the German Empire is a newly formed unit with ever-increasing centralisation. Over there exists a growing spirit of particularism or of provincialism, a constant effort to snatch something from the hands of the central authority and to make Maria Theresa's monarchy a mere legend. With us, on the contrary, the creative energy lies more in the Imperial than in the State Governments. To use an old phrase, Germany develops daily from a confederation of States into a federal State, whilst Austria and Hungary are growing out of a single State into a confederation of States, or rather, into a union of two States, one of which is almost a confederation of States, whilst the other is an attempt at a national State, but of a most difficult composition. With us political talents and aspirations are Imperialist, over there they are frequently provincial, separatist, or nationalist, but not centralising.

The German Empire is founded on the German national ideal, and finds its justification therein. The foreign-speaking portions, and especially Prussian Poles, are indeed a difficult problem for statesmanship, but they are neither so numerous nor so powerful as to come into consideration as partners in the Government. Austria-Hungary, on the other hand, has dreaded for the last hundred years the national spirit of its peoples as a decentralising power. Hence its political thought is more colourless. In the place of a central nationalism there is what the French term *étatisme,* the mere machinery of government: monarchy, bureaucracy, army.

Austria-Hungary is older; it had long been rich in land and honours when Prussia had still to seek recognition of its royal dignity; it was one of the European Great Powers before the North had any serious word to say; it was not so broken as the North either in the Thirty Years' War or in Napoleon's time; it has followed a prudent course through the centuries, and has many more traditions to uphold. The German Empire, on the contrary, is the most recently founded of the European great States, an intruder in the royal company, less inherited than fought for, a child of the nineteenth century. It is like mixing the eighteenth and nineteenth centuries to think of working up Austria and Prussia into a single historical entity.

The German Empire is more northerly, colder, more uniform, more technical. Austria-Hungary is more southerly, more brightly coloured, more a natural growth, more romantic. The difference noticeable within the German Empire between North and South Germany is in a yet higher degree the difference between Germany and Austria-Hungary.

The German Empire is more western, Austria more eastern. The same differences which we know as marking the districts east and west of the Elbe occur in more defined form in Central Europe, so soon as the country between the Theiss and the Carpathians joins the countries, distant to them, on the Mosel and Lower Rhine.

The greater part of Germany is Protestant, most of Austria-Hungary is Catholic.

Germany is much more capitalist, and consequently much more socialist, than Austria-Hungary. For us Germans of the Empire a union means a reopening of the already half-settled disputes of the preceding generation; for Austria-Hungary it means a rapid transition to conditions and problems which are there only slowly and gently approaching.

The rhythm of life is different. We work more methodically. We think more in terms of money, are more punctual, more businesslike, hence also poorer in homely comfort and the art of simple living. This is carried so far that each country secretly regards the other with something of pity and forbearance, because each lacks just what the other regards as essential to civilisation.

Austria-Hungary possesses more past because it is the older organisation, and more future because it has more undeveloped land and labour power. It has less present, because it has held itself back with long hesitation from the technical skill advancing from the West, and is not so rich in sea-coast, coal, iron, and organising energy.

Germany is a country of large towns, and daily grows more so; Austria, and still more Hungary, will for a long time yet be a country of forest, arable land, and pasture. With us the factory takes precedence of the estate and the workman's quarter of the country village; there the relation is reversed, as it was with us a good forty years ago.

Berlin and Vienna, two different temperatures, more different even than Vienna and Budapest!

．　　．　　．　　．　　．　　．

The amount of sentimental resistance and the number of opposing practical interests are considerable, hence it is not surprising that the question of Mid-Europe is approached with much criticism from both sides. Here, truly, is no case of love at first sight. Rather is there evasion and refusal, a shrinking with instinctive fear from new and boundless complications. Known evils are better than unknown. Hence it is necessary to go more closely into the reasons for the foundation of Mid-Europe, and to refute opponents by showing that there is no other possibility for either Empire. We shall begin this inquiry from the standpoint of the German Empire, and undertake to discuss without reserve all unfavourable arguments, since only thus can they be met.

Bismarck's policy in its first stage separated the Prusso-German Empire from Austria-Hungary; in its second stage it established between the two Empires the treaty connection which still holds. Taking Bismarck's standpoint, then, a development and intensification of the treaty connection may be equally well desired or rejected according to whether we side more with the younger or with the elder Bismarck. The younger Bismarck, up to 1866, agreed with the " Lesser Germany "[1] party and successfully maintained the " Lesser Germany " ideal policy in opposition to Austria. This was the starting-point of all his subsequent immense successes, successes which were beneficial both to us and to Europe. Is it surprising, then, that there are still many of the " Lesser Germany " party amongst us, and especially in Prussia?

So far as I can see, there are two principal forms of " Lesser German " opinion: an Old-Prussian and a Liberal capitalist. The conservative, despotic Old-Prussian at the bottom of his heart regards even the German Empire as a watering down of his Friedrich's State, and secretly distrusts the South Germans, whilst liking and esteeming them in other respects, as not quite capable of creating a State. He wants clearly defined terms of authority, and this for their own sake, although he sees quite well what material and military advantages the extension of the Imperial German markets and authority has brought. He might, and indeed does, also recognise advantages, of which we shall speak later, in a closer union with Austria-Hungary. But primarily his traditions and political class lead him to feel any kind of joint government with Austria and Hungary as an infringement of his personal importance, and this in spite of the doubled area of territory to be jointly governed. The Prussian noble and his adherents are strongest in the Prussian Landtag, less strong in the Reichstag, and would probably have even less influence in any future Mid-European representative assembly, should such an assembly arise out of the present beginnings. Since he has witnessed the development of the German Empire he has grown prudent and inclined to take to heart the phrase, *principiis obsta!* To call these principles of his merely selfish is inapt, since for him political ideals and his personal interests are so intermingled that it is unjust on historical grounds to deny his ideal aims. Devotion to his country makes him instinctively suspicious of all extensions that change the character of the State.

[1] *Kleindeutsch, Grossdeutsch,* terms applied in German politics, 1848–66, to those who wished (*a*) to leave out, (*b*) to include, Austria in the reconstruction of the Empire.— TRANSLATOR'S NOTE.

His political opponent, the Liberal capitalist, is of quite a different character. For him everything centres round the undisturbed development of industry and commerce, because he regards these as the means to national prosperity and a financially powerful State. The economic union with Austria-Hungary appears to him as a drag on progress, a leaden weight on the foot. Partnership with Austria-Hungary will probably mean that the German Empire must live through again the last thirty years of its domestic policy, and there is no security that the second experience will be as fortunate as the first. It might be that we should remain involved in an agrarian economic policy against which hitherto we have fought with good reason. Economic union with Austria-Hungary signifies prolongation of the policy of protection, strengthening of middle-class efforts, difficulties in the way of joining in English international commerce, and a drag on modern enterprise. The Liberal capitalist, of course, knows well that the Mid-European union will, on the other hand, bring advantages to him also, since it will widen the market protected by tariff and will increase considerably the possible openings for his capital. As a Liberal he fears that an undemocratic spirit may be introduced by Austria, and more especially by Hungary, for Austria-Hungary has, it is true, many Parliaments, but all the same there is little effective Parliamentary spirit in Austria, and in Hungary, with a rigorously worked out Parliamentary system, there is little of universal democracy.

With these two " Lesser Germany " types is associated a third, " Greater Germany," [1] party, which for national reasons seeks the closest sympathy and union with the Germans in Austria and Hungary, but wishes to admit no foreign-speaking section into the German State, since it already finds our Poles, Danes and French a heavy burden. Certain members of this group, for reasons based on the principle of German nationality, are indeed counting even today on the approaching break-up of the Danubian Monarchy, and would gladly bring about a purely German State extending from the North Sea to Trieste, " the German port."

[1] See Translator's Note on page 23.

This, at least up to the outbreak of war, represented the opinion of many Pan-Germans, whilst others among them always accepted the Danubian State as a given existing whole, and reckoned with it as such.

Obviously in actual life very varied combinations and gradations of these three modes of thought are met with. Any one who regards Mid-Europe as something to aim at, must come to an understanding with them. So far as this understanding is economic, or concerns domestic politics, we shall defer it to later sections, but here we shall speak of what is common to all three, of the desire to maintain German power. We believe that they will all recognise at bottom that this power is in itself more important than either the maintenance intact of the Old-Prussian despotism, or the rapid development of industrial capitalism, or the setting up of the purely national State. By them and by us all it is accepted that the Fatherland is worth more than any individual interests however well founded. The question is then, whether the German Empire can face the future confidently without an alliance with Austria-Hungary, whether it is perhaps even true that we are stronger without Austria-Hungary than with it? It is this that we deny.

We have already said elsewhere that the German Empire is too small by itself to defy permanently future general attacks. This statement is an undeniable inference from this war up to the present, and needs no further support, for if we suppose that Austria-Hungary were merely neutral, then we should have to face all the Russian army corps alone; but if we picture Austria-Hungary as one of the crowd of our enemies, then the position of Germany becomes a military impossibility. Hence the German Empire, for its part, can only give up the idea of a strong and binding alliance with Austria-Hungary if another equally safe and equally natural alliance can take its place. This is, however, difficult to imagine after all that has happened in the war. An alliance with France, as we have already said, would be very advantageous both to us and to the French, but what French Government could conclude it now? An alliance with England is still theoretically conceivable, notwithstanding the mutual "songs of hate," but who would vouch for its permanence? And how much would even a friendly England help us in the face of a second Seven Years' War on the Continent? An alliance with Russia offers less security for the Empire, and is less in accordance with national sentiment than union with Austria-Hungary, and its permanence could only be attained at the expense of a joint partition of Austria-Hungary. It must not be forgotten that according to Bismarck's *Gedanken und Erinnerungen* the traditional understanding between Russia and Prussia was broken off from 1876 onwards, because Bismarck, with the approval of the whole of Germany, was prepared to offer our lives to protect the position of Austria-Hungary as a Great Power! This was the decision upon which the present war depends; this was the policy at the height of his creative work, of that master whom we ought all to endeavour to follow. The die was cast then in favour of Mid-Europe.

Think for a moment, please, whether it would be endurable if our Secretary of State for Foreign Affairs returned from the Peace Congress with the news that we were again in the same position as before 1876; that is, faced by the choice between Russia and Austria! We should all know what that must signify: the future sacrifice of the Danubian Monarchy! This is where the "Lesser Germany" ideal leads us if it is logically carried out. Of course this final result would not be openly spoken of at the outset, but in Austria and Hungary a slackening of our friendship would at once be understood in this sense, and another alliance would instantly be sought at whatever cost. The international situation is such that no half security will serve Austria-Hungary. There a firm footing is essential. Moreover, the Germany which deserts its comrade after such a stupendous war would later on be betrayed in its turn by its fresh partner! This is of all things the most certain. We shall discuss later on the economic aspects of association with Russia or England.

.   .   .   .   .   .

Strong opposition to Mid-Europe is also to be expected on the part of Austria and Hungary, and so far as I can see in the following five typical forms:

The Imperial privy councillor, well proved in the service of the Crown, has contributed largely to the maintenance of government in that country of complicated race problems without always meeting with the recognition he deserved. But he has grown up in such intimacy with the idea of the ancient Austrian dignity, and so full of dislike for Prussian forms and informalities, that he will admit Prussia as little as possible into his sphere of activity. That North German embodiment of unrest would do more harm than good in ancient Austria, where delicate handling is required; and he simply does not believe that the Prussians would ever allow him to have any say in the matter. He regards the Prussian system as a strange machine, whose efficiency is not to be denied, but whose noise and mechanical accuracy make him shudder. He himself prefers to go on with good hand-work in the old style; even if it wastes time it is at any rate more human.

The Austrian, and also the Hungarian Slavs (Tzechs, Poles, Ruthenians, Slovaks, Slovenians, Dalmatians), as well as the Hungarian Roumanians, do not as a matter of course expect very much benefit from any fraternisation with the German Empire. For the most part they keep up a continual quarrel with the Germans living in their communal and provincial districts; consequently they look on them as their domestic enemies and are accustomed to judge the whole of Germany by them. Fortunately they like the Russians even less, as a rule, than the Germans, and they are glad to remain Austrian, only they deplore that arrangement of the universe which compels them to live between two great bodies of people who are so alien to them. They will endeavour in various ways to take the opportunity of the foundation of Mid-Europe in order to secure special national advantages for themselves, since, as born particularists, they are only interested in a minor degree in its formation; their first thought is for their special nationality.

The Magyar Hungarians are in a very different position. Their authority depends on the defeat and restraint of the Russians, for it is evident that one of the first principles of a conquering Russia would be to humiliate the Magyars for the benefit of the Hungarian Slavs, and perhaps even of the Roumanians. The Magyar State can only continue to exist, in its present form, as an independent political factor, in alliance with one of the non-Slav Great Powers. This is what binds the Magyars of almost every shade of opinion so firmly to the German Empire. They are well aware that Austria alone cannot protect them from the Russians. So far then as a German-Hungarian friendship is concerned we and the Magyars agree perfectly, but when it is a question of the Mid-European constitution, which will sooner or later become necessary, it appears that the existing relations between Hungary and Austria are far too vague to admit of a new Mid-European adjustment being based without difficulty on the Austro-Hungarian *Ausgleich*. And since the Magyar is by nature and tradition a stickler for "State rights," and often more of a theorist than an opportunist, he may, even with the best intentions, prove a serious obstacle at some given later time. Since we must discuss these matters more in detail in another place, it will suffice here to direct attention to them.

The Austrian German, perhaps also the German in Hungary, and more particularly the German in Siebenburgen, is naturally eager to obtain any sort of political unity with the German Empire. But in many cases he asks for something rather different from what we Germans of the Empire could grant him. Hundreds of times the Germans of the Ostmark, left outside Bismarck's Empire, have called to us: "Come over and help us!" Equally often they have been answered: "It will not do, you owe your political allegiance to Austria or to Hungary and we must not interfere!" With us in the German Empire, thanks to Bismarck's training, State policy comes before the policy of any nationality, hence we do and have done nothing which could seem like incitement to a German Irredenta. Italians, Serbs, Roumanians, or Russians from one side of the frontier are continually calling to and tempting their race-fellows on the other. But we, respecting the connection made by the alliance, have often been obliged to let our brothers call in vain. This has produced a definite feeling of annoyance; to what purpose is my Fatherland so powerful, if it cannot stretch out a helping hand to me across the border? The Germans in Austria have, in a difficult situation, done much for the German race and for the Austrian State, for which they receive no tangible reward from either side. Even now, in the Great War, they supply comparatively the largest number of soldiers in Austria; suffer, as they tell us, the most severe losses; subscribe relatively the most to the Austrian war loans; and yet are not certain for a single day that, after the war, when the Parliamentary majority becomes effective again, they will not be excluded from a share in the government and, in spite of this, have to bear the greater part of the cost of restoring Galicia. In this state of abandonment they once more stretch out their hands to the German Empire to demand that no fresh treaty be made with Austria which does not afford them guarantees against political exclusion and oppression. From their point of view they are not unjustified, but it is by no means certain whether the German Empire is in a position to delay its new Central European treaty of alliance until the very necessary regulations for the nationalities within Austria and Hungary are completed. And if they are completed, the question will still be a domestic affair for Austria and Hungary. The German Empire might indeed discuss it in a friendly manner, but certainly must not come forward from outside like a dictator, lest the whole movement for unity, so essential for all, be endangered from the outset. I know that one section of our German brothers in Austria were in such a position before the war that they would then rather have given up Austria for lost and have preferred to be included in the German Empire. But I believe that during the war insight into the coherence and responsibility demanded by all the evidence of history has so developed among these very Germans that they will now realise in future, better than before, that it is a national necessity for Germany to continue Bismarck's policy of 1876 and 1879 of maintaining the integrity of Austria.

Moreover, in many cases the racial impulse towards the German Fatherland is oddly counteracted by the Austrian interests of the German industrials. Of course there are a great many non-German industrials, but nevertheless the Germans form such an important and outstanding group among the rest that they must be counted here as a separate type. As a rule the German producer, as a man and a German, desires the closest possible union with his great and beloved home country, but as a man of business he occasionally remarks: "God protect me from my friends!" This feeling is very different in different branches of industry. Often the competition of the German Empire constitutes the greatest danger for Austro-German industry, or is at least so regarded. We shall go into details later, here we only wish not to overlook the tendency altogether. Non-German industrials, too, may be possessed by a like anxiety.

Of the relation of the Crown and of the supreme command of the Army to the Mid-European scheme we shall purposely avoid speaking here, because this is beyond the range of our knowledge, and discussion might perhaps do more harm than good.

Of such a mixed, if not more mixed, nature is the reception given to the concept of a Central European union in Austria and Hungary. But here, too, the ultimately decisive consideration will not be what advantage or disadvantage this or that group hopes or fears, but whether or no it is desired to maintain the Dual Monarchy as a State. Whoever desires this must also desire the Central European alliance, because an Austria-Hungary without allies would be even more wholly lost than a German Empire without allies; and because no other alliance in the world can give the Dual Monarchy the necessary support.

We have before mentioned it as theoretically possible that, in the case of a weakening of Bismarck's alliance, which Graf Andrassy concluded for Austria-Hungary in 1879 with the assent of his Imperial master, the Danube Empire, remembering the Seven Years' War, might some time range itself with Russia and France. In fact, we admit that there are individuals in Vienna, or in the Slav districts who do occasionally think something of this sort. This is the only effective threat which Austrian statesmen have available for us, for a bare alliance between Austria-Hungary and England would be just as platonic as a war waged by the Dual Monarchy alone against England. It is conceivable that a Franco-Austro-Russian union against the German Empire might be a serious danger, and, in fact, almost must be so. It is questionable, indeed, whether the Austro-Hungarian Crown could rely on either its people or its troops for a new Seven Years' War of this kind, but we are willing to admit this, with some important reservations, for the sake of theoretical accuracy. What would Austria-Hungary gain thereby in the end? Even in case of victory she would be reduced to the level of a crumbling Balkan State dependent on Russia's goodwill, crumbling because the Slavs would be pulling with all their might towards Russia, and the Germans towards Germany. An Austria which adopted this course would have lost its eastern frontier, its future in the south, and its task in the world's history, and therewith its inner unifying force. Such a policy might be contemplated in case of need for psychological reasons, but not from political considerations. And since the old Austro-Hungarian Monarchy possesses a wealth of political feeling such as exists practically nowhere else in the world, we may safely reckon that if a choice has to be made it will be founded not on temporary humours, but on more fundamental laws of development, which means that the Central European alliance will be, in fact, supported and maintained notwithstanding all the politico-legal and other difficulties connected with it.

Many readers may think it scarcely fitting for us to discuss at all such grievous and dismal possibilities. But in a political discussion of this kind all imaginable cases ought to be reckoned with, because it must always be presumed that each such case is being taken into account somewhere or other. Such investigations do not make cheerful reading, but it is not our business to make an inspiring appeal, but rather to discuss in a manner intelligible to doubters and opponents. Before two Empires bind themselves for better or for worse they must have a thorough preliminary stock-taking. Austria-Hungary is as independent as the German Empire, has absolute freedom of action, and has the moral right to make any use of this freedom which offers permanence and prosperity to the Danubian Empire, even if it is displeasing to the North German Empire. Austria is concerned with Austrian policy, and Hungary with Hungarian policy. We do not dispute the formal right to adopt the position of opponent, we only assert that a dissolution of the permanent alliance by Austria-Hungary would and must be a kind of suicide. From the Austro-Hungarian standpoint the alliance with Germany is less a sentimental obligation than a pressing necessity for self-preservation.

. . . . . .

But we have not yet got to the bottom of the matter. One final and most difficult question still remains to be examined: Whether the Danubian Monarchy can be kept in existence at all with or without an alliance? This question is actually discussed both within and without the black and yellow boundaries, and we must not overlook it, because there are serious German politicians who will hear nothing of the Central European union, for no reason but that they consider a split in the hitherto federated Dual Monarchy to be historically unavoidable, and because there were or are serious German-Austrians, and also members of other nations in Austria and Hungary, who agree with them. We, for our part, do not share this opinion. If we did we should not write about the future of Mid-Europe. We are optimists. But since pessimists exist, their opinions also must be examined.

Pessimists are no new phenomena in or out of Austria. When Maria Theresa, a queen unsurpassed by the ablest men, and founder of effective home government, ascended the throne, the doubters said that it was beyond human power to breathe life into the State. And from that time onwards the whisperings and mutterings about a fatal illness have never ceased, but the sick man has gone on living passably well all the same. There have been almost always symptoms of disintegration, but always new signs of life too. And the course of the present war speaks much for the possibilities of life in the Hapsburg State federation. If

PARTNERSHIP IN THE WAR 33

we Germans of the Empire find here and there less concord than we should wish, yet experienced and reliable Austrians tell us that the mobilisation, the conduct of the war, and the administration have gone on much better than they would have thought possible. Strife ceased, pettiness disappeared, slackness vanished, a sense of duty showed itself, the will developed, the State was at hand.

This is not the place to go into all kinds of details about unfortunate experiences during the war of which we hear in private, if for no other reason than that these assertions cannot now be checked. At the end of the war Austria will have the depressing but unavoidable duty of conducting an inquiry into loyalty and disloyalty to the State. Granted that as a rule, after the first mobilisation, it was harder to keep the army up to strength in the non-German and non-Magyar districts than with us, yet we must remember all that has already been said about the position of the Slav in Austria. If we take the past into account in regard to those matters, we shall say in spite of everything: the unity of the State has proved beyond all expectation! What notions England and Russia had about the progress of the war! They imagined whole nations coming from the Danube to join them. There has never been the slightest sign of this.

The most severe trial of the Dual Monarchy is, of course, connected, both now and in the future after the war, with the ideals of nationality. Without entering here upon an investigation of the nationality question we can yet assert that the highest tension in the disputes concerning it is now relaxed, and that the war is proving a stern master and educator in moderating the demands of the nationalist particularists. The impossibility of sovereign small States with mixed populations is obvious. This does not mean that the different nationalities will forget all their quarrels, but they will regard their disputes as a matter of home and not of foreign politics. They will recognise that a Tzech army, or a Croat General Staff or a purely Magyar Foreign Office, or a Slovenian economic policy or a Galician State Bank must be counted as impracticable. Centralised Management will emerge from the Carpathian campaign heavily burdened yet greatly strengthened. Even the Hungarians, who during the war have occupied prominent positions in this Central Management, will be obliged to recognise this. They do not contemplate abandoning anything of the principle of Dualism, but they are sufficiently keen-sighted to see that centralisation is technically unavoidable for reasons of political necessity. If the Government makes use of its present favourable opportunity it will re-create and extend what Maria Theresa brought into being, political consciousness! Nothing will help more towards this than joint work at the new and important task of fashioning Mid-Europe: begin a fresh epoch!

So long as the Austro-Hungarian Central Government or the responsible representative of the dynasty has nothing else in view but to maintain the existing state of things with the help of small reforms, there will be little to grip the imagination of the youth of all the nationalities owing allegiance to it. But when once it raises the banner of a new epoch its gates will be thronged by able men. Austria-Hungary undoubtedly possesses amongst all its peoples proportionately numerous talents and noble and effective gifts. But hitherto political employment has offered too few tasks demanding a broad outlook, to attract ability. This may and shall be different now. A new State-creating enthusiasm will be wrung out by force and necessity. It rests with the Crown to awaken all spirits by the watchword, Mid-Europe, and to let the fight for trivialities appear indeed trivial. It rests with the Crown whether there shall be Spring or Autumn after the war. It is optimistic to believe that it will unhesitatingly choose Spring, but there is surely no cause to give up hope.

An old State can endure much provided its foreign defences are assured. Turkey offers a remarkable instance of this. That Turkey lost one piece of territory after another was due to her old-fashioned army and the doubtful status of the advisers and instructors from the rival countries. Now that the Young Turk movement is beginning to revive in virtue of the Prussian reorganisation of the army, matters are rapidly beginning to look more favourable. But Austria-Hungary was always more stable than Turkey, and has never become so weak from a military standpoint. Hence usually the area of the State has been maintained, even in the most difficult times, and hence, too, there is no reason now to regard the further salvation of the Danubian Monarchy as improbable. There is no natural law asserting that a complete cure will be attained, but it may be attained, and we desire to attain it. We Germans of the Empire must desire it.

The Austrians, however, must not take it in bad part when I remark that it is largely their own fault if pessimistic opinions about their country are too widely prevalent in the world. There is a special sort of political criticism in Vienna which thinks itself interesting and important when it paints gloomy pictures. This, in Vienna, is done with no very serious intention, but is rather like the daily grumblings of an old lady who would not feel it quite the thing to acknowledge that she had eaten and slept well. This artificial melancholy is, in fact, purely æsthetic, and has very little to do with politics, but foreigners attach a political meaning to such expressions of weariness. If, for instance, it had been rumoured in Paris before the war that the Bavarians were on the point of separating from the German Empire, we should have raised our glasses and cried, " Good luck! " But if the news appeared one evening in the *Corriere della Sera* or in some other foreign paper that the Tzechs were threatening the Austrian State and had ready ears for foreign whispers of intrigue, the Vienna cafés would have sighed out, " Just what we expected of those Tzechs!" No doubt there is occasionally reason to sigh, but it need not be done so openly or with such satisfaction. If Austria herself will recognise her attacks of pessimism for what they really are, that is for æsthetic politics, then foreigners too will begin to respect her as more healthy. We have confidence in you, have confidence in yourselves!

· · · · · · ·

The outcome of our inquiry, so far, has been to show the necessity for a close union of both Empires. Meanwhile we have assumed in various places without further argument that the new alliance must be richer in content than the present one, but we have not yet been able to explain why the existing mutual alliance will not suffice longer.

The present Dual Alliance, called for a time the Triple Alliance, and then again the Dual Alliance, which dates from October 16, 1879, was a defensive alliance in the event of one of the two Central European Powers being attacked by a third party. How and when exactly such a case would arise cannot be gathered from the text of the treaty. Indeed, so far as I can understand it, the event referred to in the treaty has never, in the strict sense of the text, actually occurred, indeed hardly can occur, for by the time the fact of being attacked is, so to speak, juridically evident, any readiness to help would be too late. The really effective content of the Dual Alliance was consequently in part more and in part less than a treaty. More in so far as mutual goodwill was genuinely ready for any sort of complication that might arise. But less in that any compulsion to recognise the event referred to in the alliance was lacking. We have seen in the case of Italy, the treaty with which in any case differed somewhat from the German-Austrian-Hungarian treaty, how pliable a carefully drafted text becomes in this respect if an ill will undertakes its interpretation. Since each new case is different in form it must, as a matter of course, be discussed as new by the two Cabinets. This is in the nature of things so long as there are two Foreign Offices with different aims, methods and leaders. But the two Foreign Offices must be retained, as we shall explain more carefully later. The consequence is that political treaties concerning defensive alliances cannot be regarded as in themselves binding on a nation.

When, for example, in 1911, in connection with the Agadir demonstration, we were in danger of a Franco-Russian war about Morocco, without its being possible for us to assert an actual attack by the French, it remained, so far as we knew, an open question whether the Austro-Hungarian army would help us at all, since it was not bound to do so by the text of the treaty.

When in the summer of 1914 the heir to the Austrian throne

and his wife were murdered by boyish criminals at Serajewo, the German Empire was not obliged by the clauses in the treaty to trouble itself at all about the matter. That the Emperor Wilhelm and his advisers did take action was in excess of the treaty obligation. Germany offered her life-blood to Austria-Hungary, and the latter thereupon accepted the enemies of Germany as her own. The Great War is thus much more than a treaty war, it is a partnership of sentiment, as though we had already grown into unison.

Suppose now that the two Empires simply return to the old relation at the end of the Great War; that would be something less than what now exists during the war. Less just because this brotherhood of blood was not legally demanded of us, and we all know this well enough. But how ought the future relation to be put into words? We have forebodings both in North and South that the future will bring us face to face with yet more difficult matters, that the world will remain for us full of dark and strange dangers. How then can we mutually safeguard ourselves, lest one day, for whatever human reason, the partnership should prove non-existent?

The safeguard certainly does not consist in mere political treaties. No treaty can be formulated between two sovereign States which has not its loopholes and omissions. The safeguard lies in a community of life in its many aspects, political, economic and personal; in the voluntary, systematic interchange between the two countries, in the community of ideas, of history, of culture, of work, of legal concepts, of a thousand and one things large and small. Nothing less than the attainment of this common existence will bind us really securely. But even the will to attain it is of immense value. And this is the spirit in which we proclaim Mid-Europe as the goal of our development.

. . . . . .

In trivial matters, and those of minor importance, it is possible to draw up and determine upon complete plans or estimates, but for a scheme of the magnitude and difficulty of this in regard to Mid-Europe, such a proceeding would be most unprofitable.

Nothing is easier for the expert than to enumerate ten or twelve points in a programme. Something as follows:

> The same recruiting laws.
> Mutual military inspection.
> Joint committee for foreign affairs.
> Joint boards for railways, the control of rivers, etc.
> The same coinage and measures.
> The same laws for banks and commerce.
> The same assessment for military expenses.
> Mutual liability for national debts.
> Equality of customs tariffs.
> Joint collector of taxes.
> The same factory laws.
> The same laws for companies, syndicates, etc.

This sort of thing might be continued for quite a long time, but it is meaningless. In real life problems come up in succession, and no one can tell beforehand in what order or in what selection. Even for political parties the list of demands in their programme is more often a source of weakness than of strength. On the one hand people are deterred by the list because they cannot tolerate one of the points enumerated, whilst they keenly deplore the absence of another. On the other hand the party leaders themselves tie their hands unnecessarily, and often are quite unable to accomplish what they have pledged themselves to. They desire and ought to be judged by their deeds in each case as it occurs, and they ought to realise, step by step according to their best judgment, the common ideals and aims of the party. This practical conception, resulting from party experience, applies to a yet greater extent to the State. It is true that an able Minister President may be able to make one or two promises which can be redeemed in a comparatively near future, but he will never lavishly make all the promises that he would carry out were he a Zeus. If, then, a new and important political structure comes into the sphere of practical politics, a kind of super-State over other States, an Empire of Empires, it would be a direct sin against the ideal of this new creation to try to stuff it to overflowing from the outset with tasks that would occupy ten or twenty years. Each item on the programme given above will require years of work to accomplish. Many will be attempted in vain. Others, to which to-day we give no thought, will become urgent to-morrow. Politics are a work of real life done for the sake of that life.

It would be better to attempt to indicate from the outset those departments with which the super-State must not interfere, but we know from the history of the German Imperial Constitution how elastic the boundary-line between Empire and individual State has remained after more than forty years. We shall refer in the chapter on constitutional problems to some of the principles of division which are relevant in this connection. The essential thing now is not an academic general authorisation lasting through one or two lifetimes, but the establishment of an effective starting-point for the new institution itself. We shall investigate further, later on, how this may be done.

Nor must it be thought that Mid-Europe can be called into being merely by laws, regulations and penalties. It is at least equally important that the boundary between the federated States shall be non-existent for all important groups of intellectual and material interests, as is partly the case already: community in banks, syndicates, trade unions, craftsmen's guilds, agricultural conferences, meetings of economists, historians, lawyers, doctors and many others. Hitherto such super-State groups have generally only extended from us to the German-Austrians, but it is necessary that a common atmosphere should prevail throughout Mid-Europe. All this must not be hindered secretly or openly by the Government, but must be definitely promoted, so that a community of life may develop from above downwards as a result of comradeship in the alliance.

.   .   .   .

The cry comes to us from the midst of the war: "We must be a single nation of brothers, inseparable in adversity or danger!" This sublime call from living and dying is the key-note for the coming epoch. Not, indeed, that there has been no friction in the conduct of the war! Such friction has occurred, and does still occur, and often seems so disturbing to those most closely affected that they have no great desire to let their neighbours become too intimate. Officers and soldiers of the German Empire who have come back from the joint fighting-lines often speak bitterly against the Austrians and Hungarians, condemning them for want of punctuality, lack of marching efficiency, and inaccuracy. In these matters the difficulties of the polyglot army are often much too little considered. People forget, too, that the Austro-Hungarian army missed the schooling of 1870. These Imperial German military critics do not realise that the new portions of the German army in 1870 were of varying values, and needed first of all amalgamation with the efficient Prussian army. Moreover there are mutual complaints occasionally in the German army itself. This does not mean that any doubt is felt of the indomitable courage of every section of the Central European Army. Even the severest critics praise the genuine and unreserved devotion of the Austrian and Hungarian troops in the face of danger, and their good and faithful comradeship. On the other hand, both Austrians and Hungarians complain of the German, and especially of the Prussian, want of consideration and overbearing manners, and so on. On both sides there has been some stupidity, and disagreement in details has often gone deep. But all this only signifies a succession of incidental events. Comradeship in fighting and death is a much greater thing than these unpleasant matters, to which we only refer because they are more harmful if unexpressed. There is no progress without friction. And indeed such half and secondary tones are never absent from human endeavour. Even in the army of a single individual State not a single day of the war passes without collisions between transport wagons, without conflicting orders, without omissions and wrong judgments. Can it be expected that two armies that have not fought side by side for a hundred years should at once act like Siamese twins? When at last the guns are silent and those who return home are at work once again in house

PARTNERSHIP IN THE WAR 41

and shop, then these transitory happenings will sink into confused impressions and ideas, but the vital will endure: so many nationalities faced by one death in one struggle! After the war only our common victory will illumine us.

And if once again, which God forbid, the storm-bell should ring for Central Europe, this war will form a memorable background; fathers will tell their sons how they were carried from the firing-line by trusty comrades with whom they could hardly speak. We do not yet know how different all we Central Europeans shall have become after the war. We have experienced the full weight and harshness of international politics, we have lost more brothers and children than any one generation before, but we have also received more help from God and man than ever did heroes of an earlier time. We are losing much of our social harshness in the war, the class war for individual interests is relaxing, former enemies find themselves loyally united heroes, nations who formerly only looked askance at one another are mutually friendly. It is our high fate to experience what to later generations will seem like a sacred legend. With this war behind us we could remove mountains. Now or never the lasting unity between East and West will develop, and Mid-Europe will stand between Russia and the Western Powers.

CHAPTER II

OF THE PREVIOUS HISTORY OF CENTRAL EUROPE

IF an historical entity is to be made of Mid-Europe, a fresh historical consciousness must grow up, for economic considerations, however serious they may be, will not of themselves suffice to arouse the necessary enthusiasm. Of course a scheme of this nature cannot be carried out without numerous calculations as to material advantages and disadvantages, but it is a false rendering of history to believe or wish to believe that great political transformations can be accomplished by the spirit of calculation alone. Each new social creation has its birthplace in the human soul, and this soul is never merely economic; from time immemorial and still to-day, it is compounded of impulses and desires, material and ideal, definite and vague, variously mingled but yet pressing forwards.

A revolution in thought is needed comparable to the change of soul which preceded or followed the founding of the Empire by Bismarck; a re-estimation, not indeed of all, but of many accepted values. If we go nowadays into our German Reichstag we notice that it is only for certain minor affairs that Prussians, Bavarians, Saxons, Württembergers, Hessians, Hanoverians or Mecklenburgers sit together. Our political parties have throughout lost their provincial character in relation to general questions of State: they think Imperially! During the war this Imperial consciousness has shown itself with especially remarkable power. There may indeed still be daily conflicts of interests among us Germans, but there is no spirit of separatism. Things are naturally somewhat different in the case of our foreign-speaking fellow-citizens, but they too hold their own in the war with courage and endurance, for the unity of the Empire. This complete agreement

PREVIOUS HISTORY OF CENTRAL EUROPE 43

in principle is the greatest triumph of Bismarck's work as founder; for when the German Empire was "constructed," as people used to say in those days, the Prusso-German spirit of unity existed only in desire, not in fact. In those days the individual States still had their own history, their own pride and their own sensitiveness. Many centuries of quarrelsome and turbulent individual history lay behind them. Often the trivialities of their mutual relationships are hardly to be called history. The Germans were a non-politically minded race of good fellows and servants, intellectually active, but with little mind for the interests of the State. They went each his own way, like sheep without a shepherd. But in the interval, out of all this rusticity and confusion a Prusso-German tradition has developed, that is, we have each saved out of our very chequered pasts something that we as Germans can carry on with us as our joint inheritance, whilst we have let much sink into oblivion of the old quarrels and envy and injustice. Some wounds, indeed, are not yet quite healed, as we see in the case of the Guelphs. But who still deplores nowadays that Prussia deprived the Saxon royal house of its most fertile territories? Who nowadays gives a thought to the fact that nearly all the federated States took the field against Prussia in early days and again in 1866? Who now objects to the fact that Frankfurt-on-Main was annexed in those days? The whole nation is conscious, without putting it much into words, that no progress can be made as an historical entity without a cancelling of old bonds. The past is past! Let the dead bury their dead. They have served their age as we wish to serve ours. Honour to their name and to their ashes!

The political spirit of Mid-Europe, if it is to be of much value, must now take possession of us to the extinction of numerous old disagreements, for there have been many harsh, acute and cruel wars between Austria and Prussia, and between Austria and Bavaria. Here, too, the rubbish of centuries needs to be cleared away before the new building can be put up. Silesia, Bohemia and the Tyrol have witnessed amazing struggles. We are not at present concerned with the fights with and about the Tzechs, the Hungarians, the Poles and the Serbs, but are considering in the first instance the battles waged between the old German Austria and the equally German Powers, Prussia and Bavaria. Our ancient banners have all been carried in opposition to one another throughout the old German Imperial territory. We will leave them hanging peacefully on the walls, for no stalwart regiment is ashamed of its earlier bravery. But we may well allow some dust to gather on these symbols of bygone strife, for new banners are now coming to the front, honourable insignia of our indescribably great common war. Let us act on the principle: to understand all is to forgive all. We, for our part, can understand how the golden kingdom of Austria had to resist the rise of Prussia with all its might. You can understand that the energy existing in the North German States had to work out its course. We can both understand that the politics of the eighteenth century were the politics of conquering princes, and that under the conditions of the time it could not be otherwise. You went to Upper Italy as conquerors just as King Friedrich II. went to Silesia. A hundred wars, little and big, were fought out within the boundaries of what is now Austria so that it might become Austria; a hundred fights were necessary so that Prussian-Germany might come into existence. This was and is the way of the world. To-day we can hardly realise how at one time neighbouring towns and princedoms could contemplate feuds with each other. Formerly they laid siege to one another, now they talk and eat together. Now, too, the honoured successor of the Empress Maria Theresa can receive the descendants of King Friedrich II.: we are partners in victory; your enemy is our enemy!

We must extinguish between North and South the feud that existed before Napoleon's time, that showed itself during that time in bitter misunderstandings, and has since embittered the common life. Looking back we shall see both Friedrich II. and Maria Theresa as two splendid warrior types of the same periods, souls in the same Valhalla, sovereigns inspired by a like spirit of uncompromising foresight. We shall even accept Metternich and Baron von Stein as part of the same picture, far apart though

PREVIOUS HISTORY OF CENTRAL EUROPE 45

they were in real life: the one a scientific statesman full of a facile, industrious elegance, the other a prophet inspired by a difficult national morality. We of the German Empire will purposely forget the suppression of the joyous youth of our national movement in the Conferences of Aachen, Karlsbad and Vienna, we shall know no more about Olmütz, or about the pressure on the Frankfurt Federal Diet; we shall be patient when we think of the negotiations against Prussia which Beust in Vienna carried on with France, for all this is past and has an adequate explanation in history. In like manner, too, Austria will forget that at the Vienna Congress Prussia was ready to take the field with France against her, that the Customs Union was directed and carried on by Prussia against Austria, that in 1859 Prussia did not help Austria against France and Italy. Both sides must shelve the irritations roused by the Crimean War. Our common frontiers, formerly so often overstepped, are from henceforth to be permanent boundaries, no longer frontiers dividing two foreign Powers, but inland boundaries between federated countries. And the Emperor Wilhelm I., dead a quarter of a century ago, will figure in the history of our Central European union as a brother of the Austro-Hungarian Emperor and King Franz Joseph I., who, by a miracle, still dwells among us, to pronounce the blessing of a revered and beloved old age upon the new epoch, after so many ancient quarrels, an Attinghaus of the newborn and saving peace of nations.

Were Bismarck, hero and centre of many combats, to appear amongst us again for the peace negotiations after the Great War, not only would he be hailed with infinite confidence from all sides and by every party in the German Empire, but all the peoples in Austria and Hungary would meet him enthusiastically. Notwithstanding his fight at Königgrätz, he would appear to all of us, from the North Sea to the Bosnian frontier, as the creator of Mid-Europe, the man who dispensed mighty power and justice throughout the centre of the European continent. Would that he were here!

· · · · · · ·

Forgetfulness is not, however, enough in itself to awaken the new sentiment for Mid-Europe, it will merely be a preparation for further spiritual progress. We must learn to discover the germs and tendencies, the prophecies and strivings of the future in the past. New tasks demand new eyes. This is a very important chapter and merits all the care and devotion of young historians, for historians are ultimately the educators of the people. Their responsibility increases with the democratic interest taken by the people in the State. Cabinet policy in the old style could be fashioned in case of need without historical ideas, by bribery, calculation, political technique and intrigue. But since the masses have become influential in determining the fate of the world, they need to have ideas and aims and meanings with regard to future happenings. It is true that not every one can read the writings of a Treitschke or a Friedjung, but the stream of their knowledge flows through a hundred channels of speech, school and newspaper, to the cottages of the citizen and voter. Hence it may be allowable to insert here some special discussion in outline of the people and of the nature of its history.

In speaking in such a connection of the historian as a political educator, I see on his right hand the philosopher and on his left the poet. I regard him not merely as a seeker into the memorable events of the past, but as an exponent of the discoveries made by himself and his fellow-workers. In the first instance, indeed, the historian is concerned entirely with facts; he determines what has happened. That is the absolutely indispensable basis of his art, as necessary as the daily renewed inspiration of nature is to the painter. He who loses the discipline of reality is worthless as an artist. But when he has stored up material round him like the stones for a mosaic, he has then to show whether he is more than a collector, whether he has the power to reanimate, to command his material to take form and live. He must breathe something of himself into his material. This even applies to a certain extent to descriptions of ancient and long-past peoples and periods. When Mommsen wrote his Roman History, it was a German history of the Romans, a Roman history expressed in

German, a breathing upon the stones so that they cried out. This he was able to do because through his experience of the rise of the young German State he could live out the times of the first ancient Empire of the West. But the historian who portrays our own ancestors, so that we can inherit and carry on their traditions, must have even more sympathetic insight than he who describes far distant times. Out of the thousand things which he might relate he selects those which seem to him to promote or obstruct, from the standpoint of his ideal of life. The painter Max Liebermann once said to me, " Art is omission." By this phrase he distinguished mechanical copying which indeed leaves out much, but only such things as chance not to come on to the paper, from artistic inspiration which can recognise the essential matters and their accessories, which deliberately omits non-essentials, and emphasises what it is imperative to take into account. In the pursuit of truth this can never happen from petty and sophistical motives, but must spring of itself from a rare " world-philosophy."

Bismarck himself read much history, and that history or historical poetry of the finest type. Living in what he read he finally proved in his *Gedanken und Erinnerungen* an unrivalled exponent of statesmanlike ideals. The last and best thing he bequeathed us was his account of himself: very intimate and not without omissions, mistakes and partialities, but teeming with the penetration of wisdom. He sang the swan song of his own epoch of empire-making, and uttered notes in so doing which will only be properly heard when the next new epoch dawns. He wrote for us and for our times.

However, I shall not speak at present of his wonderful testament but of the historians who were his predecessors and escort. There was a school of historians of the foundation of the Empire in the stricter sense of the word: Arndt, Raumer, Dahlmann, Gervinus, Häuser, Baumgarten, Droysen, Sybel, Treitschke.

The men differed among themselves, but they were essentially of the same family. They helped themselves and many others to an understanding of the coming National State. They, with their wave of German national Liberalism, reached further than the Old Master Ranke, who in his survey of the whole of Europe embodied the older internationalism of the pre-Napoleonic Christian and aristocratic culture. Many of them have not survived their own period because they belonged to it all too completely. But in the golden days of the Prusso-German State such thinkers and poets were needed, their task was accomplished then. Mid-Europe will need such people now. It will need more than statesmen to think it out aright. The statesman is essential in his own place in the forefront of the political scheme. But in the background there must be a whispering and rushing from the far distant past; visions of ancient knights, of a passionate people, of battles lost and won, of a common emergence from bog and forest. The evolutionary basis of history needs to be discovered, the Will which controls matter, before and above any description by Reason.

The historians of the period of the foundation of the German Empire can be divided into two principal groups, the Mediæval-Imperial and the Protestant-Prussian. It is true that I have tried in vain, with the help of an experienced friend, to classify every separate case under these heads. There are noticeable intermediate types: yet at bottom the distinction holds, Mediæval-Imperial or Prussian! The contribution of the first group has just now, at the beginning of the Mid-European epoch, a renewed freshness of effect, for our mediæval period is common to all types of Germans, whether in North or South or East. But the second group, the Prussian historians, have imbued us Imperial Germans with something which cannot equally be regarded as a unifying possession for the Germans of the Danube. For this second theme owes its origin to the fight of separation between North and South. Hence, if now during the Great War we turn our steps towards Mid-Europe, we are in perpetual conflict on the way with these teachers of our own youth, especially with von Treitschke, Sybel, and their colleagues. For if they are absolutely and permanently right, then Bismarck was wrong in 1878. But they were only absolutely right for a time. They remained reliable in much for a longer period, but the game grew more

PREVIOUS HISTORY OF CENTRAL EUROPE 49

extensive, the complete vision out-distanced their revelation, and, as we recognise their limitations, a new spiritual country opens out before us. We must here enter into this point rather more at length, because without some definite study of this portion of history, the Mid-European ideal will seem merely like an old guide-book showing a few new railway connections. There is also much food for thought in the fact that the historians of the last decades are all more or less removed from the Empire-making history. They are occupied either, like H. Delbrück, with purely organising and military statesmanship as such, or like Helmolt and Schäfer, with overseas international politics, or like Gumplowicz and Lamprecht, with the history of social and psychological culture, or above all with the calm critical estimation of past struggles, like Friedjung in Austria.

. . . . . .

All earlier history is primarily a history of princes. The most determined republican is powerless to alter this, for in those days political feeling was as yet non-existent amongst the governed. It will prove a vain task to attempt to write a history of the civilisation of the nations without princes or popes. Such a history is constitutionally defective, since every servant's coat has first been worn by a gentleman, and all household furniture has first had its place in the rooms of a princess. And even nowadays the rulers remaining to us out of the multitude of early sovereigns still serve as our models in many things in life, and are supreme over our great armies in war and peace. Theories to the contrary notwithstanding, this is the fact! Thus we must look upon the German mediæval period as a history of the Emperors in the first place, before we can pass from them to the people.

The early German Emperors are Central European figures in the fullest sense of the word, and the type is thus only now becoming recognisable again. The "Lesser Germany" party are indeed unable to understand the greatest of the early Emperors. Since 1870, it is true, people have sung much in praise of Barbarossa and Wilhelm I., but the real inner connection between the two characters was lacking. To-day, during this war that extends from the Alps to Anatolia, to-day Barbarossa rises up out of the River Selef in distant Turkey.

Our people only know particulars about the most important of the early German Emperors: Karl the Great, Heinrich I., Otto I., Heinrich III., Heinrich IV. (Canossa! Friedrich Barbarossa, Friedrich II., Rudolf von Hapsburg, Maximilian I., Karl V. But throughout Central Europe, and wherever the German language prevails, a notion is rooted firmly in the hearts of the people that already in those days there was a Mid-European World Power. Even if the coherence of the Empire was often feeble in those days of overgrown forests and poor communications, even if at times the elective imperial dignity seemed hardly more powerful than the old elective monarchy in Poland or Hungary, yet, throughout the Middle Ages there existed in essence a desire for a united Power ruling from Jutland to the Adriatic Sea, and even to Sicily. Even apart from Karl V.'s Burgundian and Spanish inheritance, the western boundary of Central Europe ran about where the Germans and French are now entrenched. It began at Bruges and Ghent, extended southwards almost as far as St. Quentin, included Verdun and Toul, and in the most vigorous times took in Besançon, Lyon, Vienne, and even Avignon. The eastern boundary certainly varied very much according to whether Pomerania, Bohemia, Hungary and Croatia were joined to the Empire or not. North and south of the Alps, however, a supreme authority was exercised with but few intervals from the time of Karl the Great to that of Karl V. This authority was indeed in the characteristic mediæval way not always obeyed, but it was recognised as existing in principle. It will from henceforth be easier than before to regard as our forerunner this ancient Empire, extensive and, on the whole, powerful as it was. Neither Imperial Austria nor Royal Prussia, when separated from each other, were quite in a position to carry on the Imperial tradition, because each only possessed a part of the original whole. For centuries the Empire of the Carolingians, the Ottos and the Hohenstaufen, has been non-existent and will be so until it is born again out of the union between the Hapsburgs and the

PREVIOUS HISTORY OF CENTRAL EUROPE 51

Hohenzollerns, between the Frisians and the Illyrians, between the Prussians and the Tyrolese. In the more distant past vague feelings of community have already subsisted between them. There was even a time when Warsaw and Cracow were counted as belonging to the Hansa League. People from all parts of Central Europe travelled and rode to the Reichstag. Knights from every department of what is now the German Empire and of the Austro-Hungarian Monarchy journeyed with Friedrich Barbarossa to the Holy Sepulchre. There was, in fact, in mediæval Central Europe a peculiar community of life and culture which differed somewhat from anything in the still confusedly intermingled kingdoms of England and France, and had no analogy whatever among the Byzantines, Tartars or Varangians. The Germans occupied the centre of Central Europe, but they drew in the neighbouring peoples on all their borders: the Holy Roman Empire of the German nation. Now, during the Great War, this ancient Empire is striving and pushing under the earth, longing to return after its long sleep. Every aspiration after unity during the many confused centuries that have intervened has been an after-glimmer of its light. And when, a hundred years ago, the wars of liberation against Napoleon united all the German races for a short time, the prophets, with poetic reminiscence, sang, as of old, of Emperor and Empire: Germany shall be one! Are you not conscious, in this superhuman war, of the spirits of our ancestors? Do our sons go side by side to their death merely because of a written treaty, or is there something behind? Did not the clouds mass themselves in the sky over the Carpathians and over Antwerp as though in an attempted greeting of knights and war-horses of old? All this was once one Empire! Now it is only the dream of an Empire. What will it become?

. . . .

Of all the mediæval Empires, Central Europe remained longest in its amorphous and unorganised condition. Whilst France and England on the one hand, and Russia on the other, grew comparatively quickly and easily into single coherent political entities, the centre of the Continent from Sweden to the Neapolitan kingdom remained a territory of innumerable small States. One important reason for this appears, as we have already noticed, to lie in the fact that the Emperor was elected. In all States where the monarch is elected, it is a matter of experience that the electing portions develop to excess at the expense of the whole, for each election multiplies their particularist claims. Besides this the physical character of Central Europe has from the outset encouraged numerous subdivisions, and there was no mediæval capital. The Eternal City of Rome was always looked upon as the Imperial City of the Western World and the earlier Emperors generally had itinerant Courts. Hence north of the Alps no resident Government was established or encouraged. Central Europe produced nothing north of the Alps that could be compared with Rome, Constantinople, Moscow, Paris or London, for all our mediæval towns lacked the crystallising power of a ruler. Neither Cologne, nor Mainz, nor Frankfurt, Augsburg, Nürnberg, nor Hildesheim, Lübeck, Leipzig, nor Prague, Graz, Vienna, was a European metropolis. It was only with the rise of the Northern and Southern Ostmarks in the later Middle Ages that the older Vienna, and in still more recent times the more modern Berlin, grew up: two centres neither of which was in itself the recognised capital of Central Europe. Perhaps the reader has seen in scientific books an illustration on a large scale of the process of celldivision: one cell acquires two nuclei, and loses its form more and more as these two nuclei recede from one another. It was something the same with Central Europe after the time of Karl V. Or to put it otherwise: the controlling authority moved from west to east and split into two halves, which fought each other. But at the same time there remained an undoubted connection, which could be stretched, and at times also broken, between almost all the sections which had once been united under the Ottos or the Hohenstaufen. The result is a withering up of the Imperial idea on the left bank of the Rhine, and as compensation a forward pressure of Germanism into Poland, Lithuania, Bohemia, Moravia, and even into the Southern Slav provinces under Turkish rule.

PREVIOUS HISTORY OF CENTRAL EUROPE 53

It is indeed not quite verbally accurate, if we express it so briefly as we have just done, to say that both the new centres of authority became the means of spreading the energy of Germanism into the East. Berlin has done little more than concentrate the effects of work done earlier in East Prussia, Pomerania, and Mecklenburg. And Vienna has generally been more occupied with extending its authority towards the East than with spreading German influence. After all, the main point is this: the two leading Powers that were advancing eastwards were hampered by a formless structure: the German Empire, a country full of splendid cities and cathedrals, with golden crops and precious vineyards, but without military strength of its own and without political feeling. Whilst both struggled forward to the East they quarrelled on their van about Polish territory, on their flank about Silesia and Saxony, and on their rear about all the absurd trivialities of spiritual and worldly princes, about the continual lawsuits over the inheritances of the nobility, about the regulation of the boundaries of the pigmy domains, and about the war subsidies of the French and English. This was the pitiable condition of German affairs when, finally, Napoleon I. burst upon them with threats and disturbance. Nowhere else could he have founded the Confederation of the Rhine. But the Confederation of the Rhine was the end, the final complete end of the history of the ancient German Empire. The old Crown was laid aside. *Finis Germaniæ!* When and how shall it come again? In what intermediary form and by what stages?

. . . . . .

With the Napoleonic period the second stage in the history of Central Europe begins, the stage in which we are still living. The old Imperial drama had been played through to the end. Central Europe was full of historical rubbish, and was pressed backwards and forwards between West and East. The effective power at the beginning of the nineteenth century was in the hands of Napoleon and Alexander I. of Russia, behind whom were the English. This is not the place to discuss the personal characteristics of the Tsar Alexander, but for the purposes of this sketch he may be regarded as the embodiment of the Russian power and as the predecessor of Nicholas I.

There are two principal advances in the Napoleonic War: one from Paris to Moscow, and one from Moscow to Paris. In both cases Central Europe was pushed, first eastwards by Napoleon, and then westwards by the Tsar Alexander.

The advance from Paris to Moscow (1805-1812) might have been held up on the Rhine if "the Empire" had had any real significance; the advancing army would have been pent up before the Böhmerwald if the two leading Powers had fought in partnership instead of letting themselves be defeated separately, but there was no community of feeling. It was in Napoleon's "great army" that the Austrians and Prussians first learnt to march side by side. In June 200,000 French, 45,000 Italians, 79,000 Bavarians, Saxons, Hessians, Württembergers, etc., 34,000 Austrians and Hungarians, 32,000 Prussians, 50,000 Poles, advanced on to Moscow. This was the first occasion on which Central Europe acted in concert.

The advance from Moscow to Paris (1812-1815) presents the reverse picture. In August, 1813, 160,000 Russians, 130,000 Austrians and Hungarians, 180,000 Prussians, 20,000 Swedes marched from East to West. The further the allied army pressed onwards towards the west after the Battle of Leipzig, the more it arracted Central European troops to itself, so that finally all Germany crossed the Rhine. This was the second occasion on which Central Europe acted in concert!

It is important to picture to ourselves thus briefly the events of the Napoleonic period, in order not to be left buried in the history of individual States. In the schools of the German Empire we foster a presentation of history which lays all the emphasis on the Prussian struggle for national freedom, and we know that in Austria much more weight is put on the clever diplomacy of the Court which under difficult circumstances saved what there was to save. The first important common experience of the two States is not thought of as "common" in history, because people on both sides are afraid to admit unreservedly that a hundred years ago

Napoleonic France could not be repulsed without Russia. When the three rulers of Russia, Austria-Hungary and Prussia stood on the King's Hill at Leipzig, the Russian was the strongest of them because he had already freed his own country. When Alexander advanced on Paris in triumph, and the Central Europeans accompanied him and did what he wanted, they still went on quarelling amongst themselves, and begging the great man from the East to be their friend and arbitrator. Baron von Stein accomplished his work for his passionately loved German Fatherland more by the help of the Russian Tsar than by that of the Prussian King. The events of the Vienna Congress require this background to explain them.

The Vienna Congress re-established Central Europe under Russian protection. We will not absolutely condemn the German Constitution as then drawn up. In spite of its obvious weaknesses and faults it was yet the first attempt at the task with which we are now occupied afresh. This task demands a much more careful study, before the new Peace Congress which is ahead of us, than it has received for fifty years. With it will begin the struggle about the future form to be adopted by these provinces and peoples, who now defend themselves independently and successfully against East and West, against France and Russia, and faced by the opposition of England. Formerly Central Europe was a mass of rubble, now we see it hardening into stone before our eyes. The difference is immense. A century has wrought wonders. We now hold the centre by our own strength against Russia, France, and England, and a few others besides. If only Baron von Stein could see it!

. . . . . .

The Napoleonic period has a special significance for the soul of Central Europe, because it planted a political and democratic spirit in the people. Napoleon appeared as the personification of the French Revolution, and as a personal dictator made great reforms both directly and indirectly. The completion of the liberation of the serfs, so far as it could be accomplished in face of the opposition of the old landed proprietors, was the result of Napoleon's subversive influence on all conditions of life. What Maria Theresa, Joseph II., and Friedrich II. liked to confer as a favour to the people from above, now, amid the gleam of weapons, took the form of a popular demand. The temporary reestablishment of Poland had a nationalising effect on its neighbours. The rise of Prussia displayed a king urged forward to victory by the popular will. Universal conscription in Prussia made subjects into supporters of the State. The fragile nature of kingdoms, both great and small, was obvious. Everywhere there was fermentation and effervescence. A new epoch was striving to emerge, a national epoch. But the new still lacked form and was without tradition and without technical skill in Parliamentary politics, so that at first, in the lassitude following on the unspeakable labours of the war, it remained weaker than the practised skill of the old Governments. The Governments made many promises to the developing peoples, without carrying them out, partly because they were unwilling, partly because they could not. The best of the soldiers, like Blücher, hung their swords upon the wall discontentedly, because this peace and this congress did not repay their efforts. Mid-Europe had desired to come into existence, but had not done so. Nevertheless the new seed remained in the ground. There was now a period of secret growth from 1815 till 1848. The ideal of a free German Empire in its ancient strength and splendour developed, and, too, the nationalist demands of the frontier peoples developed, hopes, difficulties and possibilities developed. All this happened whilst officially the two Central European Powers were allowing themselves to be led and checked by Russia. Indirectly, first Alexander I. and then Nicolas I. was the Regent of Central Europe. The German provinces lay at the Tsar's feet like superior Balkan States, which had obtained their freedom from Russia. The East had conquered in the struggle between West and East, and made use of her victory.

Things went on in this way until in 1848 a fresh wave of democratic feeling surged out of France in the West up to the frontiers of the Russian Empire. The Paris Revolution concerned

PREVIOUS HISTORY OF CENTRAL EUROPE 57

all Europe. It affected Central Europe as far as Warsaw and Budapest, almost like Napoleonism without Napoleon. The soul of the West swelled up against the authority of the East. This authority was more severely shaken in Vienna than in Berlin, because Vienna had offered less scope to the spirit of the wars of liberation than Berlin, and because the national principle in Hungary risked its great and vigorous passage of arms on this occasion. The middle classes and the townsfolk in Germany and Austria now wanted to put in their word, the educated class demanded a share in general politics, the tax-payers claimed to be consulted about their money. Every little street and square resounded once again with German problems, citizens' rights and constitutional demands. But once again the new spirit lacked the energy of definiteness, for it was non-military. Wrangel in Berlin, and Windischgrätz in Vienna, proved stronger than all the popular riots. In Hungary alone did the revolution appear on the scene with its own army; Austria was too much undermined to suppress the Hungarians, and, therefore, summoned the Russians across the Carpathians, the same Russians who are now pent up in these same passes, and resigned to the Tsar Nicolas I. the task of protecting its tottering authority. Nothing is so characteristic of the condition of Central Europe at that time as this proceeding.

But although the revolution had, and could have, on the whole, no triumphant result, yet it led to essential progress as compared with 1815, to wit the beginning of Parliamentary life in the representative assemblies, such as they were, and the renewed attempt to work out the Central European problem of the Vienna Congress with fresh energies in St. Paul's Church at Frankfurt-on-Main. The constitutional content for the new structure of Central Europe which was thus attained was indeed of small importance in political law, but it was in itself a great matter that, in 1848 and 1849, a Parliament existed in which Central Europe, in so far as it spoke German, was represented. Wise things were said in St. Paul's Church about all the Central European problems, ranging from Italy to Denmark, from the French frontier to Poland and Hungary. The spirit was stirred, the political atmosphere was favourable to the debate, nothing was lacking but what we now have in the war, the pressure of foreign events and the strength of the army. What was said was by way of prelude, a mere testing of the instruments. But then everything Central European was submerged again, and the Bundestag held once more in the Eschersheimer Gasse in Frankfurt, those meetings which we know so well from Bismarck's letters and reports.

. . . . . .

In the course of the Frankfurt discussions there was a painful and grievous divergence between the " Greater Germany " and the " Lesser Germany " views. At the voting for the election of King Friedrich Wilhelm IV. of Prussia to be German Emperor, 290 members voted for the Prussian hereditary Emperor, and 240 members refrained from voting. The German-Austrians had in part withdrawn, the Tzechs had not got beyond considering the possibility of attending, the other sections of the Central European peoples were absent, because it was a question of establishing not Mid-Europe but the German Empire. Thus in this combination there existed a strong minority who did not wish to adhere to the views of the Prussian " Lesser Germany " party, and who still believed in a joint federal State since they hoped for a " rejuvenated Austria." The majority tendered the Crown to the King of Prussia, but he refused it. In this way the whole political problem of Germany and Central Europe was disposed of, and no one knows how and with what results it might have been reopened had not Bismarck, acting on other assumptions, adopted the " Lesser Germany " view and carried it through. The Frankfurt majority started with a fixed desire for German unity, and for its sake had come to terms more or less willingly with the idea of the Prussian King as Emperor. Bismarck, on the other hand, took Prussian power as his starting-point and adopted the German view in order to advance this power. He was in no sort of sense a German revolutionary, but, on the contrary, a decided opponent of the popular movement; nevertheless in order to carry out his royalist policy he was obliged to take up the nationalist demands of the time.

It is essential for our purpose to grasp Bismarck's attitude as well and as comprehensively as possible, because it is a point of critical importance for the Mid-European scheme whether it be carried through with or in opposition to the spirit of Bismarck. In the latter case it would be condemned to futility. We must, therefore, inquire more closely what induced Bismarck to enter upon the war of 1866 and to bring into being a "Lesser German" State on a monarchical basis.

Even before his days of triumph he lived more in an atmosphere of foreign than of home politics, and as a young man was unusually familiar with the contemporary fluctuations in the balance of power in Europe. Moreover he had an absolute genius for things military. Hence it came about that he had no confidence in any German unity which was indefinite from the military point of view, nor consequently in the Frankfurt Constitution. How could an effective military unity be established if small States, incompetent in the military sense, had an important voice in the Federal Assembly? We must not forget that the Prussia of 1850 possessed much less territory in Germany than the Prussia of 1867 as enlarged by Bismarck! The corresponding chapters of the *Gedanken und Erinnerungen,* like the earlier notes made by Bismarck in the fifties, are interspersed throughout by military considerations. After the humiliation at Olmütz when, owing to anxiety about the Austrian army in Bohemia, Prussia had to give up her claims to Kurhessen and Schleswig-Holstein at the demand of Schwarzenberg, the Austrian Minister-President, it would have been impossible for her to carry on a "Greater Germany" policy if, simultaneously, she wished in the first instance to attain military importance as a North German, non-Austrian Power. Then, in addition, came the influence of the Crimean War, of which in general we in the German Empire knew very little, but which Bismarck lived through with his full powers of sympathetic interest. The Crimean War freed Austria from Russian guardianship, and secured its inclusion in the existing group of Western Powers. It is possible now, after the event, to think that it might have been better in fact for Central Europe if as a whole it had joined with the West to attack Russia in the Crimean War, had freed Poland and had driven back the Russians. We are much inclined just now to form a retrospective wish of this kind, but at that time Prussia still retained in its blood too much of the fear of the unmeasured force of the French Revolution; for 1870 had yet to be lived through, and the Prussian king was used to Russian supervision. He remained a trembling neutral like the present King of Roumania. Under these circumstances Bismarck learnt the helplessness of the German Confederation. Was there, then, any other aim for his unusual, overpowering and abounding energy than to establish his Prussia and to secure for it by military means the control of the German Federation? Only so could there be any foreign policy for him, which really deserved the name of policy. The strong man must first make for himself a theatre or arena, he must build up a position for his sovereign so that there might be place for purposive action. And the course of events up to 1866 showed that he was right. He created what the majority in St. Paul's Church, with their military unpreparedness, had merely put forward as a pious wish. He created it differently from anything imagined by these learned men, but still he created it. It was he, together with his sovereign and with Moltke, who completed the work of Friedrich II. of Prussia, and who, at the same time, carried out the popular demands of the " Lesser Germany " party in St. Paul's Church.

But as soon as the revolution in the condition of the German army was completed, and after the victory of Königsgrätz, he began at once and without reserve to consider the preservation of Austrian inviolability, and extorted it from the Prussian king and his generals. Thus it appears that he and he alone at bottom thinks in terms of Central Europe, taking that as his environment whole. His own account of the Bohemian deliberations is a most weighty document in connection with our train of thought. He does not want a German Empire with Hungary, Galicia, etc.,

PREVIOUS HISTORY OF CENTRAL EUROPE 61

excluded, nor a purely German national State with no counterpart in historical experience. But he does want to retain permanently the possibility of a union of the two Great Powers lying between East and West. He never forgot that France and Russia might conceivably attempt to crush a centre that was not indivisible. All his later policy was implied in his dispute with King Wilhelm at Nikolsburg over the "shameful peace." In case of doubt he was always more Austrian than Russian. His considerations read as follows:

"If Austria were seriously injured, she would become a confederate of France and of all opponents; she would sacrifice her anti-Russian interests for the sake of revenge against Prussia. On the other hand, I can imagine no future acceptable to us for the countries which constitute the Austrian kingdom, supposing that the latter were destroyed by Hungarian or Slavonic rebellions or were reduced to a state of permanent dependence. What could take that position in Europe which the Austrian State has hitherto occupied from the Tyrol to the Bukowina? Any fresh States formed in this area could only be of a persistently revolutionary character. We could make no use of German-Austria either in whole or in part, we could not secure a strengthening of the Prussian State by the inheritance of provinces such as Austrian Silesia or parts of Bohemia, no union between German-Austria and Prussia could be successful. Vienna could not be governed as a suburb of Berlin."

Thus, in his old age, Bismarck subseqently described in writing his position in 1866, and thus does he wish to be regarded by posterity. On no account does he wish to be registered in the memories of later generations as the destroyer of ancient German unity and of the Central European alliance. And in fact he succeeded in making his policy understood by Austria and Hungary in the course of a few years and during his own lifetime. In 1866 there was an alteration of the centre of gravity, but no destruction of the germs of that Mid-Europe which is now at last coming into being.

· · · · · · ·

The Franco-German War of 1870–71 meant the final liberation of Central Europe from France. The present generation hardly knows what an extensive influence France exercised before the war in Southern and Central Germany, and how much inclined Austria was to wrest from Prussia, with the aid of France, what had been gained in 1866. Hence nowadays people pass lightly over those passages in Bismarck's *Erinnerungen* where he speaks of the danger of a new Confederation of the Rhine. To us to-day the Rhine Confederation is a distant and barely conceivable tradition, but then it was still in the region of practical politics. Central Europe stood between East and West, and as yet on no independent footing. I remember a trivial experience of my boyhood: the leading townsfolk in our little town in the Saxon Erzebirge were talking together in July, 1870: "We Saxons are all right; now we keep in with Prussia because we must, but the French if they come will know that we did not want to do it!" This, or something like it, was what a good many people were thinking. The French magic spell had first of all to be completely severed, and was in fact splendidly destroyed. In this way Bismarck fully reaped the advantage of 1866: Southern Germany joined the North German Confederation, and the German Empire came into existence. Now there was a North German Emperor. Without any fresh injury to Austria the lesser German Empire arose, a triumphant victory for those who as early as 1848 had looked forward to this and this only; as yet, however, the prophecies of Untersberg and Kyffhäuser were not completely fulfilled.

Those were wonderful days when North and South Germany conquered France together. That was a victory without Russia's aid, though with her acquiescence; that was the victory over all forms of protectorship in the West, the chance to be free after a hundred years of a complicated dependence! Even Austria, in spite of all despondency, felt that she too would gain her freedom by this war. The *Wacht am Rhein* was sung even on the neutral Danube. The Battle of Leipzig was repeated in France in 1870 without the help of the Tsar. By the blessing of God, what a change!

In attempting to formulate the results of the Franco-German War from the Austro-Hungarian point of view we must reckon it a loss for Austria that "the Empire," and in particular the South German States, came under North German leadership for all time as far as could be foreseen, so that the ancient Hapsburg period of Empire was now for the first time completely at an end for the rest of Germany. Austria-Hungary had now no longer an indefinite background in the west, she possessed her own borders and nothing more. But at the same time she gained a strong and victorious friend who could strengthen her strength and compensate for her weakness. Intelligent people in Vienna and Budapest understood this at once, and under the leadership of Graf Andrassy and with the consent of the Emperor Franz Joseph they acted accordingly.

It is most instructive for Germans of the Empire to read the history of the year 1870 in Wertheimer's book: *Graf Julius Andrassy, sein Leben und sein Zeit* (Stuttgart, 1910). There we learn to look from an outside point of view at events which as Germans we have experienced from the inside. At the beginning of the war Andrassy was in favour of neutrality, because he cherished a hope that France and Prussia would weaken themselves in a mutual war, and that hence the critical part of arbitrator might fall to Austria-Hungary at the conclusion of peace. Beust, the Austrian Minister-President, wished to join in against Prussia, but the far-sighted Hungarian insisted on neutrality, and the unexpected Prusso-German victory justified him. He may be called the saviour of Mid-Europe, for if at that time Austria had attempted to settle her accounts with Prussia again, then whatever the immediate outcome, no common future would have been possible. Thus Andrassy, in 1870, showed himself to be the same man with whom later Bismarck was to conclude the treaty of 1879. If we ever succeed in giving a political shape to Mid-Europe the portraits of Bismarck and Andrassy ought together to be wreathed with laurels of gratitude and honour.

. . . .

The western limits of Central Europe were thus fixed in 1871, a settlement of boundaries on the Russian side had to follow. In the autumn of 1876 Bismarck received a telegram in code from Livadia, which demanded on behalf of the Tsar a statement as to whether or no the German Empire would remain neutral if Russia went to war with Austria. Never was there a more fateful question. After attempts at delay had failed, Bismarck answered that we could tolerate it if our friends merely lost and won battles against each other, but not if one of them was so severely injured as to endanger her independent position as one of the influential Great European Powers. In virtue of this answer Russia came to an amicable understanding with Austria about Bosnia and Herzegovina and entered upon a Russo-Turkish instead of a Russo-Austrian War.

The outcome of these events was the Berlin Congress of 1878 and the Dual Alliance of 1879, and with these events the traditional alliance between Russia and Prussia was practically at an end. The impression produced by the King's Hill at Leipzig had faded. Bismarck did indeed preserve a certain connection with Russia in the shape of the counter-insurance treaty, but the partnership between Russia and Prussia was dissolved. The die was cast. Dual Alliance was formed in opposition to Dual Alliance: Mid-Europe between East and West. It may be said that the present war had its beginnings in 1876. The Russians for their part, it is true, proposed a Russo-German Alliance even after 1876, but the German Empire was bound, it was married to Austria-Hungary for life and for death. And thus both the Empires have passed through the last three decades together, thus today they are fighting shoulder to shoulder and thus will they continue.

This alliance agreed to by Graf Andrassy and Bismarck in 1879, and which constituted Andrassy's last important act, is in no sense to be looked upon as the temporary outcome of a fluctuating political situation. After the Franco-German War Bismarck indeed originally wanted to re-establish a triple alliance, in accordance with old custom, between Russia, Germany and Austria; the triple imperial alliance of the manarchical system in opposition to all western disorganisation. With this object in view he arranged various meetings between the three Emperors from 1872 onwards. But these grand visiting days did not prevent the fateful question of 1876. The statesman of Central Europe was obliged to renounce the dream of the King's Hill, and to say definitely, very definitely, whether or no he wished to uphold Austria-Hungary at all costs and in every danger. Any one who now wants to dissolve the German-Austrian-Hungarian alliance throws us back politically, as we have already said, to before 1876, and obliges us to consider over again all the pros and cons of the Russian question of that date. This reconsideration will do no harm, for it must inevitably lead back to Bismarck's decision, which was certainly not adopted lightly or without the most exact knowledge of all contingencies.

When dealing with the formation of the Dual Alliance, Bismarck mentions the following reasons for hesitation: changeableness of Hungarian opinion, uncertainty as to the behaviour of the Germans in Austria, danger of Catholic ascendancy over Protestantism, anxiety about Polish desire for dominance on the Austrian basis. A treaty of alliance would be of little avail against all this. All the same he concluded the treaty with Andrassy and stated his reasons in a letter which he wrote in September, 1879, to the then King of Bavaria:

" Should no agreement (connection by alliance) be arrived at, Austria could not be blamed if, under the pressure of Russian threats and in uncertainty about Germany, she finally sought a closer understanding with France or even with Russia herself. Should the latter occur, Germany, owing to its relations with France, would be left in complete isolation on the Continent. But should Austria draw closer to France and England as in 1854, Germany would be thrown entirely upon Prussia, and, if she did not desire isolation, would be involved in the, as I fear, mistaken and dangerous methods of Russian home and foreign politics."

These words are still true in essentials to-day. He who will not think in terms of Mid-Europe, because the doubts existing in 1876 and 1879 have grown greater instead of less, ought to consider somewhat with which country an alliance can be entered upon if we finally abandon Bismarck's policy.

. . . .

Whilst working this out we have spoken frequently, very frequently indeed, of Bismarck himself, but for nearly thirty years politics for us meant Bismarck. As long as he lived people might fight for him or against him, but it was he who had the last word. All Germany's political negotiations up to the Great War are either a perpetuation of his potent influence or weak attempts to break away from it. He was a Hercules. The Austrians have had no such man, but he is theirs and ours too. I think that I have made it clear that he laid the foundation of Mid-Europe. It rests with us to carry on the work. All the cares which perplexed him have been amply justified by the Great War! Shall not his hopes also bear fruit?

It is true that after Bismarck's retirement all possible efforts were made to change the policy of the German Empire. The Emperor Wilhelm II. took, on occasion, every conceivable pains to secure better and more permanent connections with France and England. But nevertheless when the universal tempest broke, Austria-Hungary alone stood at our side, though subsequently Turkey too threw in her lot with us both. What Prince Bülow, as Imperial Chancellor, did by the "faith of the Nibelungs" was an important prophecy for Mid-Europe. The century's history has first driven us apart and then thrown us together again. The probation time of our interconnection is over. It now remains to build up our common future. What else in the world could we do in virtue of our whole history?

If the German Empire enters into alliance with Russia it means a return to the position of Prussia under Friedrich Wilhelm IV. From the economic point of view, as we shall show later, this may have certain advantages, but politically it will be the death of our independence. And the German people will not endure this permanently, for it would imply joint responsibility for

PREVIOUS HISTORY OF CENTRAL EUROPE 67

everything Russian, as we have already pointed out in an earlier paragraph.

If the German Empire allies itself with England, which, after this war, is hardly conceivable, but which before it appeared to be possible, it will become the military partner of the first Sea Power, and must fight Britain's battles on the Continent. Such a position may have much in its favour commercially, but as a national policy would bring to an end our individual share in the world's history. We have already mentioned other grounds for hesitation.

In both cases the period from 1870 to 1914 would become a mere interlude in German history, an episode full of splendour and self-respect, a brief golden age such as that of Holland. An individual course is only possible to us in union with Austria-Hungary.

And how do matters stand on the Austro-Hungarian side?

Any serious attempt to enter into the traditional feeling in the Danubian monarchy will enable us to realise at once that a binding connection with the Prusso-German Empire will be regarded there as a very serious step. For without doubt it involves, in spite of all the consideration which must be shown to Austria's right to determine its own action, a bond which may, under the circumstances, be hard to tolerate. To speak quite frankly: Austria will be assenting finally to that shifting of the weight of gravity which took place in 1866. She will renounce all future claim to be the chief ruling Power in Central Europe, as she was in her ancient days of splendour. There is no formal dependence involved, no curtailing of sovereignty, no giving up of inherited power, but all the same there will be an actual acknowledgment of the existing position of forces. We shall speak elsewhere of the most complicated legal-constitutional questions, here it need only be stated, as the result of previous history, that a situation has arisen, owing to the founding of the Empire by Bismarck and its justification of itself in the Great War, in which the German Empire has become the first of the two leading States in population, military efficiency and unity. This situation exists now, and is already far from new, but all the same it will require resolution on the part of Austria to acknowledge the fact in a political arrangement.

It is obvious that Austria-Hungary, too, will examine all other possibilities before the permanent Mid-European union is decided upon. We have already said something about this, but it seems necessary to reassert, in connection with our survey of past history, that Austria cannot stand by herself in the world, because she is no match for a simultaneous attack on her various frontiers, and that she has no other natural partner in alliance except the German Empire. A Russian guarantee that the Austrian State shall retain all its present territories is absolutely impossible so long as the pan-Slavonic revolutionary movement is predominant, and an English guarantee would be ineffective. Even more certain than the statement that the German Empire needs the union, is the converse statement that Austria-Hungary is bound to the German Empire for better and for worse. This is a fact! If this alliance is dissolved the Balkan provinces will turn towards the north! If it is dissolved the German-Austrians will lose their footing in the Dual Monarchy! Austria-Hungary may and indeed ought to stipulate for every necessary condition and safeguard for herself in the union, but she cannot prevent that union even should she wish to do so. Thus speaks past history, for Mid-Europe arose in the first instance out of the Prussian victories, and especially that of 1870.

History of the past, wonderful chaos, crowd of forms, we pray thee lend us thine aid! If thou willst thou canst destroy everything! If thou willst, thou canst make everything easy! Come hither, ye learned counsel of our historical Muse, ye interpreters of the developing fate of nations, open your minds to the search, so frequently obscured, into the genesis of Mid-Europe! Hide nothing, and veil nothing of the past, but make prominent those things that are seen for the first time by those alone who begin to muse on and seek for Mid-Europe! To-day all ears are open to your words! The nations in the midst of the Continent, all the peoples between East and West, desire to know their future. Speak and we will hearken!

CHAPTER III

CREEDS AND NATIONALITIES

CENTRAL EUROPE is at the present time a geographical expression which has so far acquired no political or constitutional character. But Austria, too, was once merely a geographical expression, and Prussia was a provincial term denoting only the most easterly portion of the kingdom. It is not so very long since it was said that Germany was only a geographical concept, and what a content this word has acquired in the interval! The word " Mid-Europe," which has not hitherto been used in history, has, at any rate, this great advantage, that it carries with it no associations of creed or nationality, and consequently does not from the outset awaken feelings of opposition. We shall have quite enough and more than enough to do with such feelings of opposition, for if ever any territory on the inhabited earth contained within itself a superfluity of passionate discords and frictions, it is this Central European country of ours!

It may, indeed, be said that the more recently colonised countries, and especially the United States of America, have to deal with intermixtures of opinions and races of an even more marked and violent nature. But the inhabitants of such countries have essentially less traditional obstinacy. The ocean lies between them and their old home, and during the long voyage across they have made up their minds to accommodate themselves to new conditions. This ocean voyage is lacking for us in old Europe! Here it is not our ambition to be or to become the most modern country in the world, but on the contrary we are fervently defending old rights, old customs and old boundaries, whether they are good or bad. The very radicals with us are in this respect often the most conservative of all. But it would be an excellent thing if people could be inspired on their entrance to Mid-Europe, with some such joyous and impressionable voyager's humour, the cheerful courage of those who, after superhuman battles, believe more in the future than in the past. Ill-humoured ancestor worship will never bring us to our goal. We stretch the hand of fellowship from the North to the South to all who will march with us forward.

But, of course, all objections and special demands must receive attention. Mid-Europe can only come into being through millions of discussions about the interests of every component group and tendency. It is of no use for any one to think out a theoretical scheme of union between the countries concerned, and in doing so purposely to ignore all religious and national difficulties. Let us agree at the outset, that if any one be so "enlightened" as to have lost all his own natural colour, he still cannot deny or mistake the force of innate and inherited traits of character without making himself ridiculous. Churches may mean nothing to him, yet all the same they are realities. He may be a mere railway traveller without country, but nevertheless those who cultivate the soil from north-west to south-east, those who dwell in towns, large and small, those who tend vineyards, those who work in mines, have all their own insuperable mass of peculiarities. Our Central European wealth and vigour, as also our daily political and social difficulties, consist in an incredible and disquieting abundance of characteristic forms.

I have visited most parts of the Central European country, and am familiar with people from every district. Shall I picture them all to myself? Then in thought I am in a peasant's cottage in Lower Germany, in a country house in Upper Germany, in an Alpine inn, in a little town in Bohemia, in the industrial region in Upper Silesia, in a shop in Posen, in an hotel in Tatra, with friends in Budapest, at the port at Triest, at home in Berlin, in the splendid old cathedral of St. Stephen in Vienna, in the silence of the Böhmerwald, on the shore at Rügen; and so on continually forms arise of men, women and children, and I hear every German accent, from the broad Frisian Plattdeutsch to the Tyrolean Mountain German, from the softness of the Lower Rhine to the sharpness of East Prussia, from the Mecklenburg calm to the Viennese liveliness, and in addition there is the sound of Danish in the North, French in the West, Italian and Croatian in the South, Tzechish in Bohemia, Magyar, Roumanian and Polish in the South-East and East. The whole is alive like a mighty forest with tall trees and undergrowth, with evergreens and fir-copses and a thousand small bushes and flowers. It is like a sea in which all kinds of fish disport themselves. And nowhere are limits or divisions sharply fixed. All is in flux, pushing and pressing in confusion, whispering and shouting, pleading and scolding, praying and calculating. Unless all these people are willing, the Archangel Michael himself cannot mould them into his heavenly legion. To reduce this crowd to political efficiency, to produce from it an army and to make it a vigorous, united, organic State — this is something almost superhuman and at the same time splendid, a task for the ablest of statesmen, who possess the soul of the nations, and whose thoughts are guided by the spirit of history. He who takes up this work must have nothing petty about him, and must excel in will, in power, in goodness and in patience. For this work we want to summon our best men and women from all parts of Central Europe, or rather we want to express the summons to them in the words which Providence addresses to all of us in this war: Become a united people! Remain united after such terrible slaughter!

· · · · · ·

In government there is a conservative type of forbearance and a liberal type of forbearance, and the two must co-operate in the genesis of Mid-Europe. The conservative forbearance has sympathy with what has been. The liberal forbearance pleads for freedom of movement for what is striving to be. We must learn better than before to separate off that coercion and law which are State necessities, from those things in which free play may be allowed to individual tendencies. As the maxim puts it: *in necessariis unitas, in dubiis libertas, in omnibus caritas* = in the requirements of State, coercion and equality; in personal matters, freedom; in both, comradeship! The powers of the State confederation, of the States, of the subordinate States, of the Circles, of the Communes, of the geographical districts, of the national communities, of the religious associations, of the economic organisations, workmen's societies, trade unions, learned societies, parties, must be flexibly graduated, so that Mid-Europe, with perfected organisation, may be the spacious home of free movement. All abilities now employed in the leadership of State and commune in North Germany, South Germany, Austria and Hungary must be combined together, so that a tradition may be formed, which will perpetuate itself with ever fresh vitality, and will carry on amongst our children and grandchildren the work that we are beginning with hesitation and effort.

Central Europe can be treated neither as barracks nor cloister, neither as public meeting nor as factory, neither as farmhouse nor as suburb, neither as bank nor as workshop, but all must have a place therein: discipline and independence, threats and rewards. We need to ponder over this, for it will not come about of itself. We must raise the character of the peoples by our directing reason.

And what is the object of it?

The history of the evolution of nations shows us a development of human types which is the result of many centuries. We know what is meant by an Italian, a Frenchman, an Englishman, a Russian, an American. We know also what is meant by a German, a Magyar, a Pole, a Tzech. But our Mid-European type is not yet fully developed, he is still in process of formation. Frenchmen and Englishmen are complete after their kind, but we Germans and the smaller nations surrounding us have not at present acquired that degree of assurance in the conduct of life and in tact, nor that political training and æsthetic habit, which would suffice of themselves to guide us in matters great and small. In comparison with the two western nations we are still young. When the French had already lived through the most splendid period of their monarchy we were just beginning to imitate Romance culture. Our forefathers learnt French and went to Paris in order to find out there how to behave and how to dress and what constituted good tone. From the English we borrowed sport, habits of travelling, town-planning and many other such things. We are still not quite out of our schooldays. To confess this calmly is no shame, even in war time. We possess, it is true, old and honourable traditions and primitive elements of temper and character, and in addition many an efficient and long-used method, and many a new invention. But old and new, primitive, mediæval and modern, are still unbalanced. We are, if I may so express it, historically a half-finished product, and we are still awaiting the day of completion. This gives us a touch of the primitive and of something still capable of improvement. I should not choose to be occupied with any other human situation than this one, because it involves such wonderful problems. We have much background and many good qualities, we have also ability to work our way through, but now our high school period ought to begin. Round and about the German spirit will grow up a Mid-European culture; there will develop a human type which will be intermediate between Frenchmen, Italians, Turks, Russians, Scandinavians, and Englishmen. Let us search out these Mid-Europeans! But indeed it is difficult for us just because we are in Mid-Europe: in the land of passage for all the migrations of the peoples, in the battlefield of all the great intellectual struggles, in the region of religious wars, of fights about nationality, of an endless succession of economic periods, in a region which neither affords nor can possess inward ease because it is too full for mere classification. Taking the region as a whole we are too much occupied with futile efforts, and frequently even full of despair about things in particular, but nevertheless we have plenty of optimism about things in general. We are familiar with the despair of those who do not gain their victory, and with the optimism of those who take up the old problems afresh. Let us, in this mood, speak in the first place of the old and still influential religious struggles of Central Europe, of the many attempts, doubts, broodings, advances, falls, of suffering and death, and the song of the holy angels.

. . . . . .

From ancient times onwards, Central Europe was an object of dispute between the two portions of the old Roman Empire. To express it otherwise: the greater part of Central Europe, since it was Christianised and civilised, was fundamentally dependent upon ancient Rome, the immortal Italian capital of the material and spiritual world. But in the Carpathian districts and on the Lower Danube there was always an ebb and flow of Byzantine influence. The pre-Turkish orthodox Rome of the East attempted as occasion offered to gain a footing amongst the Magyars and Bohemians as well as amongst the Poles. But Constantinople made its furthest thrusts to the north-west when it was Turkish and Mohammedan. The Turks were twice before Vienna, they had possession of Graz and Istria and advanced on the other side as far as Galicia, they conquered Lemberg and Przemysl and galloped over the Carpathian passes which now again have been the scene of our battles. They imposed upon the conquered peoples an often oppressive system of political and military suzerainty and of taxation, but did not enjoin their conversion to Mohammedanism. Hence, even under Turkish rule, the earlier spiritual connections with the Eastern and the Western Rome continued within approximately the same geographical limits. In course of time, by material and spiritual means, Western Rome pressed its eastern boundary far forward up to the Vistula. Eastern Rome receded towards the east and south. To-day Mohammedan districts are found only in Bosnia and Herzegowina; there are Eastern Orthodox Christians in Serbia and on the borders of Dalmatia, Croatia, Slavonia, and especially in the Roumanian districts at the junction of the Theiss and the Danube, round Siebenbürgen and in the Bukowina. A section of the Roumanians and almost all the Austrian and Hungarian Ruthenians on both sides of the Carpathians are Greek-Catholics, that is, their religion is Byzantine in origin but Roman and papal in organisation. But

CREEDS AND NATIONALITIES

all the rest has been a part of the permanent whole adhering to Western Rome since mediæval times, and hence it experiences all the powerful inner convulsions of this great spiritual community.

. . . . . .

The separatist movement away from Western Rome, which began with the Cathari, the Waldensians, the Wicklifites and the Hussites, and reached its climax in the German and Swiss Reformation, was lived through in the German-Slav-Hungarian districts of Central Europe with terrible force and counter-force. The violent and injurious struggle raged on from 1517 until the Peace of Westphalia, and disturbed the organisation and wellbeing of the mediæval State almost to the point of destruction. On and around German soil a volcanic spiritual experience was consummated, the results of which were felt universally wherever there were children of distant Rome; but those who were the earliest forerunners of the movement often thereby sacrificed themselves and their country. People's hearts were in a state of ferment. Nearly all the territories which now belong to Germany, Austria, Hungary and to what was once the Kingdom of Poland, were first gripped by the new teaching, then again reconquered, and often changed their ruler and their faith many times over, until at last, after much bloodshed, the spirit and the ability to resist were exhausted and creeds were regulated according to authority and normal conditions. All these immense struggles in nearly every town, borough, county, diocese and electorate have become of necessity almost incomprehensible to our present generation of men. In the interval we have gained something which four hundred years ago, at the close of an epoch in the world's history, the most enlightened intellects hardly dared to think out. And this something is the personal freedom of the individual from the enforced bondage of religious opinion. This freedom of the individual appears as a result of the Reformation, but at first both the German and the Swiss Reformation were, according to their own intention, only a transition from the old universal community of church life and affairs to a new and special territorial one. Even Luther and Calvin desired coercion, and insisted on the axiom: *cuius regio, eius religio:* the ruler determines the faith! The age of constraint required fixed forms and discipline of the inmost soul. This had not been so in the later days of the old Roman Empire, but as soon as the Romish faith became in the North a missionary religion and a religion of the masses, and especially after it penetrated to the German Franks, it became a constituent part of public life. Out of that wonderfully free, lawless, spiritual and personal Sermon on the Mount there developed a sort of spiritual militarism, without which no social or civic order seemed possible. Thus Luther and Zwingli did not wish to infringe upon discipline as such, but to mould their spirit again more closely to the Biblical model and to advance personal piety and individual experience in religion. This constituted their sacred task, which seemed like presumption, insubordination and a misleading of the people to the representatives of the ancient and long-since systematised community of souls.

This account of the Reformation movement in the Church may seem superfluous here, but I am anxious that we in Central Europe should get a grasp of history in which Catholic and Protestant are conceived of as constituent parts of a joint past without surrender of their spiritual value and reputation. For it cannot be denied that the union of North and South may be attended by a passionate outburst of feeling in this very sphere of religion. In its religious evolution North Germany has, as a rule, conducted itself differently from Austria; and Austria, Bohemia and Poland have again behaved differently from Hungary; consequently everywhere remnants of bitterness have persisted which may be reawakened at the slightest provocation. Almost the whole of North and some important parts of South Germany have gone over to the Protestant established Church, whilst the counter-Reformation, the forcible suppression of the new form of faith, was most violent in the Hapsburg territories. There, under King Ferdinand I., the Jesuit Canisius, called by some the "Hammer of heretics," and by others the "second Apostle of Germany," carried on his work. From thence at various times Protestants migrated from house and home, and numbers of these were taken in by the Prussian rulers. The result of this is that the Protestants of the German Empire often still have a conception of the violence of the Austrian Catholics, whilst the pious Austrian Catholics have a horror of Prussian godlessness and denial of everything sacred. Any one who travels in the Tyrol and goes to church on Sundays will hear something of this. This division in opinion gives a sharper character to the struggles for political power between North and South, and thoughtful people are apt to ask themselves what spiritual and religious consequences a closer union may have for both parties.

． ． ． ． ． ．

This type of question is not new. In the middle of last century, when the "Greater Germany" party separated from the "Lesser Germany" party, the factor of creed, whether expressed or unexpressed, had its share in the matter. And von Treitschke, Bismarck's historian of the new German Empire, traced an almost direct connection between Wittenberg and Berlin, between Luther and Bismarck, when he wrote his account of the previous history of the founding of the Empire. Luther introduced German Christianity and this led by way of the great Elector Friedrich II., Kant and Hegel, to the German Empire. To us, who have grown up with this point of view, it seems so evident that we find it difficult to realise how strange it must appear to the Catholics even in the German Empire. No doubt there is in fact much truth in it, for the devotion to the State which characterised the Prussians was of no Catholic growth; but this way of putting it is inadequate as a complete explanation of the German Empire. The Empire is by no means merely the outcome of the Königsberg influence of Kant, and moreover it is only in a strictly limited sense that King Friedrich II. can be regarded as a Protestant Christian. But, above all, this purely Protestant presentation of history, whether it be true or not, cannot be persisted in as a primary Imperial tradition since all parties have given up the *Kulturkampf* and it must not and will not be reawakened. When Bismarck's Empire made its peace with the Pope and the Party of the Centre, the Protestant character of the Hohenzollern

Emperors became an unofficial private affair of those who, as wearers of the crown, were above creeds. From that time onwards the German Empire, as such, has had no special creed, and it can have none after the union.

Thus whilst at one time the Prussia of Friedrich the Great was honoured as the "leading Protestant Power," Austria was regarded as the political embodiment of the Papacy and the Jesuit Order. In contrast to the freethinker Friedrich II., his great opponent Maria Theresa, splendid in her austere and harsh devotion to the Church, appears as the founder of a State Church system which has not yet entirely disappeared, and under which the Protestant minority in Austria, whether German or Slav, has much to endure. But this point of view too, however correct as a whole, certainly admits of exaggeration, for this same Maria Theresa sent Protestant colonists, both Lutherans and Calvinists, to Galicia and elsewhere, and was more gracious to them than many later sovereigns.

But the essential thing is that in a partnership between Germany and Austria-Hungary the German, and with them the Hungarian, Protestants would be in the minority. This weighs heavily upon the minds of some Protestants, however well they appreciate the historical and political necessity for the union. They argue somewhat in this way: "Of course the union, will not directly change anything in the existing position of the religious creeds; nor is it likely that provincial administrations which have hitherto been Protestant would be induced thereby to adopt another religious policy, but the closer the Central European union became in course of time, the greater would be the danger for us Protestants of becoming, so to speak, historically unrepresented. For a papal party might easily be formed which would engross the whole of Mid-Europe and would secure religious privileges in different States in exchange for international or commercial activities, and which would give Germans a Catholic instead of a Protestant character in the eyes of foreigners." People are even heard to say that in the united Empire the Protestants would be treated somewhat as they now are in Bavaria, that is, not injured but pushed aside.

I too acknowledge that my historical mode of thought leaves me in some anxiety in this respect, and all the more because the war has greatly weakened the bond between Protestant England and Germany, and we cannot tell whether or no fellow-feeling between the German, English and American Protestants will be quickly revived. It is true that no organisation has been broken up in this connection, since none existed, but any one who knows Protestantism is aware how little it depends upon its organisations and how much upon informal fellow-feeling. Protestantism is weak as a Church, but strong as a union of convictions. Protestants recognise each other as such all over the world, but — will they so recognise one another again during the next decades? The war injures us Protestants more than the Catholics, for the papal centre, in spite of its geographical position in Italy, has remained outside the war owing to the behaviour of the present Pope. Amongst us, Protestant neutrals do indeed try to preserve the Protestant community, but they are not sufficiently powerful since they themselves formerly derived most of their spiritual guidance from Germany and England. Hence, when we are concerned about the future of Protestantism as a whole and its missionary work in foreign parts, it is no very simple matter to be obliged at the same time to enter upon an intimate and indissoluble union with a Power which is Catholic both in theory and practice. We are forced to it by all the independent reasons that have been adduced, but we may be allowed to state frankly that it involves for us a definite sacrifice from the religious point of view. Others will have different sacrifices to make, as is unavoidable in concluding an alliance.

. . . .

The considerations which make it difficult in some degree for us as Protestants to set our faces towards Mid-Europe will in the same degree render the transition easier for the Catholics. But here, too, things are less simple than may appear from a merely statistical point of view. The Central European Catholics are far from forming a completely united body. They are united before the papal chair, but not always with one another. It is much easier to combine the Protestant minorities in Austria and Hungary with us than to mould the Catholics of the German Empire into a unity with the Austro-Hungarian Catholics of every tongue. To mention one important point, the Catholic clergy in Hungary have been an independent body since ancient times and are not political in the same sense as the Viennese Christian Socialists or the Cologne and Berlin leaders of the Centre. In Hungary the almost Calvinistic Protestantism of many leading families is actually of much more importance than appears from statistics alone. Moreover the strong Jewish element among the educated classes helps to safeguard the Hungarian kingdom from religious parties. Certain attempts have been made at a clerical policy but with little result. In the Polish districts of Austria, however, the Catholic clergy, like those in Prussian Poland, are Polish Nationalists rather than universal Catholics or political Central Europeans, and go their own way. The same thing is notoriously true of Croatian, and especially of Southern Slav Catholicism, and indeed of the Tzechs as well. They are certainly not all adjusted at present to any notion of a Central European Great Power, and it will be a good time before they are. Besides the German Centre has passed through a lengthy schooling, from which it has learnt that excess in one case leads to opposition in others. This is perhaps not always noticeable in the campaign speeches made by either party, but it is quite evident in parliamentary tactics. And we must not forget that there are no small number of Catholics in Austria and Hungary who trouble themselves very little about their Catholicism!

It must, of course, be understood from the outset, that indeed neither side could conceive of anything else, that Church and school questions will never, and must never, become the concern of the Central European union. Any possible influence on religious creeds arising out of the union can only be quite indirect, and will, as we hope, be balanced by the increasing political fellow-feeling amongst the united nations. The more Mid-Europe takes shape, the further we recede from the age of religious wars and the nearer we approach to the toleration which wishes to live, and to let others live, in freedom from political coercion in those very matters which are the highest and the most sacred.

I hear that some people cherish the idea that the political union may be used in order to revive old and futile hopes of religious agreement. This is well intentioned but dangerous. Peace is most lasting in this sphere when it is not too much talked about. And truly we have plenty of other things to do at present!

. . . . . .

At this point, between our discussion of creeds and that of nationalities, we must say something about the Central European Jews. In the German Empire they are regarded as a religious sect and lay stress upon their German nationality. In the Danubian Monarchy the matter is much more complicated, for here there are not only German Jews, but also Polish, Tzechish and Hungarian Jews, and they often take their place as a separate people in the mixture of nationalities, and do not first combine with any of the existing race-groups. If a Jew from Galicia emigrates to Vienna, that does not always mean that he becomes German. Moreover, the Jews in the eastern districts in Austria and in parts of Hungary live much more closely together, and in a more tribal manner; they are like a special caste with their own customs, occupations and language, and do not combine at all with the rest of the mixed population. In the long register of Austrian political parties the "Jewish Club" even figures as a small party group, whilst of course Jews appear in addition in almost all the other parties. There are quite a number of fair-sized towns in which the Jews number more than 50 per cent. of the population, and thus have direct control of the administration. We give the following places as examples: Rzeszow, Rawaruska, Brody, Zloczow, Tarnopol, Rohatyn, Stanislau, Kolomea (all in Galicia), and Munkacs in Hungary. The stability and influence of the Jews in the capital towns Vienna, Prague and Cracow are, as in Amsterdam and Frankfurt-on-Main, much greater than in

Berlin and Breslau. In Budapest the proportions existing in Warsaw, Odessa and Lodz are almost reached. Hence it would be a serious mistake to leave the Jews out of account in making schemes for Mid-Europe. They are there, and have great influence on newspapers, on economic life and on politics. On the whole we may assume that in the west they can be won over to support the extension of the economic area by the creation of a Central European economic unity. Of the views of the Jews in Galicia I can form no opinion of my own, especially now when, like all the inhabitants of Galicia, they have had to endure the harsh and perplexing influence of this terrible war.

It is conceivable that the high percentage of Jews in the Danubian Monarchy may be advanced by the Anti-Semitic party in the German Empire as an argument against the foundation of Mid-Europe; conceivable but not certain, for the same party are wont to be very good friends with the Germans in Austria, who are in part inclined to Anti-Semitism, and would willingly work with them. But their anti-semitic efforts would probably have no political result, especially since the Jewish soldiers, both in the German and in the Austrian and Hungarian armies, have done their duty during the war like every one else, and like others have in many cases ratified their citizenship by death. After the war there must be an end to every form of mutual irritation, for the trenches jointly held will lie in the background. These will be worth as much politically as baptism.

· · · · · ·

And thus we have arrived at the problems of nationality themselves. The Jewish question is more of a social than a national question in the stricter sense of the word, for nowhere in Central Europe do the Jews as such wish to appear as forming a State. The Zionist party may understand Judaism as a whole as constituting a political power within international politics, and may seek in Palestine for a centre for combined Jewish influence, but all the same this only affects very indirectly the internal situation of the Great Central European States. We can and will take these international phenomena into account in our political calculations when we are considering the Turkish Orient, and perhaps also when we remember the western districts of Russia. But there are no questions of Jewish language, Government and party on a grand scale, either in the German Empire or in Austria-Hungary. It is all local and highly provincial. All that the Jew here demands, and with justice, is recognition as a citizen, nothing more! It is his affair in which national group he seeks this recognition. But sections of nations which have in their neighbourhood greater political State entities of their own race, or which compare in memory a brilliant political past with a dismal present, will not be satisfied with this more passive citizenship. They aspire to union as a State, and even assured advantageous material conditions are no adequate compensation to them for an historical independence which has either been lost or never attained.

All the great European States, and even some of the small States, have to struggle with national difficulties of this kind. They have been overcome most completely in the Latin countries of Italy, Spain and France, because here the old language of the rulers has so far supplanted the remnants of the popular tongue that the latter only survives in provincial dialects, and is inadequate to any effective organisation. It is different with the Irish in Great Britain and with the Flemish in Belgium. But the headquarters of the racial problems is situated where Central Europe passes over into the broad Russian plains, on the Baltic, on the Vistula, in the Carpathians, and on the Danube as far as the Golden Horn of Constantinople. And the centre of all these problems at the present time is the Austro-Hungarian Monarchy, the "country of nations."

We Germans of the Empire have less to do with these troubles, and consequently amongst us there is generally very little genuine understanding of them, and little desire to go into them seriously and systematically. We have, or had hitherto, our boundary difficulties in Alsace-Lorraine and on the Danish borders, but here there was only a small minority in question, so that people thought that matters could be arranged by administrative methods, and regarded the resistance that showed itself as an unjustifiable opposition. In these two places a great deal that was mean and of which we are ashamed has been done in the name of Germanism, but the German people as a whole have troubled themselves little about the matter. They have hardly noticed the varying experiments on the live bodies of these small groups, and have considered the authorities concerned well able to decide what would make for national safety. Now, during the war, many are beginning to form their own opinions, but they often start with the most elementary scheme — forcible Germanisation — knowing very little of the many gloomy experiences which have already resulted from this method all over the world, a method still possible in Russia but already become impracticable in the Vosges and Jutland. Suppose, for example, that people were forbidden to speak French in the square at Colmar, such a decree, even in war time, would be simply impracticable, even ludicrous in its ineffectiveness. To win over a foreign-speaking section of the population to be citizens of a national State with a different language is too complicated a matter to be successfully settled by some prohibitions and the removal of a few leaders. During the war rapid military measures may often be unavoidable, but if we intend, when peace comes, to make any change in the constitution of the Reichsland or to incorporate it in the Empire, we shall have to make a fresh start in the search for a proper method of treating the population. And we must make up our minds to learn from Austria in this matter. For we may state frankly that, however imperfect are the results of the method of handling nationalities in Austria and Hungary, there is, nevertheless, much more real understanding there of this type of problem than with us, where it is only dealt with incidentally and unwillingly. There are so many departments in which the Austrians can learn from us that we need not be afraid to admit cheerfully their wider experience in the various matters in which it really exists.

The same is true in a greater degree of the Polish policy of the German Empire and especially of Prussia. Prussia took possession of the Poles before it was itself a national German State, and had then no idea of wishing to Germanise this piece of country. It was only later on in Napoleon's time that the national impulse on both sides rose high. Then in 1830 the Prussian Poles were stirred by the surging wave of the great but futile Polish revolution, the spirit of the dead awoke amongst them and tried spasmodically to re-establish a State organism which had been ruined by its own weakness and incapacity. Now Prussia recognised in Poland a national opponent, without being able on this account to release it from the political tie, because our entire Eastern frontier becomes an impossibility if a new and politically independent Polish Kingdom intersects our difficult line of defence. Prussia took compulsion in one hand and material prosperity in the other and demanded mental adhesion in exchange. She brought about much material good but discovered no way to the heart of the Polish people. Only a few of the high nobility sought to further the transition to a Prussian State, and they had naturally always been international and connected with Germany through marriage. The small group of Protestant Poles, too, was at heart royalist and Prussian, and remained so for a long time because they had need of religious support, but the mass of Catholic Poles was and is Polish Nationalist. Even in so far as they no longer believe in the establishment of a Polish State in Prussian territory and enjoy material prosperity in Prussia, a division yet remains: they are a different race. The German schools have made them useful and industrially capable bilinguists, but not Germans. A Pole remains a Pole, very often even when he goes to live in Berlin or Westphalia. Even as a travelling workman he retains his national character and dreams of other things than the German inspectors who allot him his work. It is not only, and certainly not primarily, the opposition between the servant class and gentlefolk. This plays a part too in many cases, but it can be seen how unwillingly the Polish miner lets himself be enrolled in a German Social Democratic union. Even as a Social Democrat he must remain a Pole, and insists upon his own industrial unions.

That in spite of all this the Prussian Poles, almost without exception, have done and are doing their duty in the present war, need surprise no one who has not previously believed the talk of the over-zealous opponents of Poland. The magnetic and material force of any State which rouses itself up to war is so enormous that no section can evade it. Think of the many Germans who are unfortunately fighting over there in the Russian army! They have not all been compelled. Like them the Russian Pole marched with the Russians, the Prussian Pole with the Germans, the Galician Pole with the Austrians. Since he could not fight for the vanished Fatherland of his dreams, he placed himself at the service of the Power to which he belongs. And if he dies, he dies for a Fatherland, from which he asks consideration for his brothers. In this case too there must be a great review of all methods after the war, a liberation from enforced Germanisation, and the adoption of a better interior organisation. But this in itself brings us Germans nearer to the racial problems in Austria and Hungary. We must begin to learn to understand them, we must indeed.

. . . . . .

It makes a great difference whether we approach the racial problems in the Southern Dual Monarchy merely as Germans or as German Mid-Europeans. We neither ask for nor promise any sort of colourless detachment, for this is from its nature unprofitable in such questions of political life, because it supposes it possible to classify the souls of nations in divisions which can be forced upon them from outside. We want to think out this business as Germans, but not as trivial-minded people who think only of themselves and their immediate interests, rather as members of the greatest and most weighty nation in Central Europe. From the oppressed individual German, who, surrounded by Slavs or Magyars, inconvenienced in his business by Poles or Roumanians, continually outvoted by Tzechs or Slovenians, can find no German school for his children, can get no attention paid to his needs by the district superintendent, and can have no German recorder in the law courts — from this helpless and repressed German peasant or workman who daily considers whether or no he must not sadly forsake the home of his fathers, we certainly do not expect a philosophical detachment from facts, or much fellow-feeling in an over-burdened heart for the similar troubles of all the other detached fragments of nationalities. He fights for himself and his own affairs, and when he talks to us his speech is full of bitterness and anger. In his abandonment he suffers for his nationality. He cannot busy himself with politics in company with the Tzechs, Magyars or Roumanians, for he has fallen under the wheels, and for the time only obstinacy and a tough skin will help him. But this man is not typical of the German spirit in general, he merely stands at his post as the representative of an oppressed small nation. As such he may and must talk as he does, but we feel it painful when Germans who are not in the same position adopt the same tone. This happens daily, it is true, with other nationalities, but all the same it is ungenerous. When a German representative of a big industry spoke to me in a similar way, I left him in no doubt that I was much troubled by his tone. People have no business to play the sufferer when they are not suffering! We Germans of the Empire want as far as possible to help all our oppressed brothers in Central Europe, but we avoid pleading merely German claims in every isolated language group and in opposition to every fusion up to the bitter end. Such a course, were it adopted by every one, would be the ruin of the partnership between the two Central European States. The Germans who are living over there in Austria or Hungary in isolation or as injured persons are absolutely certain of our sympathy and protection, but even they should, if possible, ponder the fact that reciprocal justice elevates a people and that the other nations too wish to live with us.

The Germans in Austria have lost much during the last century. From the eighteenth century onwards they were a nation maintaining and controlling the State; to-day, in the Danubian Monarchy, they have become one people amongst many peoples. Their important services in the past are not valued, the pains they took to raise up the small nations are not remembered. Many hundred years ago they were called in by foreign kings and bishops in order to increase industrial ability and improve agriculture. When fresh districts were to be civilised emigrants from the Eifel or Swabia or Thuringia or some other thickly populated part were tempted by all kinds of privileges and promises. They came, and were *hospites,* guests, and benefited themselves and the country which coveted their services. In this way they were intentionally scattered everywhere between the Alps and the Carpathians like the salt of the earth, and did their duty as citizens faithfully and honestly. They made roads on which others now travel, they planned schools in which the teaching is now directed against them. And, moreover, they have the feeling that they have not been overcome by any great opponent strong in himself, but that they have often been subjected to the petty makeshifts of the crowd, in defiance of those who are yet not in a position to reinstate them. This often makes their tone gloomy and bitter, which is very natural but is not favourable to future political success. Many groups of people in the German Empire have ceased to take interest in the Austrian question because they find it hard to tolerate this woeful, complaining sort of tone. In this matter, however, both sides are wrong, for the Imperial German concerned has for the most part no idea what have been the inmost thoughts of the Austrian German and of his father. He does not at all understand the older generation in the Danubian Monarchy, and in the younger he still sees no evidence of its other and more vigorous desires and of its more complete and conscious adaptation to the world as it now is.

Richard Charmatz in his pamphlet *Osterreich-Ungarns Erwachen* (pamphlets edited by Dr. Ernst Jäckh, Deutsche Verlagsanstalt, Stuttgart), remarked of the younger generation of Germans: "They are learning to think more as Austrians in the modern sense than their predecessors, without on this account being less German." This seems to us to go to the root of the matter. To think as Austrians means for them: to begin to think as Mid-Europeans. No German living in Austria will be spared this revolution in thought, nor indeed will the members of nations speaking other tongues. Other valuable points of view are to be found in the books by Springer and Popovici referred to in the bibliography. The former discusses the question as an Austrian Social Democrat, the latter as a Roumanian Austrian Imperialist.

. . . . . .

What lingers in the hearts of many of our German brothers in Austria and Hungary is the old position of affairs when the State was the property of the House of Hapsburg and an administrative district of the German Civil Service. These old days in Austria possessed their own distinctive character, rather formal, but very respectable and understandable. The German Ostmark was historically the centre of the Monarchy. With it as starting-point Bohemia was linked up, the Adriatic provinces were occupied, Hungary was set free and Galicia was annexed. The entire State was an enlarged outwork of the German nucleus. It was an administrative State which afforded to the nations linked up with it the advantages of German organisation; a police State which attempted to take charge of every one whilst regarding them all as subjects. Nowhere has the absolute State, carrying on the business of government reasonably and possessing neither nationality nor sentiment, ever existed so completely as in the old Austrian Empire. Such was the State of Maria Theresa and also of her son Joseph II., with his very different outlook.

Metternich wanted to maintain this ancient Austrian State artificially in the midst of a world grown nationalist. It possessed style and a distinctive character, but a character that of course, like everything earthly, had its limitations. But before we speak of the cause which destroyed this distinctive State we must get a grasp of its special merits, for it will only be banished finally if it has first been properly valued. This State was less military than Prussia, less purely an administrative machine than the Electorate of Saxony, less patriarchal than old Bavaria; it was in its way a civilising influence, and considering its circumstances, modern in spirit. From the military point of view it has to its credit the long and by no means easy campaigns against the Turks. It played the Great Power in Italy and Flanders, combined much vigour with comparatively few irritating qualities, and proved what a united, disciplined and well-graded civil service could accomplish in the hands of an able hereditary monarchy. This old State stood the test of Napoleonic times better than Prussia, which was more designed to achieve rapid success. It showed a surprising tenacity in the defence of its hard-won gains and is in its way a product of history which may fairly be called vigorous, efficient and imposing. The Dual Monarchy lives even to-day on this admirable, homely old Austrian State, just as the French Republic lives on what it has inherited from its monarchy. The old German-Austrian officials live there as though the ancient State still existed. It has indeed narrowed its boundaries at various times, has given up foreign provinces, such as, in particular, Italy. But its tradition is not destroyed, was not even destroyed in 1848 when all foundations were shaken, and that not only by the attacks of non-Germans but by the wrath of German farmers and townsfolk. For the old Austrian State was a German official State but in no sense a German national State. The German element in it sat in official rooms. It was as little affected by the German national movement and democracy as by any other national popular movement. It represented the old order of things in its essence. But for this very reason it was the object of revolutionary attacks from all sides alike, even from the German.

·   ·   ·   ·   ·

Metternich is principally known to us as the opponent of the progressive spirit of his time. He was in his way a Central European, but of an old stamp: cavalier, statesman, regent with no trace of democratic or national sentiment. From the Danube to the mouth of the Elbe he obstructed that new spirit to which Friedrich Wilhelm II. of Prussia reluctantly submitted himself in the wars of liberation, for he knew, or believed, that his State, the ancient Austrian State, would be broken if the national ideal triumphed. Hence the revolution in 1848 was directed against him and his system, and it affected him and his Emperor much more seriously than the rulers of, say, Prussia or Bavaria, for the Austria of that time was anti-democratic in essence.

But in what consisted the old German Democracy in 1848?

CREEDS AND NATIONALITIES

It was and is a government by the governed, logically thought out, at that time upheld by aspiring townsfolk and small farmers, later adopted by the working classes who were pressing up after them. The authority thus aspired to, of those who had hitherto been the governed, rests theoretically upon the assumption that the masses are capable of governing by elected representatives and parliamentary majorities. Against this assumption objections were and are raised, based on the nature of the masses themselves, on the technique of parliamentary business, and above all on the incompatibility of a heterogeneous population within a democratic parliamentary system. This latter was the special Austrian problem. All the other democratic difficulties were experienced in the purely national States too, and were for the most part overcome, but ancient Austria supplies the pattern instance in the world's history of the doubly complicated case of a polyglot parliamentary democracy split up along national lines; and the Emperor Franz Joseph I. has lived through this experiment in the position of leader from 1848 until now.

Democracy hands over to the population through the franchise a share in the sovereignty, under the assumption that it will understand how to form majorities capable of governing. This is in itself no easy matter for a people who have hitherto been unorganised subjects. In partially undeveloped countries they often get the franchise without knowing what to do with it. They send up to Parliament delegates without cohesion, local celebrities, orators and respected citizens, and are surprised if the Government manages this jumble of persons as it pleases. As long as a democratic representative assembly is undisciplined and without a majority, it strengthens in the main the bureaucracy, because it frees the latter from the constraint of voting taxes without itself being able to take over the conduct of affairs. This was the unexpected experience of almost all constitutional Governments after 1848, but most of all that of the Austrian Government. In spite of the altered constitution everything remained at bottom as of old, allowing for a little more effort on the part of the Government. And it would have so remained throughout the Danubian Monarchy if in one place, viz. in Hungary, a disciplined, self-contained organisation had not appeared upon the scene. The Hungarian Revolution of 1848–49 was the first occasion on which this episode of a popular rising reached the dignity of an historical event. For this revolution was more than the vague desire for government of polyglot democratic farmers and townsfolk, it was the armed rising of a national entity which was previously almost complete in itself. The Hungarian noble was a different kind of revolutionary from the Viennese artisan, for he did not merely wish to parade the streets, to protest and to bargain a little with those in authority. He wanted to rule himself, and he knew what that meant. The really serious nationality problem only arose with the Hungarian Revolution.

. . . . . .

But before we discuss the Hungarians and their influence upon all the other non-German elements, we must make some further remarks about democracy and nationalism.

Democracy, as we have already said, is the admittance of the previously governed to a share in the government. This is a lengthy process, for the man who has been nothing but mediæval serf, labourer and subject has in general no desire to govern. He must first, in the course of generations, be raised out of his torpor and enlightened before he can even conceive of becoming himself a factor in political government. This enlightenment was the work of the eighteenth century, and even princes and aristocrats shared in it without foreseeing the results of their benevolent efforts to educate the people. Without desiring it people were transforming illiterates into future revolutionists within the despotic State itself. When the old society sent some crumbs of its knowledge into the servants' hall, it was undermining itself. This had been freely done in the most innocent manner in the benevolent Austria of pre-Napoleonic times.

The people of the eighteenth and indeed also of the nineteenth centuries accepted the education offered to them from above slowly and suspiciously, because they were not accustomed to receive benefits without reservation, and because they themselves had no pre-

CREEDS AND NATIONALITIES 93

sentiment about what was given them. They could not know what sort of strength was asleep within them. The period of government by the nobility or by the cloister had lasted so long that the far-distant times of ancient general freedom and of untamed racial migrations were wholly forgotten and lost. For when before have the common people been told their own history? They saw that there were lords over them and noticed that the ruling classes used two languages, one for their European intercourse, whether knightly or priestly, and one for the people. This second language now became the subject of popular education. The stammer of the wage-earner's cottage became a written language by the help of popular education and the national school; the dialect of conquered races and the figures of their lost rulers became subjects of instruction. Out of the mouths of babes and sucklings was made ready the power, a trembling power at first, of a newly arising nationality. The national lower classes gained ground below the international upper classes, and their instinct carried them so far that the dwellers in the castles often concealed their knowledge of Latin, French or German in order to become the popular leaders of these formerly speechless masses. Old German or Italian aristocratic families began to speak Tzechish or Slovenian, not always indeed, but when they were in the country. The once despised language of the crowd became a subject of pride, a ground for obstinacy. Often the national language lived on and raised itself by means of religious contests. Tzechish was spread abroad in early days by Johann Hus and his followers. The Hungarians in castle and cottage developed a passion for Magyar when they professed Calvinism in that language. Religious movements possess everywhere the greatest democratic and national influence. Even the Catholicism of the Counter-Reformation had such an influence, when the nobility were Protestant and the lower classes Catholic. The Tyrolese and the Steiermarker people became German Catholics when, with the help of their priests, they drove out their Protestant lords. Many ruined castles bear witness to these happenings. In this way nations developed from below upwards, their individual souls, their special God, their Mother Mary or their Catechism. The deeper the faith penetrates among the masses the more provincial it becomes. The Polish heaven differs from the Roumanian heaven, and the Queen above the stars looks differently on the Vistula and on the Isonzo. These are no distinctions of creed in the theological sense, but national growths. And the spiritual beginnings are often translated with surprising rapidity into the material. National poets arise and old songs are written out. National dress, which is often only a remnant of an old discarded upper-class culture, is held in specal honour as inherited. Romanticism beautifies and enlarges the homely legends and sanctifies the old peasant style of architecture, discovering wonderful secrets in it and in the ancestral food, animals and flowers. In such a time of awakening, as in spring-time, even shabby peoples are beautiful. It is the awakening of the masses to humanity, the first steps of national democracy.

This process of development took a somewhat different course in each of the hitherto neglected and oppressed nationalities. But any one who is not familiar with it cannot understand whence comes the wonderful vitality and passion in the nations which are climbing up out of the depths. He judges coldly from a detached point of view and thinks it a political insanity that a people of this sort should regard itself as the centre of the universe. And this indeed is so if we will admit only the successful great nations as worthy of life. But every living entity and every nation desires, when the mass of its people awake, to have its own day, its sacred and sunny maytime, and strives after it so far as is in its power. This may be disturbing and absurd, but it is very human. Those who have to solve racial disputes must never forget this national spirit whose import Herder was the first among important thinkers to attempt to disclose. Herder, understanding the soul of the people, did not believe in the permanency of the Austrian State, a very natural attitude for him and for all who study race psychology without military statesmanship. Psychologically the ancient Austrian State is actually burst asunder by the birth of the national spirit, and what binds it together is the fact that it is impossible for military reasons for small sections of nations to maintain them-

CREEDS AND NATIONALITIES

selves in the world. The military State coerces the nationalities, the old Germano-Austrian administrative State binds together the untamed peoples' States of later growth.

. . . . . .

But since the Germans in North and South have each experienced a similar national awakening, they ought, properly speaking, to show understanding of all such popular agitations, even if they appear recalcitrant and antagonistic. The Germans too were overwhelmed by a Latin-French civilisation until they became genuine free Germans. But there is one very remarkable fact about the older stages of the nations, and I do not remark what follows in order to say something conclusive, but to indicate a question which is significant for the community feeling in Mid-Europe. Why did the Germans after a certain stage feel no more genuine sympathy for the agitators among the young nations following in their footsteps, and why did they themselves cease to exercise Germanising influence? The two questions are intimately connected. Only the striver can feel love and attachment for those who are beginning to strive. Whilst the Latin Franks (the French) were young they pressed forward their national boundaries almost up to the Rhine; whilst the non-Latin Teutons (Germans) were young they pressed forward their national boundaries far into the East, and by missions and the pressure of authority made distant lands practically German. But then their force of attraction ceased for no visible outward reason. Formerly numbers of Slavs or other foreign peoples had emigrated into Germany (Brandenburg, Lausitz, Silesia, Pommerania, Prussia), but then they were all at once faced by a wall. To-day they are still faced by the same wall. How admirable it would be for us to convert the Tzechs into Germans if it could be done! But it simply cannot be done. The time for it is past, both parties are too old for it. The Germans have long since lost the cheerful natural growth, the rough vigour, the childlikeness of their mediæval Germanising spirit, and the Tzechs have long since grown less impressionable than were the Sorbs, Wends and Liutitzen, or whatever else they may have been called. To overlook these changes brought by time is the tragic error of the present Pan-German party. They wish to accomplish by school and law what they are now powerless to do imaginatively and without set purpose.

It is by no means unimportant to point out in this connection that the modern Germans almost everywhere in the world are unfortunately bad Germanisers. In my opinion this is a result of our best qualities. We are thinkers, men of understanding, engineers, organisers, successful prosaic people, perfect apparatus, invaluable voluntary parts of a machine, but just on this account strange to the children of nature and to average nations. This indeed applies in a much greater degree to the Germans of the Empire than to the German Austrians. The same ability which opens the markets of the world to us and makes our armies victorious, closes to us the hearts of those who are climbing up out of the mist. Hence, in distant parts of the earth too, we only make passably good colonists. We are, if the comparison will not offend, sometimes in the position of a privy councillor trying to manage his horse; his groom can do this much better. In other words: those Old Austrian officials who were confronted with the new national movements had all the advantages of advanced political civilisation, but lacked the innate feeling for formless creative strength. They were privy councillors with all the attendant excellences and deficiencies. Thus it came about that in 1848 an unheard-of shock burst upon that well-governed Austria, which then included Hungary: the peoples, the nations moved according to their own inspiration and not in the prescribed forms. Mutterings were heard below, at the foundations of the State: the molecules were astir in the ancient stones of the monarchy.

.   .   .   .   .   .

The Magyars were the chief nation that revolted in ancient Austria. They extorted political separation, not at once, indeed, in the year of revolution, but later in 1866. They became a State, a second ruling nation alongside of the Germans. Here we are not concerned to discuss the details of their alienation from the Hapsburg dynasty, an alienation which may be traced back to the pre-Turkish period. We are only anxious that we Imperial Ger-

CREEDS AND NATIONALITIES

mans should grasp the extraordinarily powerful and undisputed part that they play within the monarchy to which we are allied. I have, indeed, often pondered over this remarkable people, neither Slavonic nor German, which dwells in our midst and is even now helping to decide the fate of Germany. They are unlike other nations, not so high strung as the Western peoples, not such deep thinkers as the Germans, not dreamy and inactive as are often the Slavs, not mediævally chivalrous like the Turks, but a wonderful modern nation, based on an ancient racial migration, self-assertive, efficient, proud, masterful, political, above all tenacious in their nationalism. To whom shall I compare such a nation? In their fate and in their character they have something in common with the Spaniards, however far removed from them they may be in race. The Spaniards and the Magyars, in West and East, are the first nations who freed themselves from Mohammedan control. They were not in subjection so long or so completely as the nations in the Balkans or Morocco, but sufficiently long to have to bear the yoke of foreign rule. They did not only, like we Germans, experience some years of Napoleonism, but incomparably more. Their whole national existence was at stake during the Turkish period, and noble, priest and people grew up cramped in the school of servitude. But the Turkish suzerainty, on the other hand, was so far an outside influence that they remained a nation. The Turks, as we have already noted, had no idea of converting them to Mohammedanism. Subdued but not broken in spirit and well trained to arms, they awaited a change in the situation, and when the Austrians, after an heroic struggle, completely freed them from Turkish control, they were very far from blending with the nation of their liberators out of sheer gratitude. The Hungarians had as little desire to be Austrian as the Roumanians, to-day, have to be Russian. But the Austrians came as conquerors opposed to Turkey, and were scarcely more liberators as such than were later the Russians. They sent German officials into the districts that had been freed of Turks, and expected the Magyars to behave like some little Slav people that had been set free. But this expectation could not be realised. The negotiations were protracted from decade to decade, the elective Kingdom of Hungary became an inheritance of the Hapsburg dynasty, out of opposition came compromises. But at last the Magyars lost patience, and made use of the West European democratic revolution of 1848 as an opportunity for their own differently constituted national revolution, which was so fiery that the Austrians could only put it down with the help of Russian troops. In this revolution the national Government of the Magyars was, in the first instance, ruined for the second time, but only in order to reassert itself with renewed vigour so soon as the monarchy was in danger and needed the Magyars. The Battle of Königgrätz was a victory for both Prussian and Magyar, although the latter did not appear as a combatant. The Saxon Minister Beust was summoned to Vienna and, with the aid of the Empress Elizabeth and the co-operation of Deak and Andrassy, this clever non-Austrian formulated the Austro-Hungarian Dualism. This put an end to the old centralised Austria, and from Budapest started the Dual Monarchy and the present State with its reorganised distinct nationalities.

.   .   .   .   .   .

But while in 1867, the year of the *Ausgleich,* the Austrians were not obliged forthwith to regulate anew all their traditions of nationality policy, the Magyars in Hungary had to settle the basis of their future relations to their own small nationalities. Here then, for the first time, the principles of racial policy had to be worked out by a nation which had hitherto been itself under the yoke of a foreign people. What success did they have?

The Hungarian Nationality Law of 1868 is essentially a language law. It is published in the collections of statutes, but its main provisions are also printed in that instructive work, *Geschichte der Deutschen in Ungarn,* by R. F. Kaindel (Gotha, 1912). Every inhabitant of Hungary is entitled to draw up memorials to the Central Government in Budapest in his mother tongue, and the Government is obliged in its reply to use both Magyar and the language in which the memorial was written. Laws are to be issued in Magyar, but translated into all the languages used in the country. In the counties the records may also be kept in a non-Magyar language if this is demanded by a fifth of the members. In the county assemblies every one may use his own language unconditionally. Private persons and communes may write to their county authority in their own language. The representative councils in the communes choose for themselves the language for official use and for their records. In the law courts every one may use his mother tongue provided this is authorised for use in the records. Nationality cannot be counted as an obstacle to appointment to an office or to the conferment of an honour. The Minister of Education has the duty of deciding the language used for instruction in the Government institutions, but he is bound to see that, in respect of primary and intermediate schools, each racial group of people living together in considerable numbers is provided with educational institutions using its own tongue. The language employed in private institutions and by societies is determined by the founder.

This law of 1868 is well planned, a great project for a contentious period, but it was much limited by later additions and became more and more adapted to the insistence upon a Magyar official language. In 1879 instruction in the Magyar language was made compulsory in the primary schools. Any teacher may be dismissed whose scholars are not proficient in speaking and writing the Magyar language at the end of four years! A law of 1883 insisted on the study of the Magyar language in the intermediate schools to such an extent that instruction in other departments was bound to suffer. The candidates for teachers' posts must do their examinations in Magyar. That hinders even the German head teachers from visiting German universities.

In respect to the law courts, too, the original law suffered from a retrograde movement. The President of the Court may decide on the exclusive use of the Magyar language. The jury are obliged to be proficient in Magyar.

The conversion of place and personal names into Magyar is officially insisted upon.

And the provisions introduced by law and regulation in opposition to the spirit of the original law were still further emphasised by everyday practice. Although "for all citizens living together in considerable numbers, of whatever nationality," intermediate schools must be provided near the district where they live, yet we read in the official report for 1911, that altogether 4102 Government educational institutions (kindergartens, primary schools, intermediate schools and gymnasia) use Magyar as the language of instruction. Of the 3299 educational institutions which are maintained by the individual political communes, 3028 use the Magyar language exclusively. Although, under conditions therein stated, the original law allowed it to be decided by resolution that the commune records should be kept in a non-Magyar language, yet such resolutions when passed are most commonly annulled by the Government authorities. German books are forbidden, German newspapers were kept out by various tricks when there was an opportunity up to the very outbreak of war.

Thus it is evident that the matter is by no means settled by what is in itself a clear and good fundamental statute. This should be noted especially by those who believe that racial peace could be magically brought about to-morrow by a wisely thought out model law. Customs and administrative usages are at least as important as laws. But all over the world these are of slow growth and involve innumerable discussions.

·   ·   ·   ·   ·   ·

We shall try to put ourselves into the mental attitude of the ruling Magyars, which is indeed not so very difficult for us, since Germans, wherever they are in power, are inclined to think in quite the same way. To the Magyars, naturally, the racial complexity of their State is always present. They know that they themselves, counted by heads, number less than half and that with equal, free suffrage, and a fair partition into electoral districts, they could always be driven from power by a combination of the remaining elements. Hence the task to which they, whose national will to govern created the State, devote themselves, is on the one hand to guard against an equalising democracy, whether openly or secretly, and on the other to increase the number of Magyars.

CREEDS AND NATIONALITIES

The avoidance of democracy, which presumes a somewhat tortuous thought process in a nation which has obtained independence by revolution, is brought about by franchise devices, the partition into electoral districts and administrative mechanism, the morality of which we shall not here discuss, but only the facts. In Prussia, too, similar things did and do occur. But all such methods have only a limited duration, for all over the world the nations are approaching universal suffrage by way of the primary school and universal conscription. This is the more true in Hungary since there people know from experience that the ruling dynasty may any day place equal franchise rights upon its programme if it believes that the Magyar aristocracy are becoming too unmanageable. It may do this, and that is enough! Hence the Magyar control of the State is only secured if in the future there are more than 50 per cent. of Magyars. Therein lies the explanation of the violent zeal to Magyarise. And in fact Hungarian statistics report some tangible successes. Between 1900 and 1910 the percentage of those who gave Magyar as their mother tongue, or who could not prevent its being assigned to them, increased from 45.4 per cent. to 48.1 per cent., and the number of those who were generally proficient in the Magyar language increased from 52.9 per cent. to 57.4 per cent. If this is continued for a few more decades a safe majority will be created statistically, and later on also in reality. When this exists universal suffrage will be less terrifying. Accordingly — gain time and Magyarise!

This train of thought has much in its favour politically, and we should not really have done justice to our business of understanding if we were prepared to trace it all back to the egoism and to the material interests of the rulers. It is obviously indisputable that these play their part, but it is disputable that they are decisive. Even with us in Prussia there are not a few Conservatives who honestly believe that the State can only be maintained by them and with the aid of the three-class voting system, and it must be acknowledged that similar views are even more natural to the Magyar politician. He is generally well instructed in political law and foresees the doubtful consequences of a polyglot and unstable parliamentary system. As we have remarked above, a polyglot parliamentary system, incapable of stable majorities, strengthens the bureaucracy, which with some skill and a few recurrent favours always plays off the disputants one against the other. The Magyars see this going on before their eyes over in Austria, and under no circumstances will they tolerate it amongst themselves, for with them there would not even exist that bureaucratic tradition which in Austria has been influential from old days down to the present. Hungary is a young State which only since 1867 has had to devise for itself a system of government adapted to the old Austrian machinery, and which is still in a state of transition between the old county administration and a modern government by State officials. The parliamentary power of the two opposing Magyar parties does not upset this still developing machinery, since both Magyar groups have a share in it, but a direct victory of the united non-Magyars would doubtless overthrow it, and would result in a dictatorship from Vienna if not in worse disasters. Thus finally there is a struggle between parliamentary rule and the democratic principle of equality, the former being Magyar, whilst the latter is the concern of the small nations, the Roumanians, the Slovaks, the Slovenians and the Hungarian Germans.

. . . . . .

But in war time all forms of political wisdom are constrained to increase their knowledge. The various speeches of Graf Tisza, the Hungarian Minister-President, show how much he is occupied with the racial problem in the midst of the international struggle. For indeed the Hungarian system of government, whose actual foundation we have just attempted to describe from the Magyar point of view, excludes small nations inconsiderately and permanently from any share in the government, and consequently there remains amongst these same small nations a measure of uneasiness which is only too easily understood. This does not show itself during the war in the case of the Germans because the whole war is carried on in such close connection with Germany, but it appears amongst the Roumanians and Southern Slavs.

The three million Roumanians are certainly better off in a material sense in Hungary than they would have been in Roumania, for the Hungarian State, in spite of many defects in administration, is in a higher stage of development. But of course in Roumania they would have belonged to the ruling nation, and here they do not. It is the same with the Serbs, but not quite with the Croats, who are half independent in Hungary. But they, too, have in their hearts their own suppressed thoughts of domination, for they are all tempted by the impressive and dazzling example of the Magyars. As far as this is concerned it is of little use to represent to the small nations that each of them would be of very small importance in Roumania or Serbia, because though this is true enough it is no consolation. It must be frankly confessed that unsatisfied aspirations will persist both here and in all similar cases in the rest of Central Europe until the neighbouring small nations, which exercise a magnetic effect upon the fragments of their race in the great Empires, are brought alongside of us into a great free Central European union, and until in the great Empires stable and universally applicable nationality regulations are drawn up and actually enforced. But even if a Central European super-State and Central European racial toleration must one day exist, this would not on the other hand portend any complete sovereignty of the small nations. This is painful, but the teaching of universal history makes it inevitable: political small concerns require support. Hence unsatisfied national aspirations will remain, disillusionments which no Peace Congress or Minister-President can turn into joy. But nevertheless the State to which these sectional nations belong has every inducement not to drive them to sullen despair, or even to passive opposition. This is the lesson that must be learnt during the war. Indulgence, for the sake of preserving the State, in the things which can be granted without danger to the State! A more friendly way of regarding nationalist minorities is a pressing need everywhere, without exception, in Central Europe. This must be the very genuine inspiration of our Mid-European State federation if the latter is to be at all prosperous. There must be much more real, palpable liberalism even extending beyond the limits of language! This is essential if we are not to shed our blood in racial strife.

. . . .

The racial problem in Hungary differs greatly from the racial problem in "the kingdoms and lands represented in the Reichsrat," that is in the principal portion of the earlier single Empire of the Hapsburgs, which remained over after the separation of Hungary. Here the Hungarian example influenced especially the Tzechs, who possessed an ancient tradition of monarchy and would gladly, like the Hungarians, have formed themselves into an independent State whilst at the same time the Hapsburg dynasty was maintained. And they have for many years abstained from any share in the Austrian parliamentary system as a protest against the German Government in Austria, which denied them their Bohemian State rights. They are the inventors of that method of fighting which employs abstinence, obstruction and street rioting to interrupt public business until demands are satisfied, a method which in the disturbed times after the Baden Language Ordinance was occasionally borrowed by the Germans, and was also at times practised by the Ruthenians and Poles.

Although before and especially during the year 1848 the Bohemians of all shades of opinion had been amongst the most active in demanding parliamentary, provincial and State representation, they were the first to risk the Parliamentary system which they had acquired in order to obtain concessions of State rights from the Government. And the same Government which a few decades earlier would hear nothing of popular representation now showed a motherly concern to maintain the forms of the parliamentary system in order to demonstrate the unity of the State by means of the House of Representatives. Of all parliamentary histories none is richer than the Austrian in storms, fights over business procedure, ill-advised behaviour, and remarkable solutions or desperate complications, for nowhere in the world has the parliamentary system to cope with more difficult tasks. This was so under the old franchise system, when the voters were divided into curiæ, and things are not very different since the great franchise reform of 1907. Readers of our German newspapers generally hear only about the uproarious scenes and the defects in the parliamentary machine, and easily forget what worrying work has been carried on between the explosions. As a rule the Austrians of all languages, as a result of the endless debates, are much better trained in parliamentary fight than we need to be with our simpler conditions. To any one who wants to understand the details of this dispute we recommend as an introduction the second volume of Charmatz's *Österreichs innere Geschichte von* 1848–1907 (Teubner, Leipzig) and then the books already referred to by Springer and Popovici. But for our purpose here we can only treat quite generally of the nature of the influence of racial disputes upon the conduct of the Austrian States as a whole.

The subjects of dispute are almost the same as those already touched upon in discussing the Hungarian separation: official language, and that both for home and foreign affairs, language used in the law courts, conditions of the appointment of officials, national industrial policy, school and university questions. The question of military language was raised too, and with this the point was reached where the ruling house, controlling all alike, could not give way. All the other points in the end admit of discussion, but of course no statesman will find any binding formulæ which will exclude all uncertainty, especially in case of mutual ill-will. There have been endless discussions and deliberations about the matter, and there must indeed be many and prolonged further discussions after the war. The struggle seems repeatedly to endanger the cohesion of the State altogether, and often the Reichsrat in Vienna as well as the Landtag in Prague have only been able to make a show of carrying on their deliberations, and a complete official despotism has come to the rescue armed with the much-discussed Clause 14. The most serious needs of the State, such as especially the Austro-Hungarian financial *Ausgleich,* have not been definitely settled, because a business which from a distance people would be inclined to regard as a purely technical matter really involved the very determination to maintain the State at all. The parliamentary system which is a product of the democratic age has become unusable because it is handicapped by nationalism, the second result of democracy. The impulse of the nations to govern got possession of the machinery for popular representation and for the time thrust aside all other points of view, demanded a franchise and provincial boundaries only according to its own need, and destroyed the legends of the all-healing force of a normal democratic Government independent of race.

. . . . . .

The Germans in Austria, so long as Galicia is represented in the Reichsrat, are, it is true, the ancient ruling nation, but they make up hardly more than 35 per cent. of the population. Hence, with the existing political limits of Austria, they are quite unable to carry out any policy with regard to the Magyars, even if they wished to do so. But who can say whether or no they do wish it? They have had none of the schooling of oppression; on the contrary they have been the most faithful and much indulged servants of the reigning dynasty. Consequently they are lacking from the outset in strength of mind and determination, which are hardly to be found in them even in the height of combat. It is difficult for them to understand that they too must educate and force themselves on their side to become a national power in the country of nations, and no sooner is the political atmosphere bearable than they relapse into their gentle calm, charming but dangerous to themselves. Many of them are much more interested in the foreign politics of Austria-Hungary as a Great Power, and in its economic and social policy, than in the contest about whether the representative of the commune or the school superintendent in a Bohemian country town should be German or not. But what use was it? The problem was there and was forced upon them. Only in actual fight could they be roused up to resentment and passion, and hence, somewhat heartbroken, they slowly and inevitably become a nation like the others in the country of nations. But how, so they ask themselves in the midst of this enforced development, can and ought a State to subsist which is solely composed of nations, some of whom celebrate their festival of brotherhood in the East, others in the North, and yet others in the South? We recall the time when the spokesman of the Austrian Germans came to us of the Empire to talk of a day of revenge which should bring about the end of all political union with Slavs. It was about the year 1888 that I, as a young student in Leipzig, heard for the first time a threatening revolutionary speech of that kind from Prague students, which was later followed by many other such speeches by older men. We remember the days when Tzechs sent greetings to Russians in speeches savouring of the clang of swords, and went to Nancy to drink a wordy brotherhood with the French; when similar tokens of a friendship dangerous to the State were sent by the Austrian Italians to Italy and by the South Austrian Slavs to Serbia. All this actually happened. People spoke openly of Pan-Slavism, of Greater Serbia, of Greater Roumania, of the Italian Irredenta, of Pan-Germanism, and of every barely conceivable eccentric sort of alliance, whilst according to the judgment of a prominent scholar a commission was deliberating in Vienna whether or no Austria should continue to be a State at all. But even as we bring all this home to ourselves, the completed picture ends by bringing us comfort, for, in the midst of all this tension and national dismemberment, the Austrian State nevertheless maintained a progressive economic life, and a military power which now during the war is showing itself more clearly the longer the test goes on. All the national groups have declared at some time or other that the State must perish, but those condemned to death often live longest, and when foreign foes threaten the old distracted Austria with death, almost all these groups take fright and take down their weapons from the wall for Emperor and Fatherland!

This real unity might have manifested itself at the beginning of the war with quite a different fortune for the monarchy if the Austrian Government had had sufficient confidence to summon the House of Representatives to Vienna in the early days of August, 1914, as was done in Berlin and Budapest. The omission to summon Parliament throws more light than anything else on the position of affairs in the country of nations. The Parliament of these disputing peoples is, even at the outbreak of war, no simple and obviously essential expression of the will of the State. It has quarrelled so much in the past, it has been so difficult to foster the majority habit there! But this neglect at the beginning of the war, due to a really unnecessary feeling of anxiety, must be compensated for at the end, for at some time the National Assembly must at least take upon their shoulders the State finances. Things will be much more difficult indeed than they would have been in August, but the day when the Austrian House of Representatives assembles will show if and how the great joint war with its numberless bloody sacrifices has strengthened the feeling for the common State among the conflicting nations, so that they all again wish to be Austrian because there is and can be no longer anything else for them. After the war, we hope, the Pan-Slav dream will have vanished, the Italian boundary question will be somehow settled, Pan-German particularism will be transformed into a genuine feeling for the union of the two Central European Powers. It will be, indeed, necessary to balance accounts subsequently with the traitors, and some very difficult national differences will burst out as soon as the guns are silent; but this will pass, the peoples themselves and the State will remain. The wounds resulting from the war must somehow heal up. And then we wish to share the experience of these things without obtrusiveness but with the active co-operation of the German Empire.

. . . . . .

Whilst the different nationalities were thus passionately quarrelling, a remarkably powerful companion to the ancient Austrian bureaucracy, the rapidly growing Social Democracy, was growing up alongside of developing industry. The tactics of the Austrian Social Democracy are both interesting and instructive, and the more so since the party has been well managed and on a definite theory, and the records of its conferences afford important evidence of its development. We will attempt shortly to describe the process. The beginnings of the Austrian Social Democracy are of German origin. At one time it was hardly incorrect for a well-known German member of the party to say to me: " In Austria we Social Democrats are the most powerful Germanising influence." Withal it was tacitly supposed that the Tzechs, Poles, Ruthenians or even the Slovenians, gripped and awakened by the German agitation, would also, in a more distant future, be weaned from their accustomed purpose by the party leaders in Vienna. It was, indeed, properly an Imperial Social Democracy. Active against capitalism, agrarianism and bureaucracy, determined in all the demands of labour, it believed that the destructive influence of nationality might be overcome by an international programme. This, as we know, was not quite successful. As the foreign-speaking children grew up they broke loose. Now the party consists of national clubs with a very loose common superstructure; even the trade unions are involved in the separation of nationalities, and in the districts where racial disputes are hottest the national unions are already organised separately. Nationalism was stronger than proletarianism. This need not always be so, but it is the existing state of affairs.

The first dictum which the Austrian Social Democrats used to turn aside racial disputes runs thus: "That is a middle-class, capitalist affair, for it is at bottom nothing but a quarrel about political advantages and political burdens." Correctly thought out from the materialistic standpoint but not adequate in practice! It is actually true that in all disputes about nationality and language certain financial or business interests are fought for too. When, for instance, the Hungarian agrarians set up their national Government they did this not without regard to the land laws, the corn trade and the regulation of wages. When the German-Bohemian and the Tzechish manufacturers quarrelled over their respective influence on the Ministry, Government contracts were certainly not absent from their thoughts. When the German provinces protested against the Galician Poles, they were influenced in no small degree by the fact that under the rule of the Polish majority they, as the richer minority, had to pay for Polish canals and banks of credit in which they had not the least interest. All over the world political power signifies also economic interests and money. And when the Social Democrats called attention to this, they as proletarians had an indisputable and logical right to do so, only they overstretched their bow by often in the course of their agitation putting forward this solution as the only genuine explanation of the matter; and this reacted on themselves. The Moravian Slovaks and other comrades did not permanently believe what the party orators said: that it was all the same to them as workmen whether German or Slovak were the legal language in Brünn. Even the simplest workman, and indeed he especially, is influenced and pervaded by the party spirit of his nationality. Moreover a polyglot party system and trade union machinery is almost as clumsy as a polyglot Parliament.

But in order to establish definitely their avoidance of racial quarrels in the face of the national movements which rose even in the proletarian class and were intentionally made use of by the opposing parties, the Social Democrats could not confine themselves to a perfectly general international creed, but were obliged to adopt an attitude towards local questions. This was so in the Social Democrats' national programme of 1899. This programme was issued some seven years before the struggle for the franchise, which has hitherto been the most effective achievement of the Austrian Social Democrats. Hence it goes without saying that universal, equal and direct suffrage were put forward as the solution of the racial dispute. We have already remarked that this healing influence has at least not taken immediate effect. It may rather be said that the growing agitation and the increased number of active members of the party has widened the division between the groups. It may be that with a thoroughgoing democracy social problems would ultimately become so important that they would overrule language problems, but certainly this is not to be looked for until definite nationality regulations have come into force throughout the whole of the country of nations as a result of numerous debates and resolutions. The social democrats demand such a regulation of nationalities in the place of the traditional self-governing bodies of the Crown lands with national boundaries. And in this they concur with the German nationalist demand for the division of Bohemia. The resulting nationalist unions must conduct their own business, whilst a general law in force everywhere protects the minority. A State language is not to be recognised, but a language of intercourse is allowed as possible. Whether this language will not ultimately be necessary for all the higher authorities and will not, in the case of the army, unavoidably develop into a State language, is not worked out in detail. Finally, the right of every nationality to national existence and national development is recognised, but it is also stated that the progress of civilisation depends on the united solidarity of all nations.

All this can be accepted as correct, although we miss any explanation of how the special rights of nationalities will combine with the necessary solidarity. Social democracy, too, must ultimately result in a number of different settlements made according to the relative strength of the several elements at a particular time, and according to general political laws. But it has an undoubted advantage over the radical popular parties in that it puts the sense of common needs which inspires social legislation much more prominently into the foreground, and this is a practical and satisfactory preparatory work for all Mid-European schemes.

. . . . . .

A section on Poland might be demanded at this stage of our work, but during the war all Polish conditions and plans are so unsettled that, although the Polish question would occupy the chief place in any discussion on the "objects of the war," it does not as yet fall within an argument as to the permanent constitution of Mid-Europe. Upon the form assumed by victory and the conclusion of peace will depend the importance of this war as a turning-point in Polish history. The Poles themselves desire, so far as I can understand, first union, and then, if it be possible, self-government. Amongst the politically instructed representative Poles only a few believe in a new absolutely independent Poland lying between Russia and Mid-Europe. A larger number hope for an Austrian Poland, which would include the greater part of the nation and would secure a sort of Hungarian independence within the Danubian Monarchy. It is difficult to believe that Prussia will alter her eastern frontier very much unless she is compelled to do so. Whether Austria will grant a subordinate autonomy to her Poles, and whether they are in a position financially to have their own subordinate state, must be discussed by both sides. There is much in favour of this solution from the point of view of the Austrian Germans. But what will then become of the Ruthenians if they stay in Galicia? Yet so much must be said during the next months in many other connections about this and allied questions relating to the eastern frontier that it is unnecessary that we should here adopt any direct attitude towards the important political questions of the day. It may very well be that the establishment of Poland will be the strongest impulse towards the creation of Mid-Europe. But this, if it comes to pass, will be accomplished in the first instance in the rooms of the diplomatists, for only there can the necessary understandings between the sovereigns be prepared for. It is, however, certain that the new Poland is hardly conceivable without a previous treaty between the Central European States.

. . . . . .

And over all these, over the Germans, French, Danes and Poles in the German Empire, over the Magyars, Germans, Roumanians, Slovaks, Croats and Serbs in Hungary, over the Germans, Tzechs, Slovaks, Poles and Southern Slavs in Austria, let us imagine once again the controlling concept of Mid-Europe. Mid-Europe will have a German nucleus, will voluntarily use the German language, which is known all over the world and is already the language of intercourse within Central Europe, but must from the outset display toleration and flexibility in regard to all the neighbouring languages that are associated with it. For only so can that fundamental harmony grow up which is essential for a Great State, pressed and threatened from all sides. We Germans of the Empire need to devote much more genuine attention and care to this central problem of the allied monarchy than we have done hitherto. And not only to the technical and political problem in itself, but especially to the feelings of the peoples who are to be allied with us for better or for worse. In this respect much has been lacking before the war, for although our interest in the fate

CREEDS AND NATIONALITIES 113

of our German brethren in Austria and Hungary was not very extensive, yet it is notorious that our knowledge of the previous history and affairs of the Hungarians, Bohemians, Poles and Southern Slavs has been still more limited. Our eyes were directed towards the West. We were studying the nations of an older civilisation, and learnt much and discovered much from them, but the developing smaller civilisations in the East were not important enough for us, just because people felt a more personal relation with the Romance cultured languages than with the speech of their companions in arms. In this respect the new generation growing up after the war will do better than the old people, so that a type of Mid-European may be worked out including all elements of culture and strength, the bearer of a civilisation of rich and varied content, growing up around the German nationality.

I think of the first days after the war. Whither shall we proceed? In the first place most of the Romance countries will be as good as closed. Journey, you birds of passage, into the Carpathians, take your mandolins with you, let the gypsies play something for you in the forest towns. Climb, you mountaineers, not only as heretofore in the Tyrol and the Dolomites, but also further east, as far as Steiermark and Karst, and then bathe in the broad sunny Platten Lake. Visit, you seekers of art, the beautiful secret corners, the castles and churches, the homely town architecture; examine the curiosities of Prague, the antiquities of Cracow, and the proud and beautiful Graz! There, everywhere you will find both Gothic and Baroque as well as many fine modern buildings. Go to Passau on the Danube and let them take you to the Kaiserstadt, and then again to Gran and to the magnificent castle and town of Ofen and Pest! If you are interested in racial matters go and visit the isolated fragments of peoples in the Zips or in Siebenbürgen, or near Struhlweisenburg. Tell your chauffeurs, you owners of motor-cars, that the Imperial roads are excellent, and try, you hunters and cavaliers, whether the Beskiden or the Bosnien are not delightful mountains for you, such as cannot be found in the over-civilised West. Visit, you wounded soldiers, the battlefields of the greatest mountain war in the history of the world! If every year a hundred thousand more Germans of the Empire would travel in the faithful neighbouring country, then in addition to the pleasure it would produce, it would also be of much political value, for there the people are franker than in the more frequented foreign countries. I remember, as I write, many glorious hours on the Polish ridge in the Tatra and as far as Dalmatia. How brilliant was the evening on the Danube travelling to Budapest! And how genuinely national was the dance up there on the Koralp in Steiermark! Well, a pleasant journey!

CHAPTER IV

THE ECONOMIC LIFE OF CENTRAL EUROPE

CREEDS and nationalities constitute the oldest and most tangible, but by no means the only, lines of division amongst the population. There are other cleavages which are more connected with economic position and occupation, without being wholly economic. Differences which we wish to express as economic temperament or economic character. These cannot be discussed with statistical data like the creeds and nationalities, which are now become stable. Here everything is still in solution, and every sort of transitional form is possible and is constantly met with.

May I first speak of the economic temperament in North and Central Germany? In the eighteenth century this North German district still possessed no economic character of its own. Its population in the agricultural districts, in the industries in the small towns, and even in the few large towns, consisted of very much the same type of people as those who were then living in Bohemia, Austria, and as far away as Cracow. They were a people the unschooled lower stratum of which worked plainly and laboriously in order that above them might be set up an educated middle-class and a landowning nobility. These were often surprisingly homely, according to our ideas, in their style of living and the absence of luxuries, but possessed comforts in food and drink and were experienced in all the finer domestic arts and customs. This was the old world at the end of its days when on German soil Goethe and Mozart appeared as its wonderful offspring. Nowadays we refer to the remnant of the former lower stratum of these fine old times as "illiterate," and with this foreign pedantic word dismiss them from the ranks of still vital breeds. In North Germany these good old people, the illiterates, have almost entirely died out; they can hardly now be found even in the most isolated Polish farm-houses; they are as dead as gypsies, three-field agriculture, tilt carts and wolves. People are generally ashamed that only a short time ago there were men amongst us here who could not write their own names, although we are well aware that the most splendid civilisations from Athens to Versailles and London have only been possible with these old unlettered folk as a basis. The normal type of the average educated man appeared in North and Middle Germany with an uncomfortable intrusiveness, a type the like of which did not exist in the older southern and western civilisations. In the Electorate of Saxony, in Brandenburg, and also on either side of the Mittelgebirge in Württemberg, the process of transformation was beginning. Subsequently the French and English, too, tried to become educated peoples, but it did not altogether suit them. Compulsory primary education always works with them rather like an imported machine. But the development of an educated people in North and Central Germany is not the same thing as the development of the capitalist spirit, which Professor Sombart discusses in numerous books. Indeed it is not at all the same, since a hundred and fifty years ago the provinces of which we are speaking were still, as far as capitalism was concerned, very poor outlying districts, and were in no sense in the forefront of the movement. As princely mercantilist territories they desired to be included in the capitalist community, but at first they were imitators somewhat as the Balkan States are to-day. Nevertheless, something developed in them which in course of time was to outdistance in method and efficiency the already existing capitalistic civilisations of earlier growth; a homely skill in the popular ability to transform dreamers into workers by the aid of letters and memory exercises. Thus there grew up unconsciously and involuntarily the basal form of the second period of capitalism: a mechanism of work based on trained and educated workers. The capitalist employer of the earlier period developed, as Sombart shows us, in Upper and Central Italy, France, London and Amsterdam, and only came

THE ECONOMIC LIFE 117

thence, like some foreign imported skill, to the Central European regions beyond. This capitalist finds and creates the chief centre of his world in London. From his standpoint there, at the height of his power, he threatens the type of capitalism that will succeed him: the new, more impersonal group form of the new working humanity which began as individualist. He looks on Berlin (and in a somewhat different sense New York) as the home of this dangerous new type. A careful investigation into the causes of the Great War will reveal, when English-German antagonism is examined, the fundamental difference between the two distinct basal forms of capitalistic humanity. The capitalism of the first period defends itself against the capitalism of the second stage, whose advent is being proclaimed, the disciplined normal capitalism of Germany. The latter is to the former in its very essence insupportable.

But for what reason have Saxony, Brandenburg, Württemberg and later in a higher degree Rhenish Westphalia, Hamburg, the Middle Rhine districts and gradually the whole of Germany become the home of this new human type which is still in process of formation? This point deserves consideration and must be understood if we are to explain the character of Mid-Europe and the part it should play in the world. What is this economic Prussianism and Germanism which to-day enforces the attention and arouses the aversion of the world, and how did it come about? What is the origin of our new social-economic creed?

. . . . . .

During the war we are all wondering why we Germans, and especially we Germans of the Empire, are so little beloved by the rest of the world. To many well-meaning and sociable people this international dislike is something quite horrible, and they rack their brains to discover what we must do in order to find favour again. But they often look for the source of the ill-will of other nations in very secondary matters, such as perhaps in the lack of social good tone in those who travel abroad, loud-voiced German tourists dressed in Tyrolese homespun, or in the theatrical sword-clanging of some discharged general, and not in the economic national type itself, because they share in the economic and mental changes in their own nation much too unconsciously. It hardly even occurs to them that we are unloved because we have found a method of work in which now and for a long time to come no other European nation can imitate us, and which consequently the others do not regard as fair. It is this to which we have just referred as the transition to the impersonal capitalism of the second stage, a process which with us has demanded about a century and a half of work and education.

In order by illustration to make clearer at the outset the distinction between the older and the newer economic creed of capitalism I will begin with a little story about London. I wanted to look at the London docks, and said so to a respected English friend, whom in spite of the war I greet from across the trenches. He replied, " No one here goes to look at the docks! " Then I inquired at the International Tourist Offices of Cook and Son whether they arranged for visits to the docks? Answer: No, because there were no London docks like, for instance, the Hamburg docks, which one could visit and inspect as a whole; the London docks are an unsystematic succession of many very big establishments, each of which belongs to a separate private firm. Thus, as to quantity, labour, money value, goods, the London shipping trade exceeds that of Hamburg; but as to unity, articulation, organisation they already represent a more antiquated form of life. Hamburg learned from London, but added to its learning quite of itself something peculiarly German, which at the outset appeared, like some chance additional characteristic, merely as stricter police supervision and regulation, but which developed in course of time into an essential feature. Why, we ask, does the smaller German sea trade possess the greatest shipping companies?

Or another example: in 1900 I was in Paris during the Exhibition and was talking to a German wood-carver (fine joiner), who had worked for a long time in France, about the difference between Germans and French. The man, so far as I can remember now after fifteen years, spoke somewhat thus: If a

French joiner has thirty workmen and can get a larger order employing more than this number, he accepts it indeed, but puts it out on commission, because he has not sufficient confidence in himself or will not take the trouble to deal with more than thirty workmen. Meanwhile the corresponding German employer would accept the order for himself, would enlarge his workshop, and by reason of this enlargement would seek further new orders. If one of the Frenchmen acts differently, then he is certain to be from Alsace or Switzerland. Thus the Germans have the greater organising ability both in medium-sized businesses and in skilled handwork.

The peculiarity of the Germans does not consist in an essentially new attribute which has not appeared elsewhere in the world, but in the methodical, trained progress in an ability which has existed and does still exist among the hitherto leading nations, but has not been so systematically and intentionally developed. From our own point of view we are still a long way from having arrived at perfection of organisation, but in the eyes of others we have already deviated far from their style of living. We are an unfree people because we have learnt better than they have how to carry out our work on a common plan and to a common rhythm. And this applies to all types of work. It is not as if industrialism were a special German characteristic, for the English are an industrial, machine-using, manufacturing nation, and were so before us. Moreover, the peculiar German spirit of which we are speaking shows itself at least as much in our agricultural occupations as in our manufactures.

Of course there are all sorts of attempts at organisation and co-operation in English and French agriculture, as for example among the wine-growers in Southern France. But when examined closely these attempts are nearly all quite feeble, whereas German agriculture, although the independence of the peasantry is definitely safeguarded, is already almost entirely managed by systematic co-operation, or at least is making daily progress towards this goal. By the joint action of agricultural boards, agricultural schools, loan banks, granaries and dairies, a strong net is woven round the individual. He has become a peasant co-operator, member of a definite profession. He can, no doubt, evade all these regulations, but it is to his own injury if he does so. For the sake of personal interest he becomes a member of an impersonal institution and works for it as for himself. This insertion of the individual ego into the joint ego is our special ability by which we attain a more intensive cultivation, a better assorted production, and better marketing qualities for international trade. Individualism is fully developed, but it is then carried up into the next higher form of economic co-operative existence.

Owing to a like intrinsic impulse our industrial life is similarly full of ideas of organisation and regulations for combines. I mean to speak elsewhere of the economic syndicates or cartels, so that here I will merely call attention to the fact that during the last twenty years our German industries have taken on an entirely new appearance. In growing they have become interlaced. By means of employers' federations, payment cartels, zone compacts, and price agreements, a complicated machinery of spheres of business and subordinations has come into being, in which the outsider can hardly find his way, but which has been created step by step as needed, and by means of which the private employer of the old style has quite gently slipped over into the disciplined, industrial community, and that in the course of one generation and even when at the outset he was quite unwilling. He has become a federated employer. The employers of the first and second generations perhaps only adapted themselves reluctantly to these developments and would rather have remained individualist capitalists in the West European sense, but the employer of the third generation is for the most part born into a combination from the outset. Thus in a certain sense he becomes the free, directing employee of a society which produces steel or yarn or sugar or spirits. The industrial basis of the age is thus discovered, and its spirit is now steadily penetrating deeper. In another twenty years we shall see before us the whole scheme of a powerful industry with its domestic regulations and its divisions of labour. The regulation of production is on the way. Things that forty years ago would have seemed like the unreal idealism of socialist and state-socialist dreamers, now appear with incredible certainty as realities which have come into being in the interval. Germany is on the way to become not merely an industrial State, but above all an organised State.

In complete correspondence with this is our experience with the wage-earners, and following their example, with all the employees in the higher groups. The old ideal of the individual who sells his working strength when, where and how he likes has almost disappeared in the social ideal of the common unions of wage-earners and workers. The non-unionist is still numerous it is true, but he is in no way the leader. And what distinguishes the German trade unionist, so far as we can see, from the older English type, is his greater coherence and discipline, which he has painfully but successfully won by fighting, in spite of socialistic law and police intrigue, against the policy of the Government and of the employers. The German masses mean to make their advance as organised groups, that is their guiding principle. It is inadequate to say that they combine in order to obtain increased wages. Any one who knows the unionists knows that calculated self-interest is only one side of their existence, and that, especially in the case of the leaders, it is the least decisive influence. They have formed their trade unionist ideal of conduct, narrow and inflexible, as could hardly be otherwise with people of moderate means who have but little scope for action in their lives, but yet firmly decided upon and definite in itself. The idea of a superpersonal economic leadership of the masses in work and in the sale and consumption of its products is prevalent and becomes a mere matter of course. In this the German working classes differ from all the Latin nations, for what in France and Italy is called socialism is indeed related in word and theory to the German workmen's unions, but has none of the sternness of inward determination which has been attained by our social democrats, or even by other unionist groups.

All travel along the same path: engineers, teachers, headteachers, scholars, doctors, even artists. The guilds of handworkers are coming to life again and adapting themselves to the altered conditions of the time. We are a uniform nation in spite of all the quarrels among the numerous associations of opposing interests; magnificently uniform in this method of organising our daily life and work. Primary schools, universal conscription, police, science and socialistic propaganda, have all worked together to this end. We were hardly aware that we desired all this in reality: this disciplined work of the second period of capitalism, which may be described as the transition from private capitalism to socialism, if the word socialism be not applied solely to a proletarian vision of great businesses, but is understood, broadly, as an ordering of the nation for the increase of the joint product of each for all.

This new German type is incomprehensible to the individualist nations, to whom he appears partly as a relapse into past times of constraint, and partly as an artificial product of coercion that belies and overcomes humanity. In educated circles in Paris and London they feel a mixture of pity, fear, respect and aversion towards this German type. Even if they could produce the same thing there, they would not wish to do so, for they have no desire for this disciplined soul, they do not desire it because it would be the death and the surrender of the individual soul. No one can quite understand this unless he has occasionally tried to look at Germany with the eyes of the foreigner. To the German who knows only Germany, the intrinsic strength of this opposition must necessarily remain hidden; he does not realise how strange he has already become to even the best men of the Western nations, not owing to any particular thing which he does but merely owing to what he is.

. . . . .

This new German character has by no means been produced amongst us in the German Empire without opposition, for it is something distinct from the old German condition of life and heart. The old German was much more natural, slower, wilder or weaker just as it happened. All our Romanticism lacks the organising spirit; it is loyal, self-sacrificing and companionable,

THE ECONOMIC LIFE 123

but it is wanting in any guiding idea of aim. The good, ridiculous Germans of former days were thus no objects of general enmity. People thought of them at times as coarse, and wished they had a larger share of French politeness, but they had at bottom nothing against the worthy bears, who let themselves be pushed hither and thither and yet laughed at it themselves. But no one ever supposed that this old, comfortably coarse, downright fellow would one day shake off his dream and stand up as the thinker of labour. Even when philosophers of the highest rank appeared amongst us foreigners never thought that this signified a practical and economic change in the German character. Indeed we hardly noticed ourselves how much our philosophers were practical prophets. They were regarded as artists in ideas and as reformers of the world, without its being realised that, emanating from them, a spirit of labour inspired by reason would transform the entire world in the course of a century. Indeed the thinkers themselves did not perceive to what purpose they were there. They thought about pure and practical reason in the sense of intellect and morality. But after them came their followers and tried to introduce the reason they conceived of into Government, Law and Administration. They were, it is true, only partially successful, but again, in the next generation, keen, highly trained thinkers about actual possibilities were found in all departments of work. Neither Bismarck nor Savigny nor Helmholz nor either of the two Siemens is conceivable without this philosopher's oil poured out for the second and third time. Our technical and agricultural schools are German institutions for thought which aims at realisation in fact, and are nowadays almost more characteristic of our national nature than the old-established universities. The " high school " with a practical object is a novelty which we first had to assimilate ourselves, and which the people of older civilisations most heartily grudged us when it appeared, because for them knowledge was more an amusement than a practical ability.

In the quite recent past, and until our character was thus transformed in this matter of technical organisation, the English were always very friendly to us Germans. The great English thinker Carlyle, it is true, understood what was preparing in the German spirit, but his fellow-countrymen accepted what they saw before their eyes: the Germans have good schools and buy English machinery! It was not until by reason of their schools they set up their own machines and offered them to foreign nations that they lost the English goodwill; for how could the learned brother on the Continent be so bold as to mix himself up in business? This learned German technical scholar appeared in all occupations like something essentially improper. The old English world was not adapted to make a systematic working alliance between thought and international trade! From the time of this memorable change onwards the educated Englishman felt himself deceived by the German and called him a dangerous competitor, as indeed he really was, and that too in virtue of the English universal watchword; free play for the strong; but with a quite differently trained strength.

How closely the new German method of work is a continuation of the German trained thought can only be realised from a comparison between German management of important undertakings by leading men and the corresponding foreign non-German management. Our financial policy has a perceptible doctrinaire tendency, but on this very account is most successful. Our military education is markedly scientific, but is not injured thereby. Our great merchants are almost economists and statisticians by profession. Our woodcraft is almost as logically thought out as a textbook on grammar. Our shipbuilding is highly mathematical, our steel plates are scientific works, our dyes are chemical inventions. Into everything there enters to-day less of the lucky spirit of invention than of patient, educated industry. Or to put it otherwise: we believe in combined work.

That connection with systematic science which we find throughout in the new agriculture and in all the more extensive industrial undertakings was and still is the peculiar quality of German social democracy. Dr. Engels, the friend of Karl Marx, said of it that it was the heiress of German philosophy, and if the saying

THE ECONOMIC LIFE   125

is not taken to mean the sole heiress, then there is a large kernel of truth in it. Of all working classes, only the German (and the German-Austrian) is theoretical in its group of instruction in the sense of pure Marxism. This instruction may often be false in details and may be far over the pupils' heads, and remote from present-day problems, but the actual fact that we possess the most theoretical labour movement in the world is part of the picture of German economic life. This working class in combination with its educated employers, with our syndicate leaders, with our Civil Service and officers, does not offer the most charming and amusing society possible, but does constitute the most practical, safe and durable human machinery. This living national machine goes its way whether the individual lives or dies, it is impersonal or super-personal, has its frictions and interruptions, but is as a whole something that has never come to pass exactly in this way before; it is the historically developed German character.

. . . . . .

We are all being much confirmed in this our German method of work by the progress of the war. From the very first days this war, which had been forced upon us, was regarded as a necessary and quite universal duty and task which must be performed. Every one looked to those in responsible positions for a planned organisation reaching even to the smallest details. As soon as it was felt that this existed, the troops and the workers at home showed themselves ready for the greatest and most exceptional efforts, without crediting themselves with this as any special merit. The war was really only a continuation of our previous life with other tools but based on the same methods. In this indeed lies the secret of success. We conquer less through individuals than through the disciplined feeling for combined difficult work, and those who take the field to amend us after their own pattern must try in battle to equal us. If our opponents like to label this intrinsic connection between the work of war and peace as " German militarism," we can only regard this as reasonable, for Prussian military discipline influences us all in actual fact, from the captain of industry to the maker of earthworks. All that we object to is the secondary implication which has associated itself with the word militarism, and which in the management of barracks in the peace years it was difficult entirely to avoid. But after the war we shall certainly remain much more closely agreed in our common esteem for the voluntary discipline of a great national, military or industrial army so long as the men are still living who have kept at their posts during this struggle. Happen what will the German spirit has received its baptism of fire: the national genius was and is a reality. Both to ourselves and to the outside world we have shown ourselves as in essence a single unit. Now it is our concern to carry through to its goal this essential German character, proved in the most sinister of wars. This will and must be set on foot directly peace is concluded.

For on this day all Imperial and State officials and all parties and societies will produce their memoranda wherein are noted the things that must be altered after the war. I wager that three-fourths of these memoranda will contain the words: better organisation! Our foreign service, our Red Cross, our hospital system, our military clothing, our military purveying, our horse-breeding, our food-supply, all this and much else must be much more rigidly thought out and calculated for beforehand, so that we shall not again be so situated as now in the ill-advised debates on food. But all organisation consists in statistics, grouping, analysis, synthesis, control and regulation, and thus there grows up from all sides a State or national socialism, there grows up the "systematised national economy." Fichte and Hegel nod approval from the walls: now, after the war, the German is at last becoming heart and soul a political economic citizen. His ideal is and will be the organism and not free will, reason and not the blind struggle for existence. This constitutes our freedom, our self-development. By its means we shall enjoy our golden age as other conquering nations in other ages and with other abilities and excellences have done before us. Our epoch dawns when English capitalism has reached and overstepped its highest point, and we have been educated for this epoch by

THE ECONOMIC LIFE

Friedrich II., Kant, Scharnhorst, Siemens, Krupp, Bismarck, Bebel, Legien, Kirdorf and Ballin. Our dead have fallen on the field for the sake of this our Fatherland. Germany, foremost in the world!

. . . .

And now let us return to Mid-Europe. The German economic creed must become in future more and more the characteristic of Mid-Europe. The military defensive alliance will thus grow into a genuine partnership. A united economic people will develop, cutting across all constitutional boundaries.

This could not succeed were it the freshly conceived scheme of individuals. But we are only putting into words what has for long been taking shape of itself; we express it in order to further a process that is already going on. The Austrians and Hungarians have already had a share in our life for economically they are of our race, even those who speak a different language. The German-Austrians sat with us on the same school benches and have supplied us with excellent fellow-workers and teachers of the same technical training and outlook. The Tzechs or Poles or Magyars may indeed often be anti-German and uncongenial to us in actions and feelings unconnected with business, but, all the same, they have not escaped the attraction of our working methods, and have not even thought of doing so. France was for them the ideal country of the finer arts, England the technical and financial queen of the world aloof from Continental struggles, Russia, perchance, the mysterious future Power of unlimited possibilities, but the economic life of all the Austro-Hungarian nations and sections of races is quite overwhelmingly of German origin. They have borrowed their international, technical and business development from the Germans, often without being especially conscious of it or desiring it. Often the German-speaking Jews have acted as intermediaries. Their co-operation is not to be underestimated, for whatever banks, joint-stock companies, means of communication, corn warehouses, wood consignments and even manufactures exist in Austria-Hungary are workable amongst all the separate nationalities chiefly because the Polish, Magyar, Tzech and German Jews are accustomed to a mutual understanding. In spite of all the protests of the Anti-Semites the Jews are an indispensable factor in the economic life of the Dual Monarchy. No doubt to most of them the kernel of military organisation peculiar to the German economic character is unknown, but they are born teachers of commercialism as such, and thus they prepare the way and make ready for modern work.

It would be quite erroneous for any North German to think himself called upon to introduce the first elements of capitalist theory to the Southern members of the union. Indeed he might put his foot into it thereby, for the Budapest corn traders, the Vienna bankers, the Bohemian manufacturers are truly no growths of yesterday. Good-natured as they may seem they are very good men of business. In all these matters the North German must not forget that though he is better organised he is no cleverer than his Southern neighbour. The two things are not quite the same. The amazing economic vigour of the North is no pure outcome of intellect if this is understood as a general versatility of mind. The successful North Germans are often not so specially active intellectually, but they are tenacious and stick to a thing and force themselves and others into systematic progress. In this lies their strength. We are concerned with the problem of combining this strength and the versatile qualities of the Danubian State into a Central European economic system to the common profit, and of developing out of nature, tradition and breeding a successful scheme of joint work.

. . . . . .

In discussing these matters with German-Austrians I have frequently heard the phrase, "You must help us." But when I have tried to translate this recurrent demand into practical measures, there was a standstill. For it was generally quite uncertain at what point and with what objects they were to be helped. Then it was, "Oh, well, you must give the starting push!" "Yes, but if we do that you will be the first to resent it!" "Oh, well, that is true, but all the same we can't get out alone." Then,

THE ECONOMIC LIFE

without further circumlocution: what is it these Austrians want to get out of?

As individuals they are quite as clever and as skilful in business and profession as any of us and they generally know our business affairs better than we do theirs. In details we could more often learn from them than they from us. All that they lack is any general manifestation of that Prusso-German business spirit described above. They do not exactly desire this but they would like to enjoy its fruits, for they see that it makes for prosperity and strength, and that for the entire nation. Individuals have become exceedingly rich as often on the Danube as on the Spree, both in the old aristocratic and in the modern capitalist periods. But as a whole there are obstacles to the economic life there, about which even the best of friends cannot be silent. The productivity of the land in Austria and Hungary is less developed than it ought to be with modern expedients and in relation to the value of the soil and the amount of the population. It is not as if Austro-Hungarian agriculture made no progress! On the contrary it does progress, becomes more productive and more varied, but it does not quite keep pace with Germany in front, nor with the pressure of the smaller, developing nations behind. Bohemia indeed is almost like the Germany on its borders, but the further one goes into the centre and east of the Danube countries the more are there leaden weights on the feet of those who try to advance. There is still much unassisted poverty, much wasted effort, much red tapeism without any proper object. All this is burdensome and is sometimes felt as a reproach, and only a few strong-minded persons can rise above these feelings and go their way boldly and successfully. Thus it appears, to me at least, that the economic system of the Danubian Kingdom is wanting less in something technical which might easily be introduced into it, than in something psychical which must first be trained, and which is needed just as much by the farmers as by the craftsmen and artisans, and just as much by the employers as by the workpeople. I should partially fail to carry out the purpose of this book of mine if, owing to a natural and easily understood caution, I were not prepared to speak frankly in this connection. Such matters only cease to be painful when they are stated in plain terms.

I once travelled with a German-speaking Ruthenian from Oderberg to Breslau, and enjoyed his ready grasp of what was to him the new life on either side of the railway. He said something of this sort: "What surprises me is that here the peasants are really human beings." Of course from the railway he could not see how many troubled and oppressed existences there were even in Silesia, and that frequently both in agricultural and town occupations, and how little the position there to-day corresponds to our ideal of the upraising of the whole nation. But all the same it is true that the people whom one sees at the station buildings over there in Galicia or in Hungary, on either side of the Carpathians, make a quite different impression as less cared for and less independent.

To express the same point in other words: A few weeks ago I heard an Austrian economist remark: "With us two-thirds of the population are beggars." He did not say proletarians but beggars, and he was well aware of the distinction between the two words. I will leave it an open question whether or no the estimate of two-thirds was exaggerated, but it remains true that almost everywhere, and of course especially in the east, one meets with men and women who, so to speak, never escape from their rags their whole life long. These people own little and can do little, they drag along from one day to another, and are remarkably moderate in their demands on themselves and on the rest of the world and society. From the economists' standpoint they and their work are not actually worth much more than the few kronen which pass through their hands, but it would be possible to make them much more valuable. This is the problem. We Germans of the Empire know this problem for ourselves, but we have already partially climbed the mountain, we have got over the roughest parts, and hence the Austrians say to us: "You must help us!"

Why do so many people emigrate? As many as, or more than,

170,000 men emigrated overseas from Austria in a few years, and many others went across the land frontiers. In 1907 193,000, even, emigrated from Hungary. It is true that a certain proportion of the emigrants come back again, but in exchange fresh troops of them are always hoisting their bundles on their backs and going to look for bread and money in Europe or America. We too have known this emigration in earlier times in East and West Prussia, Saxony, Württemberg, the Palatinate and elsewhere, and even in the last century in the early eighties we lost a large number of our people through emigration to America, but we have got over the difficulty. This final jerk over is still needed in Austria and Hungary. It must come however, for it is poor comfort that the emigrants send or bring home money. A good economic system does not need to cast out its children but acts as an attraction, and keeps the superfluous ones itself to increase home industry. The Danube country too must cease to act as a nursery for foreign nations.

A social policy is good and necessary, but first and above all there must be employment. I remember still how things appeared in the Saxon Erzgebirge when I was a child. First one family and then another could endure it no longer, and packed up their scanty possessions. And they were always the most efficient, for the under-nourished and the poor-blooded can never get away. Thus fifty years ago, healthy people were quite literally in beggary there. I tell this purposely so that no one can feel that my previous statements were made in a pharisaical spirit. Nothing is further from my thoughts. But when I think about Mid-Europe, I do not only think of kings, courts and general superintendents, but of the whole immense crowd, of our combined great nation in all its ranks, and I consult with the economists of neighbouring lands to devise how things may be improved. For it is only by means of healthier, better-educated and better-nourished masses that the military, financial and civilised Mid-Europe of which we dream can come into existence.

. . . .

It is not of much use to hold moral discussions and talk compassionately about the poverty of the masses, for they will get no better fed or stronger in consequence. Even the school is not by itself adequate to the task, however indispensable it is. The primary school transforms a homely but helpless population of illiterates into arithmeticians, letter-writers and newspaper readers. It enlarges the sphere of activity and supplies a basis for further progress, but it cannot supply work in a district where employment is scarce. The most enterprising boys often go away the farthest into foreign countries. Moreover the primary school only makes its influence felt economically in the third or fourth generation, because without home education from the earliest years onwards too much ground is lost again after leaving school. The great importance of the agricultural and technical schools has already been noticed, but in order that they should prosper they presuppose undertakings arranged on progressive lines, which everywhere demand trained ability. Hence the fact that Austria and Hungary have done much for their school system during the last decade is in accordance with their position and task in Mid-Europe and will certainly have excellent results in the course of time, but the education question must not be regarded as the only decisive factor. The first and most pressing economic problem relates to the productiveness of labour.

Suppose a hundred men complete a piece of work which could have been done by sixty, it is evident at once that the hundred must be worse clothed and nourished than the sixty. In a natural economic condition of life this follows directly of itself. Each of the latter workmen gets more corn, flax, wine or salt. And with a system of money wages and money values the same simple law holds good. All can have more to consume if all produce more. The main difference then between the economic system of the German Empire and that of Austria-Hungary — to which however a hundred exceptions may be granted from the outset — seems to be that with us, by reason of that economic character described above, the same work is on the average done by fewer persons. The North and South Germans have themselves learnt this lesson but slowly, for by nature we all, without exception, are slow and take our time. Nor is it desirable that the efficiency of labour should be increased so artificially and excessively as is demanded by Taylor's American system, because this is too harmful to the workers themselves; but however simple the matter appears it yet constitutes the primary economic anxiety for Mid-Europe: we must speed up those who are lingering in the old habits of work, so that they approximate to the labour rhythm of the progressive.

Moreover, the Government must lead the way by setting a good example, and must overhaul its official machinery so that fewer but better paid officials may do the same services as are now carried out by too many poorly paid ones. This reform in the public services will not be a saving of money but of wasted hours of work. In this respect there is much to tighten up even on the north of the Erzgebirge, but still more on the south. Professor v. Philippovich has more than once called attention to this important matter. Owing to the impressive example which the officials in town and country offer to the rest of the inhabitants, they are the primary agents in setting the rhythm. From above downwards there must be some degree of speeding up amongst them from year to year. Perhaps this will not in the first instance make the officials more amicable, but it will raise them as men, as a class, and as models for the crowd. Later on the pleasant manner of life may reappear, if indeed it exists independently in the race. Economically that State is the best which carries out the most public work with the fewest employees.

Reforms to increase production are often indeed attempted in a mistaken way, when, the pay remaining the same, a higher production is enforced by supervision and threats. The attempt is explicable but can only afford a quite transitory success, as any horse-owner can tell you from his own experience. And this course is wrong too for economic reasons, for a decrease in the number of employees acts as a decline in the general purchasing power, if the individuals do not at the same time increase their consumption. That portion of the population which is no longer to sit in the office needs to find in the increased demands of those more fully employed the starting-point of an opportunity to earn.

And here we touch upon the popular counter-argument against the systematisation of work in all departments. It is said that in this case there will be still more of the unemployed, the unoccupied and the emigrants. But each country where work is more strictly disciplined offers an obvious proof that exactly the contrary is true. Wherever work is quick there consumption is abundant, and there wages and salaries rise, even if attempts are made to keep them down, and the home market extends daily. Where much is earned and consumed there is abundant opportunity for work.

When, fifty years ago, Lassalle began his brilliant social democratic agitation among the German workpeople, he used the much disliked and much misunderstood phrase, "cursed modesty." Fundamentally however he was right. I grew up in the very neighbourhood in which he first spoke to poor home-workers. There I found that very state of things from which to-day a few districts of Germany and many districts in Austria-Hungary are suffering: badly organised work, old, rattling looms, long hours, low rate of production per hour, miserable wages, exhaustion and under-feeding. This deserved condemnation as "unworthy of humanity" in order that the working ability might be raised out of that worthlessness which was borne only too submissively, and also in order that German industry, at that time hard pressed, might be able to compete everywhere in the world's markets. The will to rise must be awakened, the call to a fresh creed of work must be sounded. Some workers may at first understand this as meaning for them that they can earn more wages and increase their consumption without increased production. But this, which is a vain attempt in the long run, is as natural from their point of view as that converse attempt on the part of the employers to pay less for better work, to which we referred above.

I am almost afraid to dwell in such detail upon these simple matters, but since in what follows much must be said of the intensity of the Mid-European economic system, it appeared doubly necessary not to hurry over these essential preliminary principles.

. . . . . .

What might not the Hungarians do with their land! I see Hungary in mental picture before me: woods on the mountains and on the edges of the plains, and in addition pastures and meadows. Both together occupy roughly half the land. But then comes the wheat district, the centre point of all Hungarian life. According to the year from 35,000 to 39,000 qkm. are cultivated as wheat-fields. How much might be grown there! What a splendid golden harvest of twice the thickness!

Of course men must not be blamed for the effects of the climate, but allowing for this we have to deplore a production acknowledged on all sides to be painfully small. Hungary with its excellent soil produces about half as much per acre as does Germany. In other words: Germany in many years produces on half the wheat land the same quantity of wheat as in Hungary is grown on double the area. Our statistical section gives more exact figures.

But besides this a hectare in Germany although it produces double is cultivated with less labour than in Hungary. This is shown if we compare the number of the agricultural population with the total acreage of arable land.

How it comes about that there is so much less agricultural energy available in agrarian Hungary than in industrial Germany is a problem frequently discussed but by no means simple. On the one hand it involves quite general sociological experiences and on the other adjustments special to Hungary. Agricultural machinery of all kinds results in a turning back of labourers out of the barn and field into the workshop. The more agriculture is done by machinery the more labourers drawn from the farms are found in industry. This has happened to a great extent in the German Empire and also in Bohemia. At the same time the more agricultural machinery is used the more the number of labourers who are permanent through the winter decreases, and thus the resident agricultural population in general diminishes. The effect is reciprocal. The machine drives out the labourer and the want of labour cries out for more machines. Not that the Hungarian large estates have no machines! I visited the fine agricultural museum in Budapest and congratulated on this occasion all those who interested themselves in Hungarian farming. There are working models there of all the most modern contrivances, and the general trend of mind will be found fully to accord with our own. Yet, all the same, many of the big estates and most of the peasant holdings are notoriously in the old pre-industrial stage. A factor which almost equals in importance the introduction of machinery is the use of artificial manures according to the quality of the soil and its requirements. Machines and manure presuppose men who know how to use them, and whose self-interest is adequately aroused. This means for the small farmer a sale from which he himself gets the advantage of his work. Here, from what I can learn, special Hungarian conditions begin to have their effect. Of these I cannot speak since I have no personal knowledge of the matter: viz. the organisation of the Hungarian corn trade.

If Hungary could so increase its agricultural output as to produce a third more, Mid-Europe would be thereby assured of an independent food-supply. The existing small production is thus a potential asset for the future. German and Hungarian interests are here in the closest agreement. I picture to myself the future Austrian and German Imperial corn-store as being in Budapest.

. . . . . .

Influenced by such thoughts as these I have attempted, in regard to various industries, to determine by means of the published evidence the difference in the productivity of the labour employed in Austria and in Germany respectively. But my results are not free from objection because the methods of payment employed in the two cases only partially correspond. In coal-mining, so far as I was able to calculate, I consider the difference to be not very great; in lignite-mining it appears extraordinary; in the production of pig-iron I obtained no clear results because here the supply of machinery is of primary importance. The nearer to the northern frontier of Austria these occupations are carried on the more

THE ECONOMIC LIFE 137

they approximate to the Saxon and Silesian enterprises. But the actual fact that the workman in Austria-Hungary does not quite attain to the average economic efficiency of the German may be taken as admitted. Amongst other troubles connected with Austrian company legislation, taxation and the freightage conditions, the Austrian employers usually put forward this difference in the comparative value of the workers as one important reason why they cannot enter upon a joint economic life with the industries of the German Empire without special guarantees. Of course it must not be left out of account in this connection that the Austrian workman gets on the average lower wages. Here too strictly accurate comparisons are hardly possible since each district in either State has its own wage fluctuations. But miners' wages in Germany, for example, are in general higher in marks than they are in Austria in kronen. The prevailing wage for unskilled work is decidedly lower in Austria than in Germany.

Whether or no economic statistics, either now or in the future, might supply better material with regard to all these very important distinctions, for our purpose here we are only concerned to get a general grasp of the state of affairs. We attempt to picture the economic life of Central Europe as a whole, and then find that it does not exist as complete in itself or comparable. But this awakens apprehensions on both sides at the thought of combination. The stronger section fears the competition of poorer and cheaper labour, the weaker section fears the more established power. These hesitations present a slightly different appearance in each department but they are nowhere entirely absent.

We frankly admit that these apprehensions will prove a hindrance to all negotiations concerning tariffs and syndicates. At the same time their importance need not be exaggerated, because we have already endured unharmed very noticeable differences of this kind in each of our separate States and in all the provinces. Within the German Empire possibilities of profit and production are quite different. The value of labour is very various in town and country and in east and west. Wages in Upper Silesia are quite different from those in the industrial district of Rhenish-

Westphalia, and the conditions of employment for private employees and for communal officials vary also. The same thing applies to Bohemia as compared with the Steiermark, to Budapest as compared with Siebenbürgen. Thus a Central European economic union would not result in something fundamentally new, but only in a repetition of a sufficiently well-known condition or occurrence over a wide area.

Moreover, in this connection everything is continually changing. What seems to us to-day a low rate of production was not long ago a high rate. It is most interesting to turn over the older tables on this subject. That stage of development which appears backward to the present-day observer from the German Empire was once our own condition, and that too in not such a very far distant past. And of course occasional alterations in the methods of collecting the published data are disturbing. If we neglect them for the moment it may perhaps be said that agriculturally Germany twenty years ago was where Austria now is, and forty years ago was where Hungary now is. But what are twenty years for such an extensive development? The same thing may be noticed in the case of industry. It is a strong argument against any pride on the part of the progressive or any despondency on the part of districts and branches of work that have gone forward more slowly. If once these things are looked at from a certain distance, the contrasts grow smaller. Central European working folk represent old and new periods in a variously coloured intermixture, but nevertheless essentially they are even now on the point of becoming a united people.

· · · · · ·

But of course it must not be thought that there is everywhere present in the Danubian Monarchy a desire to adopt the new German economic spirit with its strained energy of work and its strong organisation! With us too this spirit grew up but slowly and under much protest and opposition, and there are no small number of people in the German Empire, in agriculture, industry and small trades who even to-day regret the "good old times," and blame capitalism for having destroyed the security of their business; believers in the older economic creed, and its more comfortable rate of living! Often, indeed, it is only the old who talk in this way, while their sons are resolute children of the present, and as such belong to or incline to the farmers' union or the retailers' association or the handworkers' guild. All these economic unions with their banks, their adjustment of relations and obligations could not indeed do otherwise than demand from their members a sure turnover, increased solidity, efforts towards increased production, adaptability and work on a cash basis. In this sense they are at bottom capitalist structures in spite of their partially anti-capitalist speeches. All the unions for fixing rates of wages too, and the other societies for workers and employees have a like intrinsic tendency, and are generally very well aware of this themselves. Each trade unionist when he joins, bids farewell to the old life of unregulated work done as it happened to suit. Hence if we want to find the really old people we do not find them in the economic unions, they are the separate individuals: the normal men, now growing infirm, of an earlier vanished economic period; the numerous small millers, jobbing butchers, ropemakers, tanners, tailors or shoemakers, with whom things often go very badly, or the isolated small farmer, without instruction, discipline and assistance, or those wandering or resident traders who did not learn arithmetic and understand nothing of their own goods. Such honest but unhelpable individuals, who to-day, as sixty years ago, have learnt neither technique nor combination, live with the feeling that they are terribly ill-treated by their contemporaries, grown covetous and organised; they do not understand that the average demands on working men and on trade production must increase. People of this kind, however, appear afresh with each intermittent advance in management, and consequently will be met with everywhere to some extent, even in the most advanced industries of all. They have been incorrectly termed the decaying middle class. The term is incorrect because out of that same old middle class too all the most vigorous employers have raised themselves and are daily ascending. Whence otherwise could they come? To speak, for instance, of the joiners;

they, on the whole, make marked progress, receiving numbers of orders owing to the increased incomes of the population. But some of them cannot rise with the rest because they lack means or quality. These ally themselves to the complainers everywhere, and thus increase a social-political group which accomplishes hardly anything positive, because, or as long as, it has no ideals of education or organisation, but which may prove a serious obstacle to general progress. In the German Empire this stream of protest against the new economic creed has for the most part died out, and has largely been absorbed into forms of association that are efficient for work. If I am not greatly mistaken, however, opposing humours of the kind may be expected in a greater degree in Austria and perhaps too in Hungary, so soon as the idea of an economic Mid-Europe is taken in earnest, for here in the Dual Monarchy the olden time is still very powerful in men's minds. A Central European combination, however prudently and moderately carried out, must inevitably be followed by a period of economic protestors and romanticists who wish to hear and see nothing of all this rubbish of organised capitalism. About this we may be certain from the outset, and need not lose our heads when it happens. It will last perhaps half a generation in its passionate form and will decline in proportion as the success of the stricter, newer system becomes evident.

But as has already appeared in social evolution up to the present, these unimportant individuals who are passed over in the process of development are joined by a certain section of the nobility and clergy, from no personal necessity, but because these latter are patriarchal romanticists. To them the progress of democracy which is involved in all intensification of work is unpleasant. For in fact a man's average production cannot be increased without raising him as a person. The man who can tend a machine is to the ordinary man with a shovel as a rider is to a foot-passenger. He feels himself worth two. People must regard him in quite a different way because he can make or spoil more. This applies just as much in the villages as in the town and makes itself apparent without agitation. If there is agitation in addition it ag-

THE ECONOMIC LIFE

gravates the transition, and the patriarchal directors of the older processes of work and of the religious life naturally in the first instance regard the whole modern technique as ruin. There need, however, be no lasting opposition here, for the aristocrats learn quickly to obtain higher profits through better workmen whereby both sides gain, and the clergy make the unexpected discovery that they can well hold their own even in the new economic church. Let inquiries be made in Rhenish-Westphalia and Upper Silesia! Hence the opposition of the patriarchal upper class is neither absolute nor permanent. But it may be anticipated in every case of improvement in average technique and activity. And all sorts of good and justifiable feelings come into play here. The old economic world with its comfort and despotism, in which however, as Professor Max Weber says, "the familiar 'thou' can only be employed from one side," has its own attraction, more indeed for those above than for those below, but still it has attraction. The old castle with no factory chimney in its neighbourhood, the fallow land on which Nature is trying to set herself to rights again, the neglected swamp with all its teeming animal life, the little town with its clumsiness and credulity, all this and much else besides is like a mediæval fairy tale which one does not like to spoil. This fairy-tale spirit is much more frequent in Austria-Hungary than in the German Empire. Go into the woods for instance! Watch the country people on Sunday outside the church! Must all this indeed be disciplined into the normal, and estimated according to its utilitarian value? The Danube people think it so dull on the Elbe, because the latter has become such a much more reasonable river. These romantic temperaments are opposed to the modernisation of the economic system. They do not want to have their old spirit artificially cleaned and repaired, for —" What does it profit a man if he gain the whole world and lose his own soul?"

Come hither, dear romanticists, we want to talk together as friends! I will not tell you that people can increase their production by technique and organisation without altering themselves. That won't do. To enter the economic system of Mid-

Europe is a soul-transforming decision. That the unavoidable transformation accompanying the entrance into modernity will give more to the soul of the man affected than it takes from it, you may perhaps wish to deny, but on this point I venture really to speak from experience and observation. The old race of pre-capitalist wage-earners, small townsfolk, handworkers and miners are generally imagined by you æsthetic people as very different and much more picturesque than the reality. The reality is harsh and monotonous and poor, both inwardly and outwardly, in the good things of life! These old lower orders gain spiritually everywhere by the introduction of the new method of work, even if they struggle against the new epoch owing to ignorance and to the danger, referred to above, of an economic decline. The beautiful old culture hardly belonged to you at all. In the churches alone, and, be it admitted, even in the churches of the villages and small towns, had the resident people of the old style any share in the beautiful art of their age. The good done by the church in this respect should not be forgotten. But does this constitute the whole of what is attainable by the poor man and his family? No, it is certainly not he who loses by the change into modernity. For a time all his existing ideas totter with his growing independence, but that is a state of transition. Whatever is good in what he retains of his past soon shows itself again. But of course there is a certain section which was on the upper side, and, on the basis of this needy underworld, fostered a pleasant culture with skill in fine handicrafts and the laying out of parks. This section has learnt to demand more in the meanwhile, and uses motor-cars, lends its money advantageously to the bank, dresses in good machine-made cloth, reads daily a newspaper printed by night workmen with a rotary printing press, whilst it wishes in addition to all this to keep up the delightful appearance of comfortable grandfatherly days and to mingle the magic of the patriarchal past with the utility of the technical present, in a confused but pleasantly flavoured drink. If you romanticists really wanted to preserve the good old time, with all its attendant features, thatched roofs, loss of time and smells, then, though I should not join you,

I should respect you as privileged and interesting eccentrics. But you don't want this at all! And indeed you could not! You could not because you yourselves would be much too poor for this new pretentious present. Therein lies coercion for you too, and the more so since after the war there will be much to pay. With rising prices it is impossible to be an economic romanticist without sinking in the social scale.

. . . .

Nevertheless there is an element of justice in this anxiety in face of the supremacy of the organising business intellect. And it is in this very matter that Austria, and especially Vienna, can supplement Berlin and the North in a salutary and excellent manner. The North has created the type of successful, disciplined man. In this way a good general efficiency has been attained which can be applied in the most varied departments of work. Industrial militarism can be set up as well in forestry as in sugar production or the manufacture of shoes. But this general capability is not in itself sufficient to secure markets if taste and form are not added. For railway lines and kitchen pots indeed utility is almost everything and form almost nothing, but there are a hundred objects which are not quite complete unless the progressive methods of work are combined with a well-devised form and colour. Every one knows what efforts we have made in this respect under the guidance of the "German Work Union." But when in the last months before the war the Union held its fine exhibition at Cologne-on-Rhine, the "Austrian House" excelled all the others. How quiet the pompous members suddenly became in there, members who might easily have thought otherwise that they could do everything perfectly! That was a lasting, unforgettable success. If such splendid ability is omitted from Mid-Europe, then it will lack something invaluable and rich in future possibilities.

Thus we reject all conceptions of the common economic life as a one-sided extension of our North German agricultural and industrial methods up to the lower Danube, instead of a simultaneous interchange from South to North. Not control, but intermixture. We have more horse-power, and you more music. We think more in terms of quantity, the best of you think rather in terms of quality. If we can unite our respective abilities, then and for the first time the hard North German civilisation will secure by your assistance that touch of charm which will make it tolerable to the outside world.

As we have said before, Paris has long possessed a magic attraction for us Germans of the Empire in North and South. And fresh threads will timidly begin to spin themselves again after the war, for the home of so much delicacy and competence does not lose its power through military events of however serious a kind. But even so, something has been broken. Here Vienna ought to seize its opportunity. The whole of Germany is now more open to the Viennese crafts than ever before. The Viennese might make an artistic conquest extending to Hamburg and Danzig. There are numerous finishing trades in which the Austrians will produce quite original goods if they can only get a firm start in respect to technique and capital. This is evident enough already in the glass trade, in pottery, in paper manufacture, in hats, veils, chairs and many other things. Where intelligence prevails it will not be injured by machinery, but will only remain terrified in the corner so long as the machines are not helpful. And the world wants skilfully made things. We want to join together to supply the rest of the world, through the ports of Hamburg and Trieste, with all the beautiful things they need for their households.

. . . . . .

We have so far said little in this section of the Southern Germans of the Empire. This omission had a definite purpose, for it is only now after the problem of establishing a common economic spirit has been worked out that we wish to bring forward our Southern Germans as an example and model of success. Almost the same anxieties and scruples about a closer union with North Germany existed before 1870 in Bavaria, Württemberg, Baden, Hesse and Frankfurt-on-Main. These countries were members, it is true, of the Customs Union, but in other respects they maintained a strong and suspicious particularism towards each other and very much more towards Prussia. In culture and economic life they wished to stay as they were. In Bavaria especially the new Empire was greeted in no very friendly way as, in the upper Bavarian phrase, an Empire of barracks and Jews. The Berliner was for long an alien, and is still so in parts even to-day. Nevertheless the unification was consummated. To-day the majority of South German farmers belong to the farmers' union, and the South German employers belong, according to the nature of their business and their further inclinations, either to the central industrial association or to the German industrial union. The merchants belong to the German commercial congress, the towns to the town congress, the workpeople to the Social Democrats, the Christian or the Hirsch-Duncker unions, the employees to the union of persons with fixed salaries or to one of the two associations of technical workers, and so on. There is no separate South German working population, advancing along a path of its own, no special unions for South Germans, no division at the Main for co-operative stores or economic cartels, the whole now lives with a common breath. People are still conscious that there were differences, but they are no longer disturbing. And with all this the Southerners have certainly suffered no economic loss. What industries are flourishing in Nüremberg, Munich, Augsburg, on the Neckar from Reutlingen through Stuttgart to Heilbronn, on the Rhine from Mannheim and Ludwigshafen to Offenbach and Mainz! The South German peasant farmer has made marked progress. His profits are rising and the number of his live stock is increasing. No one wants to put an end to the joint development, no one. There are, however, people enough who would prefer to drop what still remains of separate railway authority, water authority, postage stamps and such like. The Southern German does, however, wish and intend to maintain after his own manner his strong political and social liberalism; and this indeed he wants to introduce into Prussia. Since 1870 he has had a noticeable influence in forming the German national character, and is very far from regarding himself as a mere appendage. Catholics and Protestants, Bavarians and Alemani declare this unanimously. All the earlier humours of the Confederation of the Rhine are washed away as though they had never existed. People quarrel, as is the custom of mankind, over a hundred things, but certainly not over that inclusion in the German economic system which is henceforth indispensable.

This example is instructive for Mid-Europe. We admit at once that the task now is greater and more difficult than then, because we have to combine nations speaking different languages and with wider economic differences. But then has not every one in the interval gained a wider understanding of the need for more extensive alliances? Half a century of railway communication and international commerce has educated us all. But perhaps it is the especial task of the South Germans to be available as intermediaries when the time comes for the various associations of trade and industry to seek out and discover one another across the German-Austrian-Hungarian frontiers.

. . . . . .

To unite Central Europe by mere political measures so long as the economic groups themselves do not call for unity will certainly be a futile beginning. Incipient evidence of such a call is already present, but for the most part only in the German-speaking districts. Points of contact in congresses exist in scientific, technical, agricultural and industrial circles. One quite old union is that in the bookselling trade. Amongst political parties the Social Democrats have fostered unity the most, and to some extent also the Anti-Semites and the Pan-Germans. In this connection, so far as I know, the German-Austrians are more diligent visitors of German institutions than vice versa. There is a German-Austrian-Hungarian economic union, a Central European economic association and other similar societies. These kinds of reunions must on principle be increased and systematised, and out of voluntary congresses permanent associations must be formed for common enterprises.

Any one who studies the preliminary history of the foundation of the German Empire will come across records of numerous assemblies and festivals, at which toasts were drunk, songs were sung and speeches made. Individually they may be of doubtful value, but regarded as a whole they served as practice for the joint political life, they were the "walking out" together before the betrothal. This obviously happens infinitely more easily with people speaking the same language than with those of alien tongues. But since in Austria and Hungary most of the leading men of all professions and occupations are proficient in German, language is no absolute hindrance if only goodwill is present. This will be so much the more the case with professional meetings if practical and material advantages are pursued and obtained.

From henceforth the attention of the directors of professional and other unions ought to be turned much more than before towards joint conferences. The aim is as follows: a Mid-European trade union, handworkers' union, technical experts' union and so on. These unions will, like all new unions, seem at first to be founded somewhat insubstantially and artificially, but from year to year their inner life and the sphere of their activities will grow. First there is the already existing mutual interchange of members by migration across the frontiers, the mutual recognition of membership rights which have been won, the partnership in union literature, and where necessary its translation. Then follows the closer combination of cartels, banks, insurance institutions and credit banks. In the first instance people will draw together through the adjustment of statutes, the examination of differences, the insertion of guarantee clauses, until the two machines will one day agree so closely that they could be made into one without any great shock. All that need be demanded of the Governments in this connection is that they do not hinder and that they remove any obstacles, such as legal definitions concerning the right to form unions or other difficulties of a similar nature. The people themselves must desire to combine together in their workers' organisations. If this is not the case, mere talking round the subject by outsiders will be in vain.

Will this be the case? Now, after the war, the attempt must be made. Now is the right time for it. Workpeople of Central Europe, we call upon you!

CHAPTER V

JOINT PROBLEMS IN WAR ECONOMICS

BEFORE the war we all lived in an age of growing international commerce. Each year we bought more from foreign markets and worked for and sold more to foreign nations. It is true that this was partially restricted on the frontiers and at the ports by tariffs and similar measures, but these protective or prohibitive tendencies could not stop the process of development altogether, and indeed were hardly intended to do so. They were rather intended to regulate prices than to guide economic development. When once modern means of intercommunication have been established it is impossible to prevent them from leading to the foundation of an extensive system of international exchange. Our consumption internationalises itself in regard to all sorts of materials and departments of demand, and this applies not only to the consumption of luxuries, which has always had something of an international character, but also to the demands of the masses. Everywhere, from upper and lower sections of the population, there is a demand for means of enjoyment which the home country cannot supply; clothing is worn the stuff for which is not produced by us; we make up materials which our own soil does not supply. Each of us needs only to inquire into the country of origin of the things he uses daily to show him how much of an international person he is, and how far removed he is from our simple forefathers, who dressed in home-grown woollens and ate flummery and groats. This universal progress towards economic exchange will not cease after the war; in spite of all attempts to prevent it, it will increase yet further with the age of inter-communication, so soon as our railways have again free access to all parts of the world and our ports are again loading and unloading as abundantly and actively as before.

The war has, however, signified an important epoch in this development of international trade, for it has and still does signify for Central Europe a breaking off of its world commerce. By the will of England we are almost completely shut off from our wide foreign trade. We Germans and Austrians and Hungarians have together gone through this notable economic experience; we sat, or rather sit together in an economic prison. This is a partnership whose whole significance we shall only realise when the closed doors are open again and we begin once more to trade with the world which has been shut off from us for a considerable time, and which has not had just this experience of ours. After the war every nation will have economic disturbances to relate; all will welcome the new possibilities of exchange. But we Central Europeans shall have learnt and endured something definite and peculiar, for we have actually been a "self-contained commercial State"—that bold dream of the German philosopher Fichte which has become a reality to us during the war owing to fate and our geographical position. Our enemies wished to do us an injury, but God, the God whom Fichte believed in and preached, has thought to turn it into a blessing.

It is a characteristically English notion to wish to humble and punish us by cutting off our foreign trade. England created overseas foreign trade and permits those who acquiesce in her leadership to take part in it. That is the meaning of the phrase Command of the Seas: we have in the past underestimated the importance of the English power at sea. We knew well enough that the English controlled the most ports, coaling stations, maritime routes and cables, but since we could use them all too we did not think it particularly hard that they should have practically sole command of the machinery. And the English for their part were not illiberal in the exercise of their power during the years of peace, since for a long time they themselves had been accustomed to think in terms of exchange and of international trade. According to their economic doctrine of Free Trade and the joys of commerce, the happiness of mankind consisted in access to their world-circling system of exchange. The English necessarily regard it as the greatest penalty on earth for a nation to be excluded from the felicitous system of exchange because, for England, it would in fact be fatal. Exclusion is to be put out of the sun into the shade. When the Englishman travelled round the world he was proud to belong to the nation which controlled this universally beneficent system; moreover, he considered how it might be to put a refractory person into confinement so as to reduce him to bread and water. And such thoughts occurred readily to Englishmen because they have had to record in their history the Napoleonic continental blockade, the first great economic war in the history of the world. Unfortunately all this has for long not concerned us in the same degree. We have indeed often talked about the possibility that England would one day cut us off from our access to foreign countries, but we have never seriously thought it over. Had we thought it out thoroughly we should have been economically prepared for it in a very different fashion. I remember many discussions in which, before the war, we spoke of the possibilities of exclusion. Generally the dependence of neutrals on the English system was taken for much less than it has been in reality. In general, too, only bread-corn was spoken of, seldom fodder for cattle, and still more rarely the other branches of our imports. But England, on the other hand, had a much more adequate notion of the kind of weapon that lay ready to her hand. She examined our annual imports and secretly rejoiced at the thought of the day when she would force us to our knees by threatening to cut us off from commerce or by actually doing so. It must be acknowledged that our economic dependence was better known in the Foreign Office in London than in the corresponding offices in Berlin and Vienna. Without this knowledge England would not have used for her own settlement of accounts with Germany the war on two frontiers which we had to fight out with France and Russia. She thought herself sure of her ground: to exclude imports from Central Europe must of itself bring about

JOINT PROBLEMS IN WAR ECONOMICS 151

a deprivation of food and of work! He who does not belong to the world's economic system must die!

. . . . . .

In preparing this careful and malicious plan of blockade the English were very clever in regard to our economic position, but yet they miscalculated. They omitted two things from their estimate: the powerful counter-effect of the exclusion of such a big economic area on the countries remaining in the international union, and the stores in Central Europe not previously included in any statistics. We must examine this latter point more closely because it will have further results in the future. The plan of blockade was, so to speak, abstract economics. The statistical year-books of the Central European States were looked at in London, and it was read therein how much bread-corn, fodder, cotton, wool, copper, leather, saltpetre, iron ore, charcoal, rice, tobacco, coffee and rubber we used annually. The total record was of millions of tons, milliards of marks and kronen: this represented the annual demand! This amount would not be bought and paid for annually by the Germans and Austrians, so the reasoning went on if they had not serious need of it every year! Thus, if the larger half alone could be cut off, poor Central Europe would be conquered. This manner of calculating we are sufficiently familiar with, since we have partially applied it during the war in much the same way to the question of food-supply. Our food professors, and we with them, said: there is lacking such and such an amount, and consequently we cannot hold out without the most severe exertions! In this view we were further strongly confirmed by the amazingly low estimates of existing stocks of corn and potatoes which were made by producers and owners. We had received somewhat false estimates previously, and had made mental allowances for them, but that the first direct attempt at a Government inventory of the quantity of food-stuffs should yield such false results was beyond all expectation, for we are accustomed to much greater accuracy in the case of taxes on income and property. This is only mentioned here in order to point out that an economic opinion or general rule based on existing statistical material may be correct, and yet false as to facts. According to calculation our anxieties and the English scheme were quite correct, but fortunately the actual stock of all necessary articles was much greater than any economist believed. We were not living so much from hand to mouth as was supposed by the English and by the German statisticians. Our economic system had been much more prudent than we thought and very sound in its storing up of goods. We, as a whole country, have had the experience which often, though unfortunately not always, falls to the lot of besieged fortresses, viz., that they can hold out months longer than is possible according to their inventory of goods. It was amazing what turned up out of all sorts of corners and how resourceful people became in finding out every usable material. We remember how for some time wool ran short; seek and ye shall find! Some appeared from abroad in defiance of England's threats, whether openly or secretly and with or without a gift in return, but much more sneaked out of our own coffers and bales. We thought for a long time, and perhaps still think, that copper would run short. Hence we began to notice for the first time that there was copper everywhere that could be taken and recast. Whenever a material was lacking people looked for or invented a substitute. We still do not know what new discoveries and contrivances will come permanently into use in consequence of the needs of this war, but hardly any part of its history will subsequently be so interesting as this. Just as a hundred years ago beet sugar and continental cotton printing were introduced on the isolated continent in consequence of the English continental blockade in the time of Napoleon, so an industrial resourcefulness will date from the time of this Central European war of ours, which will make us much more independent than before. This school to which we have been forcibly sent is strict and arduous but yet useful and beneficial. We are learning to stand on our feet in international commerce. Neither England nor France are learning this; this school is our privilege, the silver lining to our cloud; it constitutes a special Central European experience. Together we have accomplished something remarkable, not only from a military but also from an economic point of view. This is the introduction to the joint economic organisation we are going to have in the future. We shall emerge from the war, whether we wish it or not, like boys who have sat together on the same bench in school. From Hamburg to Trieste and Fiume our economic designs have been forced in a like direction: a system of storage and a system of adaptability with a view to independence!

. . . .

We may be allowed to enter somewhat more closely into our important economic experience during the war, even if it apparently leads us away from the Central European question. It will be seen later that we have not thereby forgotten the object of our work. In this connection we shall speak first more fully of the experiences of the German Empire, assuming that they apply in their degree to Austria and Hungary.

The English war of exclusion was based on ideas that were correct according to the figures, but were inorganic. That is to say: the individual economic events were looked at in isolation, but not thoroughly grasped as simultaneous and reciprocal in effect. The following principles are correct:

(*a*) If a nation suffers a serious and rapidly effective deprivation of raw material and markets owing to its exclusion from international commerce, violent disturbances and economic catastrophes must occur in it.

(*b*) If a nation is deprived of about one-sixth of its accustomed food-supply, and a much greater proportion of its fodder, scarcity, dearness and famine are inevitable amongst the poorer classes.

(*c*) If a nation is obliged to send a twelfth or a tenth part of its population away from their civil occupations into military service, all trades and all equilibrium between interdependent stages of work will be so disturbed that economic chaos will supervene in proportion as industrialism was developed.

Thus the German economic system ought to have crumbled up in three directions at once: want of supplies and markets, want of food-stuffs and want of work. And indeed we watched these three dangers drawing near like grey clouds in the sky. I can think of many meetings and discussions in August and September, 1914, in which people tried to devise precautions against the expected state of distress. We counted on much more disturbance and poverty than subsequently occurred. To our delighted surprise all these matters settled themselves much more readily than we could have expected because one need cured another.

If we suppose that we had suffered an economic exclusion from international trade without having war at the same time (it is merely a theoretical supposition, since exclusion would at once force us to declare war), it will be admitted that we should have had all our working ability sitting at home and no systematic imports or exports — it would have been intolerable! That would be the most serious economic crisis that can be imagined. But since the disturbance of trade happened simultaneously with the summoning of men to the army, something took place which, to use an expression borrowed from Leibniz, may be described as "pre-established harmony," as a providential arrangement; for the curve of men called up and the curve of loss of work mutually counteracted one another. That need not have been so, but it was so.

If we suppose, further, that we had suffered the deprivation of food-supplies under the laws of peace time, it would probably have led to the most extreme scarcity, usury and hunger riots. But since martial law was in force it was possible to carry out in a few months a policy which would otherwise have needed a lifetime of discussions: the declaration that all necessary stocks were State property, and the substitution of public officials and Government companies for private trade. State Socialism made giant strides forward in a single night. Before the war it was axiomatic that, "I can do what I like with my own potatoes." Now this axiom holds: "Your potatoes are our potatoes." We do not yet know how it will run after the war. The old state of things will certainly not come back again entirely since the beneficial

JOINT PROBLEMS IN WAR ECONOMICS

possibilities of the concept of State Socialism have become too obvious, and since we shall keep in mind the economic experiences of the war.

But all this involved an unheard-of labour of organisation, for the balance between the calling up to the army and the decreasing employment did not come about of itself, and the taking over of raw material and food-stuffs by the War Purchase Companies and the War Corn or Potato Companies was and is still no small trouble. In peace time Government Offices would have been very timid about both measures, but as it was they had to attack the work with half the usual official staff and it was a success. They would have been much less successful in peace time for then every one would have presumed upon his accustomed rights, but the war conferred undreamed-of powers: you must, you ought, you can! A willing people with an economic dictatorship voluntarily endured, can do infinite things. The dictatorship was incomplete, for here too previous mobilisation was lacking, but it became effective by degrees. What we see around us is certainly not exactly what, in Karl Marx's phrase, is termed "the Dictatorship of the Proletariat," but we are yet reminded of the expression in some respects: a step towards socialism under the leadership of the Government! It is an economic dictatorship of Government Offices advised and supported by those most nearly affected.

. . . .

The great and unusual changes in the economic system during the war were accomplished, notwithstanding all unavoidable friction, with comparative ease, which would not have happened if there had not been a remarkable mobility of money and labour. Neither was taken for granted at the outset, either by the calculating English or by the many anxious Germans. We had, almost without exception, no adequate idea of the demands of a modern war. We only now know what masses of material it recklessly swallows up each day. It uses much more than even the boldest imaginations had supposed, much more munitions, weapons, artillery, horses, wagons, motor-cars, tires, cement, wood, corrugated iron, wire, leather, clothing material, chemicals, field-glasses, cooking apparatus, jams and a hundred other things, which hardly any one had previously thought of as needed by an army. The Army became the most important purchaser and orderer. Like a giant turtle rising out of the water this enormous purchaser climbed up in a few months and replaced the lost foreign customers. Milliards were lacking in commerce, but milliards were paid out in compensation by the military officials. Money flowed in. Even if it flowed in rather unsystematically at times, yet the main point, from the economic point of view, is that it did flow. Only in a few trades was there a complete stoppage, in many more we experienced obstacles, rearrangements, half-time, in not a few there was high pressure with night work, overtime, high wages and great, sometimes excessive profits. The home country became, so to speak, one large factory for the war. The war was the continuation of the national economic system. The wheels rolled onwards.

It was thus that we first fully learnt the meaning of the words "national economics." We had frequently had it on our lips when we said that national economics stood between private economics and international economics. But apart from tariff questions and socio-political laws, the peculiarity of national economics as such, the supremacy of national economic ideas had not yet entered into our heads. People suspected indeed that in between private economics and international economics there existed a special and peculiar principle of organisation, but had not yet worked it out really definitely: the economic maintenance of the State. The State needed first to fight for its life before it could attain mighty independence and make itself at once the purpose and the director of the whole process of production.

That we Germans have glided into this State Socialism, or into this national economic business (for that is strictly what it is), as if it had always been our natural habit — that is what we have learnt about ourselves during this war. When we emerge from the war we shall no longer be the same economic beings as before. The period of essential individualism, the period of imitation of the already declining English economic system is thus gone by, but so also is the period of an internationalism boldly looking beyond the existing State. By reason of our experiences during the war we demand an ordered economic system: the regulation of production from the standpoint of political necessity. Similar impulses will indeed show themselves independently in the world amongst other nations, even amongst the English, but with us, in our isolated State, they have matured more than anywhere else. We brought to it the German spirit of organisation described above, and the war has wrought it into permanence. This is an occurrence of the first importance in international economics, and it will probably be much better and more clearly understood in its far-reaching significance by later generations than by us who have first experienced it.

There is in this a certain reconciliation between the economic conception of national citizenship and that of socialism. Even before the war we knew that the opposition was decreasing, since producers were organising themselves and workers were carrying out a strong and realistic trade-union policy within the existing State. Even before the war the theories of both sides were further separated than their practice. But now the practice of war has accomplished a notable work; the dispute about the management of labour and the produce of labour continues, but the process of labour itself is grasped, above all during the war, as above party and of common interest: we are a nation, and have learnt and discovered our national economics in the midst of a world of enemies and in an economic prison. This will remain as a background for everything that may befall later on.

. . . . . .

But the State, when it appears thus as a giant customer, needs much money which cannot be obtained from abroad. From the outset Havenstein, the Director of the Reichsbank, as General of Finance, took his place by the side of State Secretary Delbrück, the General of Administration. These two men have become historical figures just as much as Hindenburg and Mackensen. Had it not been for their work much trouble would have been wasted. Havenstein has enabled the German Empire to raise the loans of milliards and thus kept the war going effectively. And this he has accomplished without a moratorium, that is without permitting financial uncertainty, and without giving up the principle of a gold cover against note issue. He issued money in the first instance before drawing it in again as a loan. He issued it in the self-contained commercial State where it could not be lost to the nation. These loans would have been inconceivable without the war, for then the increased capital would have passed into buildings, machinery, fresh enterprises or foreign investments. But now that there were hardly any new enterprises, these loans proved the only salvation of a capitalism that would otherwise have been ruined. Havenstein's financial policy saved it and the Fatherland at the same time. And meanwhile, under the auspices of the Imperial Home Office the capitalism and industrialism thus supported by the State was constrained into stable paths and trained to efficient political assistance. State Secretary Delbrück succeeded in forming a national economic War State out of the individualistic economic Peace State without dispensing with the parliamentary system, and in laying the foundation lines of an economic system which will have much broader results than the majority of people dream of to-day. When our troops return home they will find another Germany, but they themselves will in the interval have experienced the life and death socialism of war, so that what they find will seem to them like their own flesh and blood.

But whilst we keep up our military power in this way by loans and organisation, we burden the future with far-reaching obligations, with the duty of passing over from a war organisation to an orderly condition of peace and with the duty of beginning a policy of finance and of taxation which will discover a way out of the debt. Both tasks are in close connection with one another, as the veriest outsider will admit. We will begin the discussion of these connected duties with the financial side.

No one yet knows how great our Imperial debt will be at the end of the war, and whether and to what extent the payment of war indemnities may be counted upon. Owing to this uncer-

JOINT PROBLEMS IN WAR ECONOMICS 159

tainty we avoid any estimate in figures. So much is, however, certain: that we shall have to raise a very large sum which cannot be met by a rise in the existing taxes. Every form of taxation carries its own limits within itself. In the past time before the war I calculated that the wealthy classes paid down, in various ways, one-sixth of their incomes to Empire, State and Commune. There were local differences, but prolonged observation has convinced me of the truth of a South German banker's remark: "We work for the State for two months in the year!" In like manner I calculate that a man living on his wages also gives, in the form of direct and more especially of indirect taxes, about one-sixth of his income to the State (and also to the classes assisted by the national tariff policy). Owing to these already existing imposts on production both sections are sensitive to any new burdens imposed in the old forms. New methods of taxation must be sought for, if the burden of the war (loans, new constructions, payments to invalids, pensions) are to be met. This is an occasion when the financial obligations arising out of the war must lead to fresh organisation. The new phenomenon which gives warning of its approach may be called either a State industrial monopoly or the taxation of syndicates, but these are in essence only two different expressions for the same thing.

· · · · · ·

Forty years ago when socialist problems made their appearance there were three kinds of theoretical socialism: State Socialism, Producers' Socialism and Workers' Socialism.

State Socialism was the concept of taking over a larger section of industrial life into direct State control, after the manner of the nationalised railways and post office, and in this way of meeting the financial requirements of the State.

Producers' Socialism was the concept of creating a self-administrating and self-governing body out of the property-owning and industrial classes by combining the great industrial and agricultural federations, and thus reducing mutual competition.

Workers' Socialism was the idea of weakening the authority of the employers by combinations of both the upper and the lower labour forces and of the consumers, and of a transition to self-government by the working masses, and thus securing for the workers the employers' profits.

Each of these three forms has made progress, but no one of them alone has become the determinative basis of the period. The air has been full of attempts at organisation without any final general concept of this development emerging. It can only be said that a more complete victory of any one of the normal types appeared out of the question. But in the meanwhile intermediate forms made their appearance, which combined two or even all three of the basal ideas: combined management, communal joint-stock companies, State syndicates, tariff union enterprises, public management with private shareholders and employees resembling officials. All this seemed to those not concerned therein to be very complex and hard to understand, but to those in the midst of things it all soon became quite easily managed and practicable. Almost all the big town councils started enterprises in combined management, gas and electricity works, tramways, slaughter-houses, companies for workmen's dwellings, in which communal socialism appeared as a pioneer in future methods of business arrangement. The best known of these enterprises is the alkali monopoly, with its imperial protection, imperial compulsion and workman's insurance. The correctness of its policy in details is much disputed, but the constructive idea underlying it has already been recognised as a new basal form. When the petroleum monopoly was under consideration people went back to a similar train of reasoning. The State does not thereby become a monopolist pure and simple, but it holds a decisive number of shares and controls its portion and also the terms of payment for employees and workpeople. An arrangement of this sort has the value of a new invention in national economic machinery, which may perhaps be compared to the invention of balloons. The apparatus of aeronautics also resulted from a combination of different existing models and technical expedients. We shall not assert that the social problem is "solved" by the combined types of management of State joint-stock companies or State syndicates, but it will be admitted that

JOINT PROBLEMS IN WAR ECONOMICS 161

herein is proclaimed something that has been demanded through long decades. This roughly was the position before the war. And the war has matured these beginnings.

Now for the time the war freed us from all the control of theoretical principles and forced us to organise solely for practical ends. And it immediately became evident that Government, producers' syndicates and workmen's trade unions are only organs of a common system of life, of the economic nation. In order to carry out the immense tasks of war economics all the usual dogmatism had to be thrown aside and people had to see how the most effective type of administration might be established with the peaceable and active participation of all required energies. Much has been left indefinite during the process, in particular guarantees to workers and employees in the combined management of national economic enterprises, but the different State joint stock companies for war purchase, for military supplies, for food administration embody evident future developments. They are present to the minds of those who have to approach the new financial problems.

. . . . . .

To put it briefly and in a way generally comprehensible: financial policy after the war must rest mainly upon State syndicates combined with guarantees for workpeople. The latter are an essential constituent, without which the State syndicate would become an instrument of class government, and without which no parliamentary majority in its favour could be secured or maintained. For our existing population a monopoly without systematic limitation of its absolute control over its workpeople constitutes an intolerable menace to personal freedom and to that standard of life which it will be difficult enough to maintain in face of the rise in prices that will probably continue after the war.

Financially the State syndicate involves the imposition of a tax obligation upon an industrial association which receives in compensation the right to be the only one of its kind. To illustrate from the case of the alcohol syndicate: the State does not of itself devise new taxes on production or manufacture, but requires the management of the syndicate to produce the required millions in whatever way they think wise commercially. The producers and manufacturers who do not at present belong to the syndicate have to adapt themselves to its assessment, which supplies a very strong motive for joining it. Should this syndicate, based upon a politically favoured voluntarism, break down or for any reason be discontinued, a Government tax on the quantities sold or manufactured will be enforced, which prospect conduces greatly to the maintenance of the syndicate. The settlement of prices and the methods of sale are the concerns of the syndicate, but the State possesses a very simple remedy in case of excess or of neglect of the workmen's guarantees: it can alter the tax if required as educational pressure. This is the easiest way for the State to secure simultaneously money and commercial pliancy. The State money will be abstracted during the process of production before it has become private money. Milliards must be raised somehow, and consequently the national economic system must be burdened somehow and at some place. Wealth must unquestionably be withdrawn, the only problem is by what method. The method here indicated has the immense advantage over all other conceivable ones in that it makes for commercial and technical concentration and improvement. The self-interest of producers' associations is made to serve the interests of the State.

The scheme for this method of supplying the much increasing needs of the State can only be completely matured in practice, and will take different forms for different industries. Alcohol exists under different conditions from sugar, sugar under different ones from iron and steel, and steel again under different ones from coal or yarn or cement. It can only be determined step by step which branches of industry will come in question. The general principle is: the more an industry lends itself to the formation of syndicates the more suitable it is for State participation.

This train of thought will inevitably provoke much contradiction and many doubts at the outset, but it will probably meet with no serious opposition from amongst the directors of the existing syndicates since through it, in the first instance, they themselves were firmly established. Now they are already not merely the deputies of their shareholders, but at the same time managers and governors of their departments of the national economic system. According to our reasoning, this will be politically recognised, and it will on the other hand be recognised that the workers, through their unions, are to be represented on the managing and financial bodies. The process of evolution moves of itself in the direction indicated, only it would all have taken much longer if it had not been accelerated by the financial need of the State. The war has made all sections of the nation much more docile about violent transformations and political necessities. Now an important step may easily be taken and — what else could we do? We ask each one who objects to this sort of scheme, from reasons and hesitations which are in themselves justified, how he himself thinks of obtaining the milliards. Mere criticism avails nothing at all.

. . . .

In addition to financial motives a second great impelling force in the same direction is the necessity for a State system of storage.

Hitherto we have luckily been able to surmount the English blockade policy by means of existing private economic stores, but this basis is much too insecure for future war anxieties. When the war is over we shall plan a State storehouse, or one controlled by the State, for the most necessary materials. This may already be described as a national demand without distinction of party. But this storage policy is essentially an interference with the individualistic economic system, for it means that in future prices will not determine themselves according to supply and demand in the old sense, but will be liable to influence in an upward or downward direction through the State storehouse. This applies to all departments. The State, by holding an available reserve of copper, caoutchouc or saltpetre or wool becomes at once a factor in the market, an agent in the processes of exchange. Preparation for an economic war thus leads here also to a kind of State socialism, and that of a very obscure and unexplored kind. As a rule the plan will not, for practical reasons, lead to an undisturbed store of material, but rather to larger trade reserves than are necessary for the purposes of a purely private commercial system. The attempt to establish the petroleum monopoly was an easily understood example: either the petroleum trade increases its reserve stock or the State establishes its own storehouse with authority to trade. Practically no material will bear storage for ten years, so that any one who has a stock must carry on sales. In a word, storage policy thus includes much more than appears at first sight: State commercial policy.

Storage obligations must be laid upon the syndicates on behalf of the State in addition to the financial obligations referred to above, and State commercial management or a State commercial monopoly must be introduced for such objects of commerce as are not in the hands of a syndicate or cannot easily be so controlled. This applies primarily to food-supplies and fodder. Here the Government and the representatives of the people are called upon to make decisions.

The elder ones among us still remember very well the time, about twenty years ago, when the "Kanitz proposal" was occupying all the agricultural conferences. It was the idea of a State monopoly of foreign trade in corn. At that time these endeavours arose from the desire to keep the price of corn, with the help of legislation, at the definite height desired by the farmers. The prices demanded then have now long since become very low. But in those days there was, in fact, much more dispute over the amount of the price than over the principle itself. The latter, indeed, might be opposed from the Liberal, but hardly from the Socialist standpoint. However, the Social Democrats treated the affair at the time almost entirely as a temporary question of price. Thus it came about that the Kanitz proposal was dropped, and was replaced by a strong and successful agrarian tariff agitation. Now all these already half forgotten quarrels are being revived, but with respect to the storage policy. The old debates are taken up again with fresh vigour under the new conditions. It is a difficult task to prophesy anything as to the result of these discussions. A useful proposal often breaks down for incidental reasons. But at bottom the matter stands thus: if an automatic method of determining prices is agreed upon as between agrarians and Social Democrats, there will be nothing left for the rest of us but to help to establish the contrivance, or at least not to obstruct the State corn warehouse. This is essentially an outcome of the war. We shall remain politically unquiet until we possess it. "National economics" demands it as a necessity of State, in order to make future wars of starvation impossible. Perhaps this is the greatest interference with private economic enterprise which will be introduced owing to the war, but here too we may ask: how could we possibly do anything else so as to avoid future anxiety about starvation?

.   .   .   .   .   .

Of course this is only a very fragmentary discussion of the abundance of economic problems connected with the end of the war. The transition from war to peace forms a chapter in itself, and might give all statesmen much to think over even to-day, although such thoughts run the risk of entangling themselves in false anxieties and expectations like a boat among reeds. It will be best to try to pick out the elements of certainty first of all.

For our economic system the end of the war will mean the draining out and emptying of all stocks of imports and materials, and consequently at the same time an unnatural abundance of some (not indeed of very many) export stocks in such industries as have wished to employ their machinery and their remaining workpeople without being able to join in the war industries. Hence it follows that there will be a great stimulus to the import trade, especially by sea, combined with insufficient facilities for transport, a fight for ship space and dock berths, a strained and heightened condition of commercial life with excessive prices, unless opportune regulation is introduced in this department. Hamburg, which has grown unnaturally quiet during the war, will be reanimated, but will need prudence meanwhile, like an invalid when he first leaves the hospital. The same thing will apply to Trieste and the other ports. And also to the Rhine navigation.

Further, the end of the war will mean at the outset an immediate replenishing of the military stores that have now become empty, since in all human probability peace will come upon the world slowly, and not without renewed risks of complications. As formerly at the Vienna Congress, and recently at the London Conference at the end of the Balkan Wars, the international position will remain very insecure, just as rubbish still glows after a fire when the big flames have been extinguished. That is to say, more loans and more war industries and works of restoration will follow the war immediately, without its being possible to count on any long continuance of these renovation industries.

The return of the soldiers to civil life at the end of the war will bring not only joy but also much trouble. Only a portion of the number returning will readily find their old posts again. The women will frequently be driven out of the occupations which they have taken over in the interval, small businesses, unfortunately, will have in part disappeared, and the question of unemployment may result in calamity after the war if there is any unwisely rapid breaking up of war formations. This need not be so, but it will be if mistakes are made or if there is a lack of precaution.

The money market will be pulled hither and thither in a thoroughly embarrassing manner, for the imposing unity of the war loan system will be cut across by a formerly unknown demand for private credit for which at first all basis will be lacking, since all savings have been absorbed into war and communal loans. Moreover, the filling of the stores of which we speak will require money, and indeed the exportation of money abroad, because imports will begin to flow again earlier and more extensively than exports. We may have to endure unaccustomed fluctuations in values, but not we alone. The whole of the international money market will be like a storm-tossed sea, and many businesses which are still holding on during the war will be carried off like wreckage on the waves.

It is to be supposed that the war will conclude with a big rise of prices in all departments, in the midst of which legal maximum prices for important supplies could only be maintained by sacrifices from the State Treasury. All the accustomed international price standards will be in doubt and must be settled afresh. Thus there will be possibilities of great profits and losses, and especially a very painful interval of social struggles, until prices, wages and salaries have again found a tolerable mutual relationship. Immense problems will confront the producers' federations and the trade unions during this period. The demand for housing too will be more disturbed than during the war, as soon as the war subsidies and the contributions of the big municipalities cease.

We do not specify all this in order to spread fear and anxiety, but only to show for what reasons that trend towards State Socialism which we have described will outlast the war. A nation that has fought through a war of such unheard-of difficulty so remarkably will not be beaten by problems of this kind. It only needs to learn in due course that the war organisation with all, or at least with many, of its consequences must be continued through the peace preliminaries. When the doors of the economic prison are opened, the prisoner needs a careful diet lest he should be more upset by freedom than by his imprisonment.

In other words, the social struggle for existence, which is now restrained by general consent and regard for the party truce, must wait somewhat longer before it can take its course with its old licence. This is unpleasant hearing for all the discontented citizens of every camp and party, for they have already collected material for the day when they can attack one another after the old fashion. But here, too, reason will remain victorious over the passion, in other respects justified, for individual interests. And thus the period after the war, between imprisonment and freedom, and before the dawn of a new future, will perhaps prove of especial fruitfulness in efforts of value for the promotion of mutual understanding. In this connection I am thinking of the question, repeatedly raised, of public labour exchanges, advised and controlled by representatives of those concerned, of a more settled arrangement for suitable arbitration procedure in wages disputes, of the organisation of house-owners and tenants, of a closer fusion of hitherto competing professional representative bodies. All this must not be entered upon for the sake of a social theory, for under the circumstances no one has time or mind for academic reforms, but in all probability the things will in practice arise of itself out of the peace difficulties. The social harvest of the war will be reaped while the party truce is still half maintained, until such time as the political heaven becomes so far clear that we can, without risk or injury, begin anew to quarrel, as belongs to a healthy condition of body and soul.

· · · · ·

When, however, we re-enter the system of world-economics after the war, we shall have been markedly changed in the interval by the pressure of our enemies. A much more compact, self-contained whole has developed out of our many-sided German system. We all think much more in terms of State economy and buy and sell much more as a whole; for it is obvious that State syndicates and State monopolies with regular guarantees for the workpeople work differently from mere competing private traders. Of course all this applies only to those parts of the German economic system which are suited to union. The manufacturers of finished goods are, as it is, less affected by the change, and amongst the small farmers house and farm will be found faithfully kept going by wife and children. The small trader, in so far as he returns home safely, remains as he is, and seeks his own markets in the usual way. Above all, the aspect of German foreign trade will be changed if the country comes forward as buyer and seller in the world's market in a much more compact shape in respect to many raw products. Foreigners will talk even more than before about German economic militarism, but we are convinced that the enforced transformation of the war period will not suit us badly. The organised economic State will be strongest when the organisation is able to go on living on itself. But it is just this which we believe we have learnt to accomplish in virtue of our wartime experiences.

Of course it is not certain that all these very complicated problems will be solved exactly as we have briefly indicated here. There are numerous byways and variations. But in essence our

JOINT PROBLEMS IN WAR ECONOMICS 169

account is probably correct. What we have described in the previous section as the German peculiarity, the vigorous and living organisability, will be immensely increased by the war. We shall appear on the scene as economically even more German than before. We shall do this whether we are alone or in partnership with Austria-Hungary.

But it is a question and anxiety for Austria and Hungary whether or no they desire and are able to tread this path with us. This is their problem.

. . . . . .

What has Austria-Hungary accomplished during the war in the economic sphere?

The first answer is as follows: Here too things have gone much easier and better than could have been expected. Austria and Hungary have had their very great racial difficulties, but as far as the economic position is concerned special distress has only appeared in districts directly affected by the war. The sufferings that we have gone through in the parts of East Prussia that have been occupied by the Russians have lasted much longer in the case of Galicia and have affected a much wider area of country. Moreover, in Bosnia and Herzegovina, so far as can be learnt, the disturbances due to the war are not inconsiderable. None of this is as bad as what the French are enduring in the districts occupied by the German troops — although as a matter of course the Germans have shown much more forbearance in respect to the economic conditions in Northern France than the Russians did in Galicia — for in North France there has been at least a year's produce lost in agriculture and very considerable industrial losses in the French economic system. But still the Austrian economic injuries are not small, and the recovery from them constitutes a very difficult war problem. In addition to the financial problems which are in any case bound up with the war, there will be the remaking of the destroyed roads, fortifications, public buildings, schools, churches, and the assistance needed by the population in country and town when they take up their systematic occupations again. Already in the wake of the advancing army precautions are taken and attempts made to help where possible, but it is doubtful how far this can go on, because the distribution of the burden of renewal cannot be definitely settled from the outset. Who will have to pay? Galicia or Austria or Austria-Hungary? Here already we come upon the consideration which we regard as a main problem for the allied States, and which crops up in the most varied directions: Are we concerned with a single economic State or with two or with several?

When the German Empire was founded, the desire to establish an economic entity was a principal object throughout the whole historic movement. It is only necessary to look in the Constitution of the North German Confederation and in the German Imperial Constitution based upon it, at the careful enumeration of the departments reserved for Imperial legislation, in order to realise how deliberately everything economic, with the exception of purely agrarian legislation, was made the business of the Empire. The economic federation was formed out of the Customs Union. Hence in individual cases it was left for future consideration, how far the Imperial legislature should take over the regulation of trade, industry, financial law, the bourse, patents, social policy and the prevention of adulteration, but the right to legislate on all these matters was firmly established, and we have seen how very extensively this right was put into practice during the next forty years. In any doubtful case the Empire is competent to act if it desires to do so; only the enforcement and the administration appertain to the federated States. But no such economic unity exists in the Dual Monarchy of Austria-Hungary, nor was it intended, but on the contrary until now it has been expressly excluded by the fundamental law of December 21, 1867, concerning the constitutional Ausgleich. The true position of the matter is sufficiently well known in Austria and Hungary, but must be emphasised for readers in the German Empire, because they are often inclined to apply Imperial German conditions to Austria-Hungary without further ceremony.

For the case immediately in point this means that according to the theory of State rights and the legal position, both States, it is true, following the provisions of the existing settlement, are answerable for their joint possession of Bosnia and Herzegovina, but not in like manner for Galicia. The chief burden of Galicia rests on the kingdoms and lands represented in the Reichsrat. But this burden may still give rise to complicated discussions, if say at the end of the war a fresh section of land that had hitherto been Russo-Polish were added to the rest of the monarchy. Who will then be liable for its financial equipment? Will it be the Polish districts themselves, and will they be capable of it? Will it be Austria? Will it be the whole monarchy?

. . . . . .

In the fundamental law of 1867 the unity of Austro-Hungarian economic policy is declared in so far as it relates to politico-commercial representation abroad, and the principle of equality is kept in view with regard to tariffs, indirect taxes, the monetary system and the construction of such railways as affect the interests of both halves of the Empire. This is all! There is no joint economic legislation, no department corresponding to our Imperial Department for Home Affairs. Hence too there is no joint war economic system.

This division of the economic life into two is most obvious in regard to the question of food-supply. Austria was approximately in the position of Western Germany: it needed to import corn; Hungary was and is the fortunate possessor of a surplus of corn. To an ingenuous mind nothing seems more obvious than that a compensatory arrangement, similar to that which exists in the German Empire between districts with a surplus and districts with a demand, will be found also throughout the territory of the belligerent Danube Monarchy. But deference to State rights produced a different position. Without being separated from Austria by tariff barriers Hungary has and carries on in the midst of the war its own policy in regard to corn, its own maximum prices, its own railway management, and the effect is indeed almost as though two foreign States were negotiating together. This situation is aggravated by the fact that any possible Roumanian supplies can only reach Vienna by way of Hungary.

During the joint war Austria is kept in sensible dependence upon Hungary. There is no object in moralising about this; the Hungarians are doubtless right in theory, they insist on their bond. They have always, even in doubtful cases, advocated a special Hungarian economic State, and are only keeping up in war time their conviction and custom on other occasions. But the economic union in war time is not a part of the Ausgleich of 1867. People are shedding their blood together and yet the corn prices in selling Budapest are intentionally higher than in purchasing Vienna.

Although an understanding will of course be arrived at ultimately, there still remains a difficult question for the future. The future preparation for war, of which we have already spoken, rests on a complete co-operation between military affairs and the national economic system, and hence the suppositions at the basis of the Ausgleich of 1867 must be re-tested in the light of military preparedness. Here the triple organisation of the army will come under consideration, but this we will not discuss at present. The underlying idea in 1867 was a military partnership with economic separation, a conception which was very explicable at that time, but which in this war has already led to all kinds of painful complications, and which will prove still more destructive when the future precautionary war-storage system is introduced.

It may, indeed, be admitted as certain that a permanent defensive and trench-making alliance between Germany and Austria-Hungary will only be possible on the basis of a system of war storage carried out by both sides. I do not say a joint storage system, because that is desirable but not absolutely necessary. A situation can easily be conceived in which two allied States keep their economic system separate, but in which, with mutual rights of control, they promise and agree what and how much each shall store up and hold in readiness. If this latter provision be neglected it will be impossible, according to the experiences of this war, to conclude any further treaty for mutual defence at all. The possibilities arising during the war without this are too serious.

JOINT PROBLEMS IN WAR ECONOMICS 173

Let us suppose then that in the first instance Austria and Hungary make the system of corn storage a subject of negotiations in drawing up the renewed Ausgleich, and then together come to an arrangement with the storage administration of the German Empire. In this case there are various conceivable ways of satisfying requirements. The starting-point of the discussions in question might be a system of Austrian State corn stores, which would collect the necessary supplies. After the expiration of the existing commercial treaty there is nothing connected with the rights of the individual States to prevent Austria from taking up, for herself alone, the State purchase of corn, and especially since Hungary has continually insisted on the economic independence of the two halves of the Empire. The system of Austrian State corn stores would in this case carry on business with the associated corn merchants in Budapest just as with other foreign corn firms, whilst Hungary would simultaneously make sure of its own State stores in case of war, not a difficult matter for Hungary. This position of affairs would be a direct continuation of the procedure adopted during the war, but is certainly not without difficulty for the partnership of both sections in other respects. We are convinced that another solution of the problem will be discovered according to which Hungary will occupy that central position in the business of providing corn for Mid-Europe which corresponds to its agricultural strength. But it would seem like interference if we in Germany tried to make proposals about a matter which is, in the first instance, the home concern of the Danubian Monarchy, however closely we may be interested in the results of this very decision.

. . . .

Nor can the remaining war-storage problems be quite decided without going more closely into the problem of the Ausgleich between Austria and Hungary. A whole number of joint economic regulations have already been taken in hand up to the present in virtue of the common tariff and the common system of indirect taxation. Such, for example, is the State treatment of breweries, brandy distilleries, mineral oil works, sugar factories, patents and joint-stock companies. In like manner joint superintendence and administration will be introduced in the warehouses declared necessary for the purposes of the new system of war storage. For instance, a copper monopoly or a copper syndicate under State influence will be unavoidable as well as a caoutchouc and rubber syndicate and State regulation of the stores of petroleum. It is impossible to say beforehand to which materials this method of treatment will be extended, nor do we wish to anticipate here the possible work of a future Military Economic Commission. We wish merely to show, and to indicate the reasons thereof, that in Austria-Hungary, just as with us, the effect of the war is to transform the economic system. Even should Austria-Hungary, contrary to our desires, not be united with the German Empire in permanent preparedness for war, the Danubian Monarchy must still, and more especially indeed in this event, in view of its risky geographical position, devote the utmost care to plans for war storage. But if, as we hope and suppose, the two Central European Powers attain to a permanent political union, joint regulation of the storage system will have much to recommend it, especially for those materials which can either be produced more extensively or further worked up in one of the two Imperial districts, because in this case partnership will ensure a wider oversight and more economy. We must set up a Central European War Provision Office as a centre from which all the store places shall be established and filled, proposed to the several governments and parliaments and inspected as to their contents. Thus the beginning of a joint economic system will grow up almost of itself and of necessity, out of the joint defensive system. This economic partnership is not voluntary in its origin, but is forced upon us by our history; it is no theoretical academical demand but is a practical precept, and its chief supporters must be the Ministers of War on both sides.

. . . . . .

But probably the further development of the financial question in Austria-Hungary will be of even greater importance for the future interrelations of the two Empires now allied in the war.

On the whole the condition of finance in the Danubian Monarchy during the war has been better than was expected. Our general statement that the Austro-Hungarian economic system had sustained the war remarkably well, applies especially to monetary matters. The loans in both Austria and Hungary have aroused surprise at home and abroad, and, considering the conditions of life, have been as much an economic victory as those in the German Empire. The Dual Monarchy has sufficient capital and also procures enough milliards for public purposes during the war. One difference consists in the fact that as a matter of course the system of a gold cover was less strictly enforced than in Germany, and that hardly any gold was in the hands of the population, for Austria-Hungary had previously withdrawn the gold from circulation or had never issued it. Consequently the reserve was necessarily smaller, which expressed itself in a sharp fall in the foreign exchange value of the bank-note. We also have had our exchange difficulties, for we need only go to Switzerland or Holland to find out at once that a German hundred mark note is no longer worth the same as before the war. But in the judgment of all the experts the decline in the value of our bank-note is only temporary, and is due to the fact that we keep back our gold whilst we import much more from abroad than we export thither, so that a stock of German treasury notes that are difficult to dispose of collects on the other side of the frontiers. After the war our renewed exports will be paid for with them, and also the interest, which will again be payable, on foreign securities. The decline in Austrian values is from its nature more serious, since it cannot be explained merely by reason of a negative balance of trade due to one-sided displacement, but is connected with the question of a gold cover. No exact estimate of the quantitative relation between the cover in specie and the note issue can be made, and hence all these matters are for the present somewhat obscure, but the disturbance in the relative values of the paper mark and the paper krone is evidence of how the state of affairs is conceived of in banking circles. No definite and permanent standard exists between the Imperial German paper money and that of Austria-

Hungary. We shall have to consider this point in our investigation into the future commercial policy of Mid-Europe, as forming a serious obstacle to any economic partnership; here we refer to it in the first instance as an Austro-Hungarian economic problem that will give much food for thought to the Finance Minister over there.

An adverse exchange signifies amongst other things that more must be paid than formerly for debts to foreign countries, that less will be obtained from foreign debtors if they have to pay in domestic money, that imported goods will be made yet dearer owing to the exchange, in addition to other general causes, that foreign loans can only be raised at great sacrifice. All this will probably make the day when international commerce is re-established a very critical time for Austria-Hungary. Not that the weakness cannot be overcome, but it will not pass without rapid and energetic financial operations. The taxable capacity of the Dual Monarchy must immediately be called upon in a marked degree if a period of congestion is to be surmounted. Austria and Hungary must make good the lack of gold, in so far as such a lack exists, by obvious evidence of the solvency — based on the products of taxation — of the State Treasury. The most severe economic trial will not be felt until then, and that will be the very moment when people would like to allow those who are returning from a war a comfortable interval in which to make themselves at home again.

. . . . . .

We know up to the present even less of course than in the case of the German Empire what forms of taxation will be selected by the various financial bodies in the Dual Monarchy. Only this much may readily be pointed out: that Austria and Hungary like ourselves will be in no position to fight shy of new and productive State enterprises or State regulated syndicates. There is an instructive little book on *Österreichs Finanzen und der Krieg* by Hofrat Meisel and Professor Spiethoff (Dunckler und Humblot, 1915), in which is calculated in a most interesting way how many millions could be saved in Austrian finance, if Government, parties and nationalities wished to economise. We take it for granted that the most vigorous efforts will be made in this direction, but nevertheless, if the war goes on for long, there will be a big, new deficit in taxation to overcome. Taxes on luxuries and expenditure will certainly play their part here, but they will not suffice. We cannot judge whether or no further types of direct taxation will be considered. Certainly, however, in Austria too it will finally come to this: the process of conversion into capital must be tapped where it is still impersonal. But how can this be done, without, as in the Austro-Hungarian taxation of shares, directly checking business expansion? Austria-Hungary too will at this stage find syndicate questions becoming more pressing than, on purely economic grounds, they are at present: the most highly concentrated intensification of industry with a view to solving the financial problems of the State!

Thus we arrive again at the position already reached in the previous section: the transition to the labour *tempo* and labour methods of the German Empire appears to be a condition preliminary to surmounting the financial burdens of the war. After the war we shall both need primarily to economise and work for a long time with all our energies and resources, in order to get free from its consequences. The more we do this in partnership the greater will be our success. We Germans of the Empire, for all the sufficiently adequate reasons cited, must desire for Austria-Hungary the greatest conceivable vitality and good management, and must do everything that we can with a view to setting our comrade in the union upon a stable financial footing. If the Austrians and Hungarians wish it, if they desire it and demand it, the German financial and organising power must be at their service. We say if they wish it, because success is otherwise not conceivable. An economic partnership accepted unwillingly and suspiciously is pointless, it would only prejudice and estrange people. Hence the energies of the German Empire ought not to make the offer of themselves. That would only arouse or increase the suspicion that the Germans wished to get through the period of stagnation after the war by means of the Austro-Hungarian business, until such time as international commerce was admissible in its old form. This suspicious notion is possible and indeed exists in certain quarters, and it is on this account that I repeat that those of us who are striving after an honourable, permanent, economic partnership in Mid-Europe feel no pleasure when intrusive advisers and speculators wish, forsooth, to use the circumstances of the union as a pretext for their selfish interests. Endless harm may be done in this matter by those who cannot act tactfully and with foresight. But we have confidence that the big Imperial banking houses and directors of syndicates will grasp the seriousness of the situation and will understand what is at stake. No oppression, no intrigue, no self-interested exploitation of any possibly existent weakness, but a frank and honest readiness to answer the call in case it sounds!

We have sat together in the economic prison, together we will break the chains and go hand in hand into the fresh air again. And if all kinds of war infirmities still cling to us, we shall help each other so that subsequently even a great matter will not trouble us. We shall all have much to do, truly very much! Shall we do it together or shall each one act for himself?

CHAPTER VI

OUR POSITION IN THE WORLD'S ECONOMIC SYSTEM

EVEN if Germany and Austria-Hungary fuse themselves into an economic unity, they will together make up no great structure from the point of view of the world's economic system, for all our notions about great and small have altered more during the war than in the whole of the previous decade. We have seen the giant States rising up to crush us. They have not succeeded, but we shall not forget the moment when Russia began to move on the West and when Great Britain called on her Indians and Canadians. The future will be even more concerned with phenomena on this grand scale, for the experiences of the European War will be studied in all Government Offices all over the world, and every Government, even as far as East Asia and Argentina, will be impregnated with new conceptions of quantity. It will not only be Central Europe that will emerge from the war with schemes for equipment and defence, but all the other States as well. Even a growing inclination among the people towards peace can do little to alter this steady preparation for coming wars, for the historical moment when mankind will combine into one single immense organisation is still far distant. Before the organisation of humanity, the "United States of the World," can come into existence, there will probably be a very long period during which groups of humanity, reaching beyond the dimensions of a nation, will struggle to direct the fates of mankind and to secure the product of its labour. Mid-Europe comes forward as one such group, and that indeed a small one: vigorous but lean!

Sovereignty, which formerly was a possession, widespread amongst the nations of the earth, concentrates itself more markedly as time goes on at quite a few places. There only remain a limited number of central points amongst mankind where government is really exercised: London, New York, Moscow (or Petersburg) stand firm. It is still doubtful whether or no an East Asiatic world-centre will grow up in Japan or China. It is at least very questionable whether or no India or Africa will ever produce such a central point of the first importance. The same thing applies to South America. The future significance for mankind of any East Asiatic and South American centres that may possibly arise is not, however, at present a question of practical politics for general history. But, on the other hand, the question whether or no a separate centre in Mid-Europe can maintain itself between Russia and England is even now being fought out with all the energies of Europe and with endless bloodshed. The human group Mid-Europe is playing for its position in the world. If we lose the fight we shall probably be condemned for ever to be a satellite nation. If we are half victorious, then we shall be obliged to fight again later. If we win a lasting victory we shall lighten the task for our children and grandchildren, for then Mid-Europe will be entered in the Domesday Book of the coming centuries.

What is meant by a satellite nation in this connection? We might also say a planet State. Such States have their own life, their own summer and winter, their culture, their anxieties and their splendour, but they no longer follow their own laws along the great paths of universal history, but add strength to the guiding group to which they belong. In this way the United States of North America seek gradually to bind to themselves all types of States in North and South America, not in order to absorb them but in order to direct them. Russia also, though in very different fashion, is drawing all the nations within its borders: Finns, Poles, Little Russians, the Caucasian races, Armenians, Turkomans, Tungsians, etc. So, too, Great Britain surrounds itself with Africanders, Australians, Indians, Egyptians and Portuguese, and now during the war is even trying to include the two Latin nations, France and Italy, in its rotation, although they themselves in virtue

OUR POSITION IN THE ECONOMIC SYSTEM

of past greatness and considerable performances would gladly still count as individual centres.

But round about the satellite States there still exists a certain mass of unorganised national material, which has either not hitherto desired inclusion, or for some reason or other has not arrived at it; asteroids or comets, which for the most part call themselves neutral because they belong to no sun. In their way they are a very old political family, much older than the conquering supernational syndicate States, for they represent the old small middle class in the family of nations. But at some time or other each of them will be swept away into the satellite relationship, for it seems impossible that an ancient small Power should endure uninjured through the centuries in the midst of a world of concentrated Great Sovereignties of immense bulk.

All these movements towards organisation are still very much in process of becoming. Practically every combination may reappear as loosened once more or as linked up together in another way. And in fact the commercial age which has called forth the World-Powers has only been actually in existence for a couple of generations, so that its effects cannot be in any sense yet determined. The period of groups of humanity has not yet arrived, though it is already at the door. The same thing applies to them on a large scale as applies to industrial syndicates on a small scale: the adhesions are still changing continually, but the principle of adhesion itself will not die out. Groups of humanity will come into being because such new technical apparatus as steam-power and electricity cannot work with State formations that are still under the influence of earlier and now vanished forms of international intercourse. What is a territory of half a million square kilometres to-day? It has become a single day's journey.

· · · · · ·

But before we discuss the Mid-European group of humanity, we shall attempt to grasp the new super-national structure in itself with somewhat more sociological accuracy. We shall examine then the three great organisms that are relatively complete: Great Britain, America, Russia. Each of these is more potent in extent and in mass than Mid-Europe can ever be. In the most favourable event, so far as human foresight can tell to-day, Mid-Europe will only be the fourth World State.

Of the three first World States which have already come into being during the preceding period, the Russian is based mostly on coercion and the American on free-will; England stands between the two. No general law can be established as to whether the compulsory or the voluntary formation is the more permanent and solid, for either principle applied to excess will break up the State. Every super-national Great State is a work of art, a venture, an experiment daily renewed. It is like a great machine which continually needs repairs somewhere or other to keep it in working order. And as every work of art is determined by the artist and the material so the Great State grows out of the leading nation and the nations that accompany it, out of the ideas and customs of the rulers and the qualities of the ruled, out of the ability of the great men and the desires of the broad masses, out of history, geography, agriculture, manual work and technique.

The psychical character of the Great State ought never to be left out of account if its essence is to be grasped. A bare, mechanical way of looking at it is absolutely useless. The greater and the more educated and the more exacting the multitudes to be governed become, the more elasticity is required in their management, an elasticity which must be passed on as inherited wisdom from generation to generation. The proper mixture of enforced unity and permitted freedom acts magnetically on the satellite portions. But no physical or organic comparison can quite express the politically formative inner condition, yet this condition must be felt in retrospect by any one who ponders in the spirit of a creator over a fresh great formation which is just coming into existence. Very many instruments must be harmonised together in the super-national Great State, so as to keep in unison many opposing human elements. This does not come about in accordance with definite formulæ, and written laws and constitutions too are only a very inadequate and incomplete expression of the manifold ac-

OUR POSITION IN THE ECONOMIC SYSTEM 183

tivity, in which daily mistakes must be surpassed by daily achievements.

The Russians, with all their crudity of nature, possess an undeniable charm which attracts half-civilised peoples to them. We find this magnetic power of the Russian spirit, a power hard for us to understand, all along our Eastern frontier, amongst all the peoples intermediate between Finland and the Balkans, all of whom waver in their sentiments as to whether or no they do not prefer the unsystematised Russian in his natural vigour, to the German who for them is quite too rational and precise. It is a great mistake to explain the Russian influence as entirely due to fear of the knout. Fear does form a part of the Government machinery of this group of peoples, but not fear alone. The Russian can really govern after his fashion, and possesses a diplomacy which looks back on a long series of successes. Here, to be sure, methods are often employed which pre-suppose very robust consciences. Gloves are worn but they have holes in them. What we despise in the Russians is what partly constitutes their vigour, just as on the other hand what in us is offensive to the Russians makes up a part of our best strength. What we previously termed elasticity, with the Russians takes the form of caprice, an official despotism softened by corruptibility and humours, very comprehensible to populations who would govern in just the same way if once they had the command. Half the Russian corruption, nay a quarter or a tenth of it, would ruin our State, but the Russian organism can stand much, very much, as the war shows. Even new revolutionary movements, should they appear, as is very possible, will indeed curb the Russian strength for a moment, and will disturb the machinery of government, but according to all historical experience they will in no sense mean the end, for they too are in keeping with the whole character.

How differently the Englishman administers his world! He requests, so long as it is possible, instead of commanding. His sea and colonial empire, scattered over all parts of the earth, is organised quite without system, just as the history of each world province and the chance process of its acquisition has brought it about. Hence monarchical, aristocratic and democratic contrivances are employed according to requirements and just as seems serviceable, as a ship is constructed according to requirements out of iron, wood, copper and canvas. The English elasticity consists in this: that what we call principles, it regards as working methods, an instructive, calm adaptability amongst its leading men, combined with an unshakable self-confidence. The unsystematic character of English Imperialism has often been pointed to as a deficiency by theoretical critics among the Germans, and people believed that the loosely constructed building would break in pieces by reason of the superficiality of the links between its many members. But the war has shown, in this case too, that loose threads, when they are properly put together, can hold fast. The Empire, geographically so varied, spread out on every coast, has remained a unity. There may be shocks in India or Egypt, and some indications suggest that these will not be altogether wanting. But a flexible administrative skill reacts even on the entirely foreign races, the subjugated masses of the Asiatic and African territories, and always successfully postpones again the moment of danger.

The great American State works in yet another way. It is the most non-military great human organism that has ever existed. A business State in virtue of a detached geographical position and a popularly intelligible doctrine of democratic principles. Its strength lies in the truly rational division of competence between municipal, county, State and Federal governments. The concept of majority rule prevails everywhere as a matter of course, and justifies itself as State machinery on the whole in spite of all the troublesome accessories which must be taken with it as part of the bargain. For with an unconditional principle of majority rule the formation of a majority becomes a profitable business, and thus, according to our feeling, commercialism enters much too strongly into politics, makes parties into business undertakings and materialises the finest ideals. But the American can live politically even with these methods of his, for, as we have

OUR POSITION IN THE ECONOMIC SYSTEM

already said elsewhere, he has the voyage across the ocean behind him, is a modern utilitarian, and wants above all neat, transparent formulæ. He is essentially lacking in political ·mysticism. His State gods too are excessively human. He will have no mysterious, moral, joint ego. His morality is private, not political. The State is a Clearing House for interests. He maintains the State by limiting the concept of State. Thus he does not easily arrive at serious internal crises, such as are still the order of the day in South America. At most these only occur over presidential rivalries. In this case the crisis signifies that one clique of business-politicians, with or without an assertion of principles, has been thrust out by another. But it does not indicate that the State itself is in question, for if it broke up to-day, to-morrow it would be set up again in accordance with exactly the same simple axioms.

These groups of humanity are thus no mere administrative districts of a homogeneous human society developing according to like rules. On the contrary the super-national structures possess something in themselves which is intermediate between nation and humanity, a specific essence which cannot be taken away from them without danger, because it is just this that forms the bond of union between the various constituent elements.

·   ·   ·   ·   ·   ·

Each of the three old Great States is intrinsically international. In them is actually expressed as much of the international idea as can be realised in the present epoch.

The international idea was in the first instance religious, an heirloom of the Roman Empire surviving in Christianity. All Christian ideas, in so far as they are not hampered by sectarianism, are directed towards mankind as a whole: "Go ye into all the world and preach the gospel to every creature!" But religious unity has not come to pass. The Papacy in Rome remains as the incomplete attempt at a spiritual union of all the nations on the earth. Christ's kingdom on earth is a concept, a prophecy and a prayer, but no tangible reality. It desired to organise what is noblest and highest in man before his material needs could be organised. The stupidity of dogmatism, the aspirations of nations not satisfied with church membership, the geographical separation in earlier centuries, the human nature displayed even in the management of the superhuman, all these have destroyed Catholic unity. Christ's kingdom has become a plurality of creeds. Only a prophetic expectation makes itself heard quite softly throughout all creeds, that some time, in the wisdom of God, and by different methods and fresh energies and in a more materialistic sense, a road will be again broken through to that goal which the splendid efforts of so many apostles, synods, councils and bishops failed to reach.

Next the international idea became a philosophical concept. Almost all great philosophers are in some degree cosmopolitan. And under their inspiration literature became impregnated with evidences, small and great, of the longing for a universal civilisation, which reached out to the goal of evolution across all historical narrownesses. But when national struggles became serious and when the spirit of nationality was awakened, the philosophers and men of letters for the most part took their stand again by the rank and file of their nation, as Fichte and Schleiermacher did in typical fashion with us Germans. Philosophical teaching, free from the churches, could not bring about what the Church had failed to accomplish. Like Christianity it embodied human desires, but bare abstract thought is too delicate and too weak to organise mankind.

Whilst, however, the philosophical teaching of humanity was still at the height of its influence the international idea was adopted by English commerce and spread over the rest of the world. The free trade concept comprehended mankind in realistic fashion as an immense but yet ultimately limited and calculable multitude of working faculties, buyers and sellers and found the purpose of humanity in the business of exchange. We have already pointed out that the English always regarded themselves as the creators and supporters of this internationalism, a fact which is bound up with the historical characteristics of this commercial type of cosmopolitanism. Moreover, this tendency

OUR POSITION IN THE ECONOMIC SYSTEM 187

contained very much pure international idealism along with its utilitarian theories: a peaceful liberation of the nations from political limitations, the repression of possibilities of strife, the raising of all through all. The results of this process of thought have become quite enormous in virtue of the machinery of exchange which set it going and accompanies it. There exists to-day in fact a world united in the economic sense, a world of steamers, railways, letters and telegrams, a world of sewing machines, grain silos, plantations and warehouses. International commerce and division of labour are established amongst the nations. All this will return after the interruption due to the war, but not in its old unbroken and unreserved character. The war has shown that exchange alone is not peace, for it possesses by itself no governing and controlling strength, no force to compel peace. The old well-established military and administrative States live on within a world of international exchange and struggle with all the means at their disposal over the profits and the supreme control of the world-machinery.

Social Democracy took over the concept of internationalism from middle-class commercial liberalism and deepened it essentially in that it sought to make an association of mankind for production out of an association of mankind for mere exchange. Since it is primarily and in origin a proletarian organisation, social democracy possesses a highly developed sense of organisation in general, and hence has been the first to get a genuine grasp of the organising character of the social epoch which is now dawning. With bold, dialectic imagination it enlarged its experiences of socialistic organisation to fit mankind, and conceived as its final aim an administrative State which should include all nations. There is something dreamlike about this, but a hundred years earlier the free trade ideal was also imaginative in much the same way. If all nations are to trade with one another, the conditions of life of the workers in every zone must continually grow more alike, methods of work must approximate to one another, goods must be classified and money values must be exchangeable, average requirements must arise and a housekeeping scheme for mankind belongs not to the inconceivable for those who think in centuries. Even to-day we have a world-corn-harvest and a world-production of cotton, a world-coffee-market, a world-production of iron, a world-demand for saltpetre and much that is similar. Most of the syndicates that have arisen locally or been promoted by a State, form associations reaching beyond the frontiers of the country and endeavour to secure the control of the whole of their department of production in all parts of the world. The great directors of the economic system have long since ceased to think in terms of single States. Capitalism becomes international through its own impulse towards growth, and socialism, being contained in it, follows in its footsteps. All this is already beginning to be actual fact and will persist. But the war has broken through this socially deepened conception of internationalism, the ideal of organisation is not merely economic, is not only made up of syndicates, markets and trade unions, but the basis of all human order and organisation, of all law and of all coercion is the State. And the State does not make the leap across from national State and territorial State to humanity, for it is no creature of thought but an organic reality, which grows according to its nature, which widens its boundaries and which yields nothing that it has earned or established unless it is vanquished. A world-organisation without political character can still only exist in the sectional spheres of commerce or finance, but States are tenacious and fight for their life, that is for the preservation of their authority within their borders, of their control of production, of their financial strength, and now also of their storage system.

· · · · · ·

But whilst the States are thus fighting, those same central points of which we speak are arising and extending their power. For the military struggle of the States is no game which is continually set up afresh on the same chessboard and with the same pieces. The demands on each combatant State increase owing to military technique, the bulk of the armies and the height of the war expenses, and any State that cannot keep up in the race will be displaced to the third or fourth rank of sovereignty. A stern, inexorable law of selection rules here. How many States have already gone under! How many are organised into federal States or State confederations! The foundation of the German Empire is a classical example of the politico-economic process of enlargement. This development is independent of all our individual wills. Even those who regard it with horror in its relation to personal and national culture are forced to recognise it as fact. There are growing States which are continually driven further forward by their own size. In them is realised a side of internationalism which is not simply commercial exchange, and even the exchange of goods submits itself on the frontiers to the commands and claims of such States. Thus, within the world of exchange, there arise great State or super-State economic provinces, which ultimately begin to formulate their economic law and draw up their demand and their scheme of management. On the way to the ultimate world-economy lie these great economic States. They begin by creating a regulation of labour for their own areas, and they deal with one another in world-exchange like great corporate businesses. They do not, it is true, realise the dreams of religion, philosophy, free trade and socialism, but they are the greatest vision of humanity that is attainable at the present time. Any one who wishes to look forward hopefully to the far distant future may regard them as the early stages of the final organisation of mankind, but that is his private affair. They themselves wish chiefly to live as independent existences and to build up for themselves first their Right and their Might. Whether or no Central Europe possesses the strength within itself to become such a world-group economic body [1] on a political basis, is our problem. This is how our international question presents itself.

. . . .

[1] *Weltwirthschaftskörper.* This and other similar terms must be read in connection with the phrase "groups of humanity" above. There are to be great world-group bodies intermediate between Nations and Humanity. The world is to be partitioned between these bodies, and they alone will count in determining its future. Hence the term *welt*. "World-group" has been used for *welt* in the compounds *Weltwirthschaftskörper*, etc., since neither "world" nor "international" is unambiguous in this connection.— TRANSLATOR'S NOTE.

It is in no sense unpatriotic to answer in the negative the question whether Central Europe is capable of becoming a special world-group economic organism, for if it is to turn out later that, notwithstanding all our goodwill, we lack the material preliminary conditions, or the spiritual energies needed, the vain attempt will, under the circumstances, mean increased difficulties in our subsequent position. At present there still exists a possibility, even after this war or perhaps on account of it, of joining either the English or the Russian system of trade and sovereignty. It may seem difficult to believe this whilst the guns are roaring in East and West, but all the public and private talk about a separate peace either with Russia or England implies at bottom, if the matter is thought out, a future economic or political union with one side or the other, for after a war imposing such sacrifices, peace will not readily be concluded for the sake of a mere breathing-space to repair weapons. After this war each nation will want to secure a permanent position to compensate for its immense sacrifice. It may be that circumstances will oblige us to ally ourselves with one side, it may be that one or other of our opponents will seek an interval for the sake of self-preservation and that we shall grant him favourable conditions for the sake of gaining strength. But in such a case the Mid-European idea, according to the position of the matter, will be either partially adjourned or wholly decided. Let us then look matters frankly in the face and acknowledge to ourselves and to others what may happen if we decide, either voluntarily or through compulsion, that we are incapable of creating Mid-Europe.

We will take as the first possibility a permanent treaty with Russia. From an economic point of view this offers dazzling prospects, for it opens a selling market of the first rank to our industry, since the French milliards, in that case lost, have during the last two decades secured the first victory over Russian economic barbarism. As things are to-day the Russian and German economic systems supplement each other wonderfully well. By a system of corn storage we can protect our agriculture from a

OUR POSITION IN THE ECONOMIC SYSTEM 191

glut in the supply, and for the rest we can make Russia the chief source of our food-stuffs and raw material, so far as the character of the country and the stage of development over there admit of it. Our capital will then quicken the further progress of Russian agriculture and the very promising increase in mining, trade and industry. Looked at purely from an economic standpoint the arrangement is the most productive of all for us if it is permanent in character — but only if! But this is impossible so long as we are the opponents of Russia in Turkey, in the Balkans and in the Slav districts of Austria-Hungary. Herein lies the insurmountable obstacle placed by history. In such a case we barter our independent political future for a temporarily great economic advantage, for through this alliance our prosperity will indeed develop but so also will Russia's strength, until finally Russia will shake us off, because she no longer needs us. We shall become a Western nation dependent on the Eastern Power, certainly not unconsidered, but not the leader. Bad Russian management will shelter behind our good name, and our technical skill and our capital will improve the soil on which millions of Russians and half-Russians will be born, who will never resemble us and will never trust us. We shall thus act as engineer to promote the military and economic victory of the Russian World-Power. A great nation with such an ascent behind it as that of the German Empire during the last century, cannot do a thing of this sort. Our conceptions of civilisation rise up against it, and our hearts will never be wholly in the business. Never! Better small and solitary than Russian!

As a matter of sentiment, and that in spite of all the war "songs of hate," it is easier for us to contemplate a permanent union with the English World-Power. In this case we shall become, as one of my friends puts it, the junior partner in the English world-firm, shall supply it with confidential agents and clerks, build ships and send teachers to the colonies, furnish English international emporiums with German goods, industriously made and well paid for, speak English outside our own four walls, enjoy English internationalism, and fight the future English battles against Russia. Our navy and submarines will in this case no longer serve any specially German purpose, for who else could wish to dispute English sea-power if we have submitted ourselves to it? All this would be regulated, after the English fashion, in quite reasonable and pleasant forms, but our German Imperial history would have become a history of a territory as is to-day that of Saxony or Württemberg. A great nation only does a thing like this when nothing else remains to it. We know that most of the nations on the globe have no choice but to seek such an alliance, on one side or another, but a greater aim tempts us in virtue of our strength and experience: to become a central point ourselves!

To many Germans to-day this dilemma does not appear to have yet presented itself. They wish to become neither Russian nor English nor even responsible for a new world-group economic organism intermediate between the two. They call their view national independence and self-sufficiency! But they fail to appreciate that our own sphere of existence is too small for the purpose. That "small and solitary" which we have ourselves just proclaimed in contrast to the possibility of a Russian alliance, is indeed, as we must now assert, in no sense the same thing as, say, when Friedrich the Great's State rejoiced in its solitary position after the Seven Years' War. In the interval the world's economic system has become so much more narrow and everywhere the principle of syndicates and of exclusion has made conditions very different from what they were in the individualistic atmosphere of the early beginnings of capitalism. He who is alone to-day will find himself outside to-morrow. In such a case we put ourselves in the position of industrial enterprises which in order to be free wish to remain isolated from the combines growing up around them, but whose freedom from thenceforth endures only in a state of continual defence against boycott and combined competition. Thus everywhere we are met by the tendency of the developing great associated bodies to round off their sphere of control. The better regulated the world's eco-

OUR POSITION IN THE ECONOMIC SYSTEM 193

nomic system becomes the less can a nation of only seventy millions go on its own economic path alone, for in its isolation it would be overwhelmed by the cries: England for the English, America for the Americans, Russia for the Russians! All the great bodies endeavour to look after their own interests within the world's system. Even Greater Britain will, if we remain in isolation, surround herself with tariffs and systematically make it more difficult for us to share in the use of her trading and coaling stations. The notion of encircling and starving out will be further considered, and calculations will be made as to how, next time, we can be hit more sharply. No doubt we shall always be able to sell the products of our labour on the English-Russian-American world markets in time of peace, and we shall be in a position to turn our military strength to good account between the great combatants, as is the fashion of neutrals. But we shall be powerless against the further rounding off of the more powerful bodies, against their tariff policy, commercial intrigues, limitation of imports, metal monopolies, cotton trusts, against their colonial dominion and world-encircling policy. We shall, it is true, be the strongest of the small nations, and hence our position will remain better than that of our weaker competitors, but the idea of a purely national independence offers no cheerful prospect to our children and grandchildren in this economic age. He who does not grow, declines. As once the Prussians were forced to create the Customs Union in order not to remain small and solitary, so must we keep before our eyes the Central European economic world-group. This is the meaning of our history whether it suits us or not.

. . . . . .

So long then as the sun still shines on us it must be our purpose to enter the first class of the economic world-group Powers. This involves the adhesion of the other Central European States and nations. Except to our comrades of German race living in Austria and Hungary, it is indeed of no special direct interest to these peoples that we Germans should sit in the upper council of universal history. It is not to be expected of them that they should share our historical sentiments, since there beats within them a heart of another race and of different stuff. They will put the question to themselves from their own point of view: whether, in the choice of German, Russian or English leadership, they wish to belong to the German world-union or not. Their position is similar to what we have just described in discussing how it would be with us if we were to join the Russian or English union, only with this difference, that the smaller nations have not the possibility of imagining themselves as leaders of economic world-groups. They have in fact only to choose between isolation and adhesion, and for them, for the reasons adduced, isolation will hardly be any longer tolerable by the end of another generation. Hence sooner or later they must anyway decide with which union they will or can range themselves, according to geographical position, production and mental leanings. This is a harsh necessity, a heavy fate, but it is the overpowering tendency of the age, the categorical imperative of human evolution. When once the powerful intermediate forms have introduced themselves between territorial and national States on the one hand and humanity on the other, struggles and complaints avail nothing. People may submit to necessity earlier or later, freely or from compulsion, but the universal watchword is spoken and must be complied with. And those who conform to it earlier will in general secure better conditions for the future than those who let themselves be forced and pushed beyond the historical moment. There is no need whatever to proclaim this to opponents with many words, for words are feeble in this connection, but economic experiences will speak. Small States which cannot carry through any tariff war, but need daily imports and exports, must in future be registered with one of the great world-firms, as soon as the super-firms themselves mutually separate off from one another even more than they had done before the war.

. . . . . .

If, however, the foundation of the Mid-European union is to be attempted in the midst of this human evolution, it must be admitted as a matter of course that Mid-Europe will be no such natural growth, no such already coagulating organism as the three great unions already in existence. The Mid-European structure must be erected with judgment and deliberation from stones already shaped and repeatedly used in building. Unfortunately it did not grow up out of the old instinct for power before the period when mankind began to make schemes for setting its house in order. This constitutes a weakness and a very considerable practical and politico-technical difficulty. The building of Mid-Europe will be even more an intellectual achievement than the foundation of the German Empire, but it will be the intellectual achievement of that nation which can say of itself without vanity that it is gifted and trained like no other for organising an economic world-group of this nature. We refer in this connection to the exposition that we have given earlier. No one amongst us or amongst our neighbours doubts that the Germans can accomplish the economic organisation involved, if it is at all humanly possible. But it is a somewhat different question whether or no we have, in addition to organisation and technique, that indispensable quality for world-union which we have previously termed elasticity, that flexible skill which we find in three different forms amongst Russians, English and Americans. We are somewhat hard, masterful, taciturn, have but little patience for our slower fellow-creatures, and demand that things shall be done precisely as we wish. All this has its good side, but in order to be a leading, directing economic nation some sort of international oil is needed, the art, the great art of managing men, sympathy with others, the power to enter into their nature and aims. Scientifically we can accomplish the thing irreproachably. In retrospect we are the most sympathetic of all nations, but practically we have not seldom been small schoolmasters of the old style or non-commissioned officers with pencil and mustachios. This indeed applies least of all to our leading merchants, but often to our trade secretaries, directors, officials. The German nation as a whole needs first to grow into its new task. But this too it will be able to do if it is necessary. It needs only to be put plainly to us in the first instance. We are still rather too young as a world-group nation, too close to the narrowness of the old provincial manners and the habits of thought of small nations, not yet free enough from the old position of subjection of the pre-'48 period, not sufficiently assured in intercourse, and hence often rude and insolent from want of self-confidence. Respect for those with whom we wish to work in prosperity and failure is not yet a matter of course. I say all this openly and repeatedly with intention because herein lie much greater hindrances than in clauses and statutes. Yet already the race of men who are now returning home from the war, and the race of women who have in the meanwhile worked like men, are more flexible and readier for great things. We all wish to begin anew, and so, and so only, not with our old positiveness, we approach our neighbours and ask whether or no they will enter into our union.

.   .   .   .   .   .

Whom must and can we invite?

At this point a section of our work begins over which more than over the others the word "caution" should be written, for we are still living in the midst of the war, must publish nothing about the "aims of the war" in the narrower sense of the word for very sufficient reasons, and cannot count everywhere upon a friendly interpretation of our statements in the passionately excited war conditions in neighbouring foreign countries. Then rather a word too little than too much!

Even now there are, it is true, in Germany as elsewhere in Europe a number of people who put no curb on their capricious imagination and talk as though the government of Holland, Scandinavia, Roumania, Bulgaria, Greece and the Turkish Empire were their merely secondary duty and they needed only to write the names of these countries on paper in order to receive them into the Central European economic world-group. Yes, there are daring thinkers who wish at the same time to attract Switzerland, France, Spain and, after a cerain purifying interval, even Italy, and so found the United States of Europe with or without Belgium. All this has only the value of a play with possibilities, but is harmful if it is read in the States concerned, because it is

OUR POSITION IN THE ECONOMIC SYSTEM   197

almost always conceived from a one-sided German standpoint, and does not take into consideration that it needs at least two, each of whom has his own interests and anxieties, to conclude a treaty. He who wants too much in this matter, at bottom wants nothing at all except to express himself. We dissociate ourselves most distinctly from this facile and superficial treatment of the problem, and on this very account have confined ourselves throughout our work up to the present to the discussion of the union between Germany and Austria-Hungary, because we are convinced that the two Central Powers must first be united before any application to a more distant State can have even the smallest prospect of success. The basal forms of the new treaties and arrangements must originate between the German Empire and Austria and Hungary. If the attempt miscarries here then other States need not be troubled at all. If it succeeds we shall know what we can offer to the others concerned, and shall talk to them with concrete numbers and in calculable values. Hence it is also a mistake to talk of a German-Austrian-Hungarian partnership only, as it were, in passing, as an auxiliary means to Germano-Turkish objects, as though the latter were the principal thing and the former only a work of secondary importance to be settled anyhow. All this will be carefully noted in Austria and Hungary and will in no sense increase the desire to enter into serious and difficult negotiations. The Austrians and Hungarians think of their own Balkan and Turkish interests, which mean more to them than ours can do, and are surprised that we Germans should, so to speak, carry on our Turkish policy over their heads. And they are right in this! They know that all German-Turkish schemes are nothing but water without Trieste and Fiume.

·   ·   ·   ·   ·   ·

The German-Austrian-Hungarian economic area, as now it lies before us, shut off by the war from the rest of the world, is obviously not sufficient for an economic world-province, for it is far too much of an area for the import of food-stuffs and raw materials, and is already much too one-sidedly directed towards industrial exports to be able to support itself by its own energy and without further additions, even in the principal articles. On this point, as formerly, we refer the reader to the statistical section of this book. A vital Mid-Europe needs agrarian territories on its boundaries, and must make the accession easy and desirable to them. It needs, if possible, an extension of its northern and southern sea-coasts, it needs its share in oversea colonial possessions. But how can all this be talked of now without getting involved in inconclusive discussions of neutrality or in the coming negotiations at the Peace Congress?

So far as the German colonies are concerned they have held out well and bravely during the war, and in doing so have everywhere supplied valuable proof to the German Colonial Government that we are not so incapable of colonisation as was believed in some places both at home and abroad. Both white and coloured people have done their duty, so far as we know, in a surprisingly splendid manner. The whites have kept up the defence till the last man and till the last possible moment and the natives have, with few exceptions, stood by them faithfully. Now, however, we are cut off from the colonies. Whether and to what extent and in what condition we shall get them back again through the exchange proceedings when peace is made no one yet knows. In our opinion we ought not at any cost to allow ourselves to be deprived of colonial activity, and if it is unavoidable we must make concessions of occupied land in Europe, in order not to cease to be a colonial nation. But all these general statements show how vague our future economic situation in the world's economy is at the present time.

And who is prepared to say where the future Central European trench-made boundaries will run? Whether they will pass on the inner or the outer side of Roumania, or on this or that side of Bessarabia? Whether they will follow the Vistula or not? Whether Bulgaria is to be included in the Central European sphere of interest or not? Whether or no we shall secure a line of railway to Constantinople in the trusty hands of allies? What Mediterranean seaports will come into consideration as the starting-point of Central European railway lines? What will become

OUR POSITION IN THE ECONOMIC SYSTEM 199

of Antwerp? How the Baltic Sea will appear after the war? Thus there are a hundred questions which will still remain to be answered. So much only is clear: that their answers will be essentially affected according to whether the German-Austrian union is, at bottom, something that is desired and determined upon or not. Here and here only is the birthplace of Mid-Europe.

. . . .

But let us suppose for once that a beginning has been made with the German-Austrian-Hungarian union and that it has been satisfactorily steered through the Peace Congress, that it has at its disposal adequate seaports on the North Sea and the Mediterranean, and that northern and southern accessions to the union are under consideration. Let us suppose further that Turkey has come out of the war intact and thus with a belief in the future, and that there devolves on us a not too small tropical or subtropical colonial territory. With these favourable assumptions, which in themselves contain nothing extravagant, an economic State makes its appearance, whose statistical position each may easily reckon out for himself in its main numerical relations, but which we shall not express in figures for reasons already mentioned. How will this economic State be able to maintain itself in the midst of the world's economic system?

Undoubtedly it is much stronger than Germany alone or Austria-Hungary alone, for it is a more powerful buyer and seller and can negotiate in a different way with foreign customs unions and economic bodies than is possible to a separated and isolated individual State. This advantage exists under all circumstances, even though we must subsequently assert that quantitative possibilities for the life and economic development of Mid-Europe remain limited even if progress be favourable.

Of course there is no simple method of estimating the strength of such a union, for political and economic energies will in general not allow themselves to be brought to a common denominator. Could the estimate be even approximately arrived at we should not need war in the history of the world. War is only unavoidable because there is no recognised measure for evaluating the claims that are put forward. If, for example, Japan, Russia, England, America and other States dispute over the extent of their influence in China, there is no recognised procedure of apportionment according to which their mortgages on China can be measured. The actual discovery of such a procedure would be pacifism. The Court of Arbitration, taken by itself, is only a proposal for a machinery of justice, but at present there is no sketch of a fundamental law for its decisions. Under these circumstances, what remains but to put it to the test of blood how highly each one who makes a claim is in a position to value it? Thus in all future international affairs Mid-Europe too will ultimately be referred back to its military strength. That this is very great the war has given satisfactory proof. But after all even the war only shows that Central Europe has been able to hold its ground, by exerting all its energies, under existing social and economic conditions. It is no guarantee that, in a later stage of mankind's development, just the same trial could be endured again. After the war people will set to work afresh to build, to plant, to gather in, to dig, to forge, to weave, to water, to calculate and to save, until the trial must once again be made whether or no the new organisation has been, on the whole, a strengthening and an advance.

We ask, therefore, whether or no the new economic world-group of Mid-Europe offers prospects of growth according to human foresight and in so far as we are able to judge. In putting this question the wish may easily be the father to the thought, but just because it is easy and pleasant to paint glowing pictures of the future, we regard it as our duty to call special attention at the outset to the difficulties and obscurities of the matter.

·   ·   ·   ·   ·   ·

We will begin then with the geographical relations of size. What is the area of Mid-Europe?

To any one who journeys, staff in hand, from the Baltic to the Adriatic Sea the country lying between naturally appears spacious, varied, broad and extensive. But he who compares it with the available areas on the inhabited earth must perforce call it very small. That is to say, if we begin to reckon in millions of square

OUR POSITION IN THE ECONOMIC SYSTEM 201

kilometres our two home countries dwindle to quite small fractions of the total available area. The inhabited surface of the earth, including the deserts but not the polar regions, amounts to about 132 millions of square kilometres. This amount contains much land of lesser value, out of which no meadows or plantations have been made in the course of centuries, but still: the housekeeping area of the world with its hinterlands and waste lands is of this size, and no one knows what metals, salts, coal and power-sources may be opened up even in districts that are now unusable. The home countries of Germany, Austria and Hungary make up only 1.2 million of this 132 million square kilometres, that is, less than 1 per cent.! By adding in a number of neighbouring European States we can make it up to about 2.5 million. Further, if we claim all European and Asiatic Turkey our share is increased to about 6.7 million by taking charge of a good many Arabs. If we add on the former colonies of the German Empire we may register about 9.3 million. If we venture to count in, to a, it is true, somewhat arbitrary extent, the overseas possessions of neighbouring States which have not yet joined us, it is possible to arrive at about 13 million. But this means that, by a very favourable calculation, the Mid-European economic body will be in a position, in some more distant future, to control one-tenth of the available amount of land. Even so, this one-tenth is still hardly above the average in its productiveness. In contrast to this Great Britain alone, with Egypt, but without its satellite States, possesses 34.4 million, Russia 23.7 million, France alone 11.4, China 11.1, the United States alone without other American States 9.4, Brazil 9 million square kilometres!

Whether we with our tenth, to keep to this assumption, can supply our own principal needs, can fill our own storehouses and keep our own economic system going even by applying all our strength and technical skill is doubtful, at least with the increase in population that is otherwise desirable. Of course we must increase our own agricultural production very much, especially in Hungary and perhaps in the neighbouring States that join us — this we shall do. Also we shall help Turkey to irrigate Mesopotamia and to induce a pleasant fruitfulness there, but the dowry of land is at the outset somewhat meagre both for Germany and Austria-Hungary.

. . . . . .

How do things stand with the amount of population? This question too can only be answered in outline, for there is very great difference between one man and another, and a million Central Europeans cannot be set against a million Indians or Tartars. But all the same the population figures give something to go by.

The population of the German Empire and of Austria-Hungary together amounts to about 116 millions according to the last census figures, which are now of course already exceeded. Then there is the German colonial population of perhaps 14 millions (various estimates). If we count in with these 25 millions of European and Asiatic Turks and about 20 millions of other Europeans with perhaps 25 millions of other non-Europeans, and this is still on a favourable assumption which we should not like to put higher at the outset, the population of the Mid-European economic world-group would be roughly reckoned at about 200 millions in round numbers, that is about one-eighth of the present supposed world-population. We need not point out again how uncertain all estimates of this kind are at the present time. The object of these figures is only to give a quite general view. For comparison it may serve to note that the British Empire was registered some years ago at about 425 millions, China at 330 millions, Russia at 170 millions, the United States 107, France with its colonies 95.

Our Central European home population would be the centre of the life of an economic body which stretched out its grasp into other quarters of the globe. It possesses an immense capital in strength if it does not stop increasing. The decline in the birth-rate which began before the war must be overcome! The first years after the war will probably decide whether or no this will succeed. After the war we must everywhere begin afresh, and in this respect more even than in anything else. Mid-Europe needs children, children, children! This is the presupposition of all prosperity both military and economic. Now that the war has shown us obviously in France how helpless and in need of help a nation becomes that has lost its taste for growth owing to insistent civilisation and to immorality; now that it has shown us in Russia what the masses signify, even with only a Russian training; now that we have lost a hundred thousand men in the war; now the urgent, heartfelt, beseeching call must resound, mingled with the ringing of the peace bells, calling to men and women in town and country: beget children! All allowances to public and private officials must estimate the father of a family differently from the mere private spender. The storage system thus accords with the policy of increasing the population, a highly sacred patriotic task. This is no party question, no controversial question, it is a duty, a vital command.

. . . . . .

Whereas hitherto we have on principle banished the relevant figures to the statistical portion of our book, an exception has been made in the discussion of area and population because here no presentation at all could be given without numbers. From henceforth, however, we shall return to the earlier practice, since otherwise our further exposition would be too difficult reading, and since all statistical comparisons between the economic products of world-group States can only be drawn with very many reservations. If, for instance, we establish the quantity of wheat produced by England with Scotland and Ireland, that has a certain importance for future submarine wars, but has only a small value for world-economics. If we add what Canada, India, South Africa and Australia produce, the picture changes enormously. But even these much larger figures are not useful for purposes of comparison since rice frequently takes the place of wheat in the British colonial territories, and especially in India. In order even to arrive at a judgment concerning the strength in food-supply of a world-group Empire, we must be able to express in figures the total of food-stuffs produced by it, add them up and divide them per head of the population. But how can this be done when both adequate statistical data and methods of computation are wanting for the purpose? The attempt at computation employed in the publication *Die Deutsche Volksernährung im Krieg* by the German professors who inquired into food-supplies under the direction of Professor Eltzbacher is very interesting, and will certainly give occasion for other kindred works. But it has not proved of immediate value to us in the war for economic schemes of national housekeeping, and without further investigation no one can transfer the method used to the other economic States. With the help of the available international surveys and the statistical abstracts of Germany and Austria-Hungary, I have done my best to compare the Central European economic area with the Russian, English and North American areas. I have, however, only succeeded in placing side by side some separate series of figures obtainable from the statistical abstracts, so that the reader may work them out further as he pleases. And in relation to the scheme for our Central European economic system the further possibilities of development must be taken into account at least as much as the present production. But in this case also any numerical grasp is quite unobtainable. In addition at each individual point we are met with the difficulty, already sufficiently discussed, that no statement can be made beforehand as to which of the intermediate and small European States will sooner or later join the Central European union. Hence we must unfortunately be content to indicate briefly acknowledged tendencies and tasks.

.   .   .   .   .   .

The English world-group Empire is the first, the oldest and the most powerful economic Power. We have discussed above its administrative methods, now we must realise the abundance of its wealth in land, its goods, powers, productions, plantations, railways and ships, its economic material. Here the Central European reader must discard from the outset an error current amongst us, that is the undervaluation of the English colonial territory. Indeed nowadays these are often no longer colonies at all but Imperial provinces, and after the war they will secure a yet greater share in the Government than hitherto. Indeed, one of the facts that have become evident in the war is that Australia, South Africa and Canada are English in will and feeling. They have their own provincial pride and their inalienable autonomy, but they wish to be independent parts of Greater Britain. After the war they will not demand separation from Great Britain but an increasing co-operation in the management of the Empire. The old Mother Country is being absorbed in the whole organism and will be a marketing province for it and the centre of finance and industry, and will no longer be the seat of all authority. Expressed in economic terms this signifies a weakening of the industrial character of the Empire for the benefit of the most powerful raw material community in the world. London will have for Greater Britain something of the value which, under different conditions, Petersburg has for Russia — it may one day be temporarily cut off without the English Empire as a whole being vitally injured thereby. The more the immediate future is affected by submarine policy the more this event will be accelerated. But this means that the industrial competition between Central Europe and Great Britain is indeed very important for the economic character of Greater Britain but is not an entirely vital question. This war is still carried on as an industrial war by Great Britain, but it is becoming apparent in the course of it that the question whether Great Britain or Germany have the lead in the production of iron is by no means a vital one for Greater Britain. Its factories will be removed much more to the overseas provinces, in so far as geographical conditions permit, and there guns will be fused and machines constructed. Out of a colonising country will develop a State of incomparable self-sufficiency as regards agriculture and raw material and with its own developing industries. This State will, as we believe, gradually set on one side the old English trader policy, will more and more leave to the Parliament in London only the domestic administration of Great Britain, and will set up a Super-Government with economic boundaries such as Joseph Chamberlain tried to introduce more than a decade ago. The watchword of the World-Empire will be economic independence, but at the same time the repayment of war debts will provide a strong inducement to the establishment of an Imperial war chest with the revenue from tariffs. Now that free trade internationalism has broken down, the English genius will apply itself resolutely to a Greater British protectionism, and, from the economic point of view, everything is ready for this except the boundaries, for this Empire lying scattered on every ocean is assailable at all its corners. Its trenches lie in the water. Sea-militarism!

. . . . . .

Greater Britain has a wellnigh inexhaustible basis of arable land and cattle pasture, more indeed than the United States of North America. It possesses forest lands in Canada and Central Africa, meadow lands in Australia and South Africa, herds of cattle in Canada and India, cotton plantations in India and Egypt, sugar plantations in India, coal in Great Britain and also in parts of India, South Africa and Australia. It lacks coffee, cocoa and iron-ore, but instead there is abundance of gold in Africa, Australia and also in India, silver in Australia and rubber in Africa. We are still without any economic work which treats this whole territory as a unity so that an inventory and balance sheet can be drawn up. Generally we can see only the demand of the mother-province of Great Britain and cannot see at the same time how far it can be met by the other provinces. We see the demand of the European Mother-Country for cotton without at the same glance surveying the cotton ports of India and Egypt. The same is true of wheat and other materials.

All exchange within Greater Britain is naturally accomplished by water routes and has consequently, as already remarked, an insecurity which can never be entirely removed. But what man can do to establish an adequate system of transport that England has done. Her merchant fleet, in comparison with the merchant fleets of Germany and Austria-Hungary together, is as 136 to 36. The command of the sea is not only a claim but an actual fact. The floating multitude of England's freight-carriers stands far above the means of intercourse possessed by all the other seafaring Powers. These carriers may be interrupted in the war but not replaced, not dispensed with.

It is necessary to give an impression of these quantitative relations, because there are too many worthy Central Europeans who

OUR POSITION IN THE ECONOMIC SYSTEM

think it a small matter to make the building of Greater Britain totter. Certainly Greater Britain suffers from the war; it trembles and alters and shifts its internal formations, but — after the war it will still be there.

· · · · ·

Even if we consider the United States of North America without Mexico and without South America, it forms an economic Power which is indeed far behind Greater Britain (with India) in population, but is full of unlimited wealth in land and of possibilities. The decisive point here is the nature of the population: there are nearly 88 per cent. of Europeans or their descendants, so that the average type of human being is fundamentally above the average in Greater Britain (always including India) in economic efficiency. But at the same time the old English leadership is much weaker than in Greater Britain, much more mixed with inflowings of another type. The displacement of the upper class in the country is indeed one of the most serious problems, perhaps as serious for the United States as ocean connections are for Greater Britain. It appears from a summary of the immigration since 1821 that a greater increase has come from Germany and Austria-Hungary than from Great Britain and Ireland, but this increase has been worked into the original old English community. Yet difficulties are increasing now that Russians, Austrian and Hungarian Slavs and Roumanians, Italians and even East Asiatics crowd in far more than do English, Germans, Irish and Scandinavians. This may not be very dangerous politically because all these elements immediately take their stand on the footing of the democratic system already briefly described, and there are no serious problems relating to the defence of the country. But from the economic point of view it involves a certain average decline to the proletarian standard, which decline is perhaps somewhat blunted by the marvellous swing upwards of the last hundred years. And after all, the foundation of material advantages, success and will power is so strong that we must still be prepared for new manifestations of American efficiency.

And whereas Greater Britain is engaged in shifting round from being an industrial country to being the leading raw material Power in the world, North America is obviously moving in the opposite direction. It is adding a daily growing industrialism to its immense production of raw material, and in this way fulfils all the necessary presuppositions of a wealthy, rising, powerful, world-group economic area. Railways here are what steamships are to Greater Britain. The American is essentially a railway man. The area employed in agriculture here is nearly as great as the agricultural area in European Russia, the forest area is greater than the Russian, the unused land is still extensive. The North American wheat area is in proportion to the German-Austrian-Hungarian as 203 to 68. The product per acre is not yet as high as our average, but is increasing. The United States cattle herds are only surpassed by those in India. The number of pigs is almost twice as great as in the central States of Mid-Europe. Above all, the United States is the leading cotton country in the world, far ahead of Greater Britain, producing more than half the total world harvest. In coal the United States equals Germany and Great Britain together. Of iron-ore it has nearly twice as much as Germany. The profits from iron exceed the total of Great Britain, Germany and Austria-Hungary. In gold the United States is surpassed only by South Africa, in silver it holds the first place. On such a basis the Americans work with the fearless, good sense of a business-like and indefatigable nation, and understand the organisation of trades and syndicates just as well as we do. Since, moreover, they are not really injured by the war, but on the contrary are making much money out of it, they will enter upon the next period of international economics in an uncomfortably healthy condition as our most powerful competitors.

· · · · · ·

And how do matters stand with Russia? Just now during the war so many wise things are said about Russia that one becomes silent. Even those to whom the country is not unknown, mostly differ in their opinions. No one knows what western frontiers Russia will have after the war. But this much is certain, that

OUR POSITION IN THE ECONOMIC SYSTEM

Russia has shown more military and organising power than many well-informed people expected. People talked to us of Russian corruption as though it were an absolute impediment to corporate action. But that is not the case: a big elephant can tolerate many insects. What we cannot form an opinion about is the effect of the war on the Russian nation. Perhaps war and defeat will mean a beginning of far-reaching reforms, which will have something of the effect of the reforms of Stein and Hardenberg in Prussia. Perhaps! But in any case there will remain immense quantities of people and material. Russia has the best increase in population in the world. If it treats its people wastefully, they grow again. In addition it has forest and arable land in abundance. Its European forest land is in proportion to that of Germany-Austria-Hungary as 168 to 33. Then, too, there are the Caucasian and Siberian forests. And forests are increasing in value, as we have already said, in world-economics. Russia's European agricultural area is in proportion to that of the two Central European Powers as 210 to 68. Russia's wheat production is in proportion to that of Central Europe as 228 to 112, but the product per hectare of the Russian land may still be immensely increased. The number of cattle and sheep is great, and above all is capable of increase. In beet sugar Russia comes next to Germany and Austria-Hungary. The number of its cotton-spindles is less than that in Germany but more than that in Austria-Hungary. In coal it ranks comparatively low, but in petroleum it stands higher than all the countries, except the United States, together. In iron-ore it surpasses Austria-Hungary. In pig-iron it ranks only a little below France, the fifth iron-power in the world. Its gold cannot be compared with the stores of Greater Britain and the United States but stands much the highest in Europe. All these materials wait for capital and labour. It is exceedingly doubtful how things will look with Russian capital after the war, but capital will come from somewhere or other so soon as materials, demand and labour power are present. To awaken, in the economic sense, this rich Russia is one of the greatest tasks of world-economics, much more tempting than even the induction of China into the capitalist system. Notwithstanding all the crises and fluctuations that are still to be expected, this awakening will sometime succeed, and then the masses of the Russian population will take on form and content. When this happens we need to be already well ahead in Mid-Europe in order not to be overpowered.

. . . . . .

The object of these three scanty surveys is only to supply the right proportions for Mid-Europe. Many of us are still far too much involved in small conceptions, and fail to appreciate the greatness of the older world-group economic areas. We can no longer work up to the quantitative measure of these three Empires, at least not in the, for us, visible future. This is no argument against the foundation of Mid-Europe; but a strong argument for accomplishing it quickly and thoroughly. If we wait another generation, the neighbouring nations and colonies that are now perhaps still attainable for us, will be lost. For the Great Powers will work onwards and will follow the law of their own weight.

The individual producer, great estate owner, farmer, forest owner, manufacturer or mine-owner asks what it matters to him whether he tries to make his profit in a small State or in a world-group economic Power, and often replies to himself that he would rather be an important man in small surroundings than a member of an almost boundless economic union. Moreover, he points to the Russian producer, who has to put up with severe oppression in spite of the extent of his markets. This latter point may be readily yielded, and it may be acknowledged that a smaller, better managed State has advantages over a larger one badly managed. It may also be admitted that more effective aid is often given by the Government of a small State than by that of a great Power, since all Great Powers have, on account of their size, something of a free trade character. But the main fact remains that extensive markets are the first preliminary condition of economic expansion and vigour. So long as the agriculture and industries of economic small States like Belgium and Denmark can share without further ceremony in the English international trade system without at the same time making themselves dependent either in the political or economic sense, the industrial producers in those States will find no occasion to think other than provincially. But as soon as the gates of Greater Britain are closed they will inquire very quickly and minutely where, in the world's economic system, they shall and can find shelter. Individual producers are often quite unable to imagine how an international economic displacement will work. I can still remember clearly how, when I was a child, the weavers in Saxony were greatly troubled when Alsatian Mühlhausen was taken into our economic union. They would have preferred to remain by themselves! And what has now become of all these anxieties? We know nothing more about them. It will be the same when Mid-Europe has been in existence for a generation.

To-day we need to get away from all such very natural anxieties; we must do so if we do not wish to be involved for all future time in economic dependence and insignificance. No farmer or manager of a business in a great Empire wishes to desert his wider sphere and go back to the old limitations. Has any one ever heard of a Hanoverian, even if politically he be a Guelph from head to foot, has any one ever heard of such a one who wishes to abandon the Prusso-German customs and economic union? There is no such person! And thus later no Hungarian and no Austrian will desire to go back again, if only the connection is made so complete that an economic world-group really comes into existence.

. . . . . .

And if now we are willing to venture on the foundation of Mid-Europe, let us examine our assets. What do we possess? In our investigations so far we have already spoken of this. We have a country which is small compared with the countries of the older economic Powers and will remain small even if it is increased by further adhesions and colonial acquisitions. But we use our country up to the last corner, and shall also bring into complete and intelligent use the land which to-day is only half employed. Our forests are looked after in rather a different fashion from those in Russia, our arable lands are grateful and responsive to industrious cultivation. Our herds of cattle are a source of pride, and will amply win back their old abundance after the war. Our Central European people know how to deal with nature and understand the growth of plants and cattle as hardly any other does, for it respects natural development and loves the individuals. Let us number the cattle and pigs that we own between the North Sea and the Balkans! Look at our wheat! Look at our oats! Look at our fields of potatoes, at our sugar-beet! These, as we have just experienced during the war, constitute a basis of life which under a reasonable system of storage will guard our joint territory from foreign dependence! And then go into our mining districts and hear there the daily murmur and rumble of work; look at the ironworks and ports. Look at the factories! Notice also the industry of the artisans, the activity of the merchants, the ability of the legions of workers! We do not want to overrate ourselves and our powers, and we wish to teach our children still better than we have learnt ourselves, but our joint population is a splendid and valuable capital. Even in a limited space 120 or 150 millions of such people are a power, when rhythm pervades their actions, and they are supported, sustained and spurred on by organisation.

It is true that we lack essential material unless we discover some unexpectedly great colonial supplement. In the first place we lack cotton, then wool, then corn to some extent and fodder to a great extent, we lack copper, iron-ore, leather, coffee, rice, tobacco, also wood, maize, jute fibre, petroleum, chemical materials and many other things. We lack more than Greater Britain and North America, we have fewer quantitative possibilities than Russia. But there exists no world-group economic area quite without supplementary requirements, and we can make and lay by in our storehouses sufficient to save us from anxiety in a serious emergency. A population that possesses such stores of coal, such machines, and can work as ours can, can also purchase, save and economise.

When we are once united we can make our common economic scheme as a part of the developing world-group economic scheme.

We shall think over what we have, what we ourselves produce, what we must buy and what we can sell; in this way all our work will become much more definite and distinct. We shall calculate for all of us together. In this matter all economic unions of producers, employees and workmen will help. This will be our practical world-group socialism.

. . . . . .

And how will things go with the people of moderate income in our Central European nations? It is obvious that the great and strong will gain when their sphere is enlarged. But how will it be in this case with the moderate-sized undertakings, the dependent energies? We have already touched slightly upon this question, which is always at hand, since a nation's future is not merely the future of its directors. But here we must once more indicate two fundamental facts which we have already experienced in the German Empire, and which we are in a position to point out to the Austrians and Hungarians in virtue of the occurrences in our own nation.

We have found that with the growth of capitalism the small independent businesses have indeed gone through a severe crisis, but are far from having been ruined in the mass, as had often been prophesied of them. There are developing and declining manual trades, and others remaining level. The butchers and bakers serve as an example of the first class, linen weavers and tanners of the second, bricklayers, shoemakers and indeed also tailors of the third. In the small trades that are endangered it always happens that a section raises itself up, whilst another and larger one declines, but the decline is generally such that the old people drop out and, frankly, often very painfully, whilst their children begin from the outset as wage-earners. But, on the whole, the great bulk of the small trades continue about level, they do not grow but they maintain themselves, for wherever there are agricultural or industrial profits, a smaller middle class of auxiliary industries grows up near the chief centres, small shopkeepers, innkeepers, clothiers, agents. To these is added the new middle class of Government, communal, bank, commercial and industrial officials. These all make their living out of the general progress of the world's economic business. When work and business is brisk they live well. For them, according to their locality, the prices of wood, corn and cattle, the bank balance, commercial settlements, salaries and, above all, wages, are the indirect bases of their existence. It is almost impossible to help them by legislation, even if people wish it ever so much, they can better help themselves mutually by comradeship. But the really important thing for them is nothing, nothing else at all, but the magnitude of the national economic business. But this business depends on the activities of the world's economic system, and hence these smaller and weaker individuals, too, are connected with the most important economic questions. A Viennese member of the House of Representatives once said: "If only our manual workers were as well paid as those in the German Empire; that is all they wish for!" But this and more besides they will never attain as long as Austria and Hungary remain in isolation.

And we have further found that with a growing economic development the working classes everywhere become not only very much more numerous, but above all better nourished, better cared for and better paid. Of course many very important and well-warranted desires remain unsatisfied and will be brought forward by the trade unions at every opportunity. But no one will dispute the fact itself, that in a developing economic State the workpeople rise. The whole of our modern labour system would be worthless were this not the case. I have heard impressive accounts by Austrian social democrats of the difficulties and necessities amidst which they work. They too use the same phrase: "If we were only as far on as you are in Germany!" In the pursuit of their own special interests these men must be the most ardent champions of Mid-Europe. In narrow conditions all labour movements remain weak; they can protest loudly but attain little. But so soon as the horizon widens, the area of passionate ardour increases and the wheels revolve a thousandfold, for in such a case even the members of the proletariat can demand their due wages for work necessary to the world-group system.

OUR POSITION IN THE ECONOMIC SYSTEM 215

The concept of a Central European economic world-group is in no sense, or perhaps only in the first instance, a producers' affair. It may even be that for some producers the benefit that is to be won thereby will ultimately vanish. No, it is a national concern, the problem of the masses: how will you rise, if you are willing to remain as you are?

CHAPTER VII

TARIFF PROBLEMS

NO part of the Mid-European economic system has hitherto been so much discussed and written about as the customs partnership: its feasibility, its consequences, and also its limitations and its questionableness. Military partnership, financial partnership, closer approach in matters of intercommunication, law and administration, associations of syndicates and trade unions, have only been spoken of vaguely and in whispers. But the customs or commercial partnership formed the subject of meetings, schemes and congresses even before the war, and has continued to do so during the war. This is readily to be understood owing to various causes presently to be discussed, only people must not be deceived thereby into thinking that a mere customs and commercial partnership by itself is feasible either from the Austrian, the Hungarian or the German standpoint. The reasons for this in each case are somewhat various, and we shall state them at the beginning of this chapter as introductory to its main subject-matter. We shall speak then in the first instance of the customs partnership quite generally as the removal of frontier tariffs, and shall leave it until later to define more closely the possible extent of this removal.

Suppose that on the frontiers between Germany and Austria in the Tyrol, in the Bavarian forest, on the ridge of the Böhmerwald, on the Erzgebirge and on the Riesengebirge, the customs officers were removed, or that only a few articles were left to them to control and on which to collect money. What might be the consequences of this for the Austrian economic system? It would not in any way injure Austrian agriculture, nor the really big industries, which already have their place in international markets, nor would it at all disturb the home market. But all those businesses that only subsist because the people in their immediate neighbourhood order and buy from them for local or national reasons would receive a blow, in the form of a new, unusual competition, which would, it is true, have to bear the greater costs of transport and distance, but which in other respects would work under more favourable conditions. This latter point is here the important thing: the frontier customs officials can only be removed if the remaining conditions of production are as far as possible equalised either beforehand, or simultaneously, or at least soon afterwards. Quite equal they will never be made, and moreover, as we have already remarked, there are considerable internal differences within the German Empire and within every economic world-group. But a certain measure of equality is under all circumstances the presupposition of the removal of frontier barriers. For example, if it costs more for a North Bohemian manufacturer to procure cotton than it does for a Saxon producer in the same industry, the latter will gain an immediate advantage from the removal of the duty. It follows that the policy relating to freights and railway rates must go hand in hand with the customs partnership. Or if a joint-stock company in Austria has to pay many more taxes than in Prussia, then, when barriers are removed the Austrian company will if possible remove itself to Silesia. Or if, owing to the diminished value of the Austrian currency, an Austrian manufacturer must pay more in kronen for his half-finished goods sent from Germany than his competitor in the German Empire pays in marks, it will be difficult for him to sell at the same price. If the Austrian, owing to a certain formalism in his Government administration, can only get his new engine-house built two years later than the German, this interval is sufficient to give the latter the advantage. We might go on talking in this way for a considerable time and the outcome of it all is: the customs partnership will only suit the Austrians if it is at the same time much more than a customs partnership!

. . . . . .

The same thing is anyhow broadly true for Hungary as well,

but Hungarian affairs are much more complicated and demand special discussion. We shall not touch upon the matter as it affects State rights until the next chapter, here we need only speak of the interconnection of the economic questions. With regard to this point we call to mind the account in a previous chapter of the two economic States united in the Dual Monarchy, and the section relating to it in the statistical portion of our book. The question is, then, how will it affect Hungary if there are no longer customs officials on the mountain ridges between it and Germany? The effect would be the same as on Austria if Hungary and Germany were bounded directly by one another on one or two important routes of communication, but since this is not the case the Hungarians will, so to speak, get the benefit of the customs partnership at second hand. This might be somewhat compensated for later on if the inclusion of the powerful Balkan countries bordering on Hungary came into question. But in the meantime, so long as only the German Austrian-Hungarian customs relations are the order of the day Hungary is actually dependent on the goodwill of the Austrian traffic administration. A very big, profitable market for its numerous natural productions opens out to it, but in between is another economic territory that also, of course, wishes to buy and sell for itself. Consequently Hungary, too, is not helped by a mere commercial partnership without further additional clauses. Like Austria it must demand a closer approach in legal and administrative matters. But besides this it needs a guarantee that the raw materials and half or wholly manufactured goods which it obtains from Germany will not be detained on the way or made more than necessarily costly, and likewise that its consignments of cattle, fruit vans, grapes, packets of vegetables and butter casks will reach Berlin as quickly as possible.

The Hungarians are distrustful in this matter, and hence would gladly go a step further and demand in the union a return to the earlier conditions of a special intermediate customs frontier between themselves and the Austrians. We shall here discuss this point, but only in relation to economics, deferring, as before, the question of its bearing on State rights. We have had to touch on similar matters already in discussing the problems of war economics. The conception of a special Hungarian economic State exists, and will possibly be reawakened by the unavoidable necessity of discussing the Mid-European commercial partnership. This must not surprise us, for the Hungarians, it may perhaps be remarked, are in general much stronger State politicians than economic politicians. Their political and national energy is very great and enforces admiration even though it may be exceedingly inconvenient to the rest of us in particular cases, but the economic ideal is less worked out, otherwise economic particularism would already be more on the decline. For if any part of Central Europe is certain to gain much from the union, it is Hungary. We have already pointed out what difficulties it must get into if it were left outside the German-Austrian corn trading system. In this case it would be in the same position as Roumania and must sell its corn at Roumanian prices. The difference in prices between Bucharest and Budapest would disappear, and this almost entirely to the disadvantage of Hungary. To put it otherwise: the economic boundaries of the corn trade between Vienna and Odessa would lie on the Leitha. The same is true in some measure in regard to cattle and other products of forest and field. As opposed to this the interests of certain Hungarian textile and iron manufactures and similar undertakings in a protective tariff will naturally be relegated to the background from the Hungarian standpoint. A country with such a big export trade in raw materials as Hungary cannot really seriously contemplate an isolated economic position when the possibility of inclusion in a country with a corn tariff is offered to it. But the presuppositions are: partnership in traffic communications, partnership in tariff, unimpeded rights of economic citizenship in the big common union.

・　・　・　・　・　・　・

Nor can the German Empire, for its part, admit a mere easing of customs duties without another and more extensive economic partnership. Formerly we had an economic treaty with Austria-Hungary as with Russia and other States with tariffs. After the war, of course, this can be continued, renewed, and altered in details according to the wishes of both sides. But in this case so soon as we mean to go beyond the limits of the arrangements and to grant specially easy conditions to the Austrians and the Hungarians the difficulty arises that we cannot simultaneously yield up to another Power the advantages which we grant to the Danubian Monarchy. We render all our remaining commercial treaties more difficult for ourselves, yet without gaining thereby anything substantial for our economic future. Moreover, the same thing also applies in a lesser degree to Austria-Hungary. In such a case we neither of us gain the advantages of the enlargement of free markets, and we hinder ourselves in all our "most favoured nation" relations in regard to the other economic worldgroups.

We must bear in mind here that of course for Austria-Hungary the trade with the German Empire far exceeds all its remaining foreign trade (imports for home consumption 39.5 per cent., exports of domestic produce 40.8 per cent.), but that this same trade is of much less importance in the foreign commerce of the German Empire (imports 7.7 per cent., exports 10.9 per cent.). Hence if we increase our exchange with Austria-Hungary, but owing to this make our exchange with other countries more difficult, this is quite a different matter for us and for Austria-Hungary respectively. For Austria-Hungary the German trade is absolutely the primary factor in commercial policy, an unconditional, vital necessity, whereas for us the trade with Austria-Hungary holds the second place indeed in exports, but only the fourth in imports. It is important enough, but is not a decisive factor in our development. It must be readily admitted in this connection that immediately after the war the mutual connection will for both sides come more strongly into evidence than hitherto. But all the same: for purely economic reasons Germany will not be able to enter into any one-sided preferential position in respect to Austria-Hungary at the expense of its relations with the rest of the economic world. For us the matter appears in this light: either Austria-Hungary is a foreign economic State like other

TARIFF PROBLEMS 221

States, in which case, with all possible consideration, it will yet in the main receive equal treatment; or it is and will remain our partner in the union and our comrade for life in the narrow and strict meaning of the words, in which case all foreignness vanishes and we take over its interests as it takes over ours. In this case we shall have no treaty, as with Russia, France or the United States, but we shall be or shall become a unity, and together shall confront all the world in buying and selling and in all treaties. It is evident that this cannot be attained all at once, but even now our first steps must depend on whether we desire this whole or not.

. . . . . .

Nevertheless a great deal, and much that is expert, has already been said and written in connection with other general Mid-European economic questions about this very point of the transaction of a special commercial treaty. And this will certainly be all to the good, for the intrinsic logic of the matter will lead of itself from this starting-point to further developments. The choice of this starting-point for the discussions has, however, a special cause in present-day facts and a special cause in history. The former cause is this: that the military, technical-financial and commercial matters connected with the union, as well as the question of syndicates, are of such a specialised technical character that each one of them can only be really surveyed and prepared by a limited number of men; whereas tariff negotiations, on the other hand, have always been the subject of public debates and have constantly aroused lively interest in Parliament and in books. Even here, it is true, the number of people who can really attain insight and an intelligent survey is not great. But the general fundamental concepts are easily accessible, and the statistical material is ready at hand. Here every figure is available whilst in questions relating to money and syndicates often the very most important points of all remain business secrets. Thus it is not merely its actual value that has placed this point above all the other matters to be discussed. And in addition there is the historical reason, that the remaining schemes for combination are new ideas which have only just arisen, whilst the German-Austrian-Hungarian customs union is a very old and already much contested problem, an inheritance from the previous century.

Professor v. Philippovich, the most distinguished representative of scientific economic doctrine in Austria, in his work, *Ein Wirthschafts-und Zollverband zwischen Deutschland und Österreich-Ungarn* (published by Hirzel, 1915), has given an excellent historical account of the earlier ideas and schemes about commercial policy. Friedrich List here comes to the fore as the most original thinker on the German side; List, the prophet of our railways, chambers of commerce and eastern colonisation. Bruck, the Minister of Commerce, was the leader of Austrian thought in this connection. List is brought conveniently within reach of present-day readers in the edition of his works now shortly to be brought out by Geh. Finanzrat Losch of Stuttgart. And Philippovich gives us an admirable sketch of the broad outlook of the Austrian statesman who was Minister of Commerce in 1850 when the tariff barriers were removed between Austria and Hungary. At that time there arose almost simultaneously from South Germany and Vienna the demand of the "Greater Germany" party for an economic partnership extending from the Adriatic to the North and Baltic Seas. But Prussia refused all these ideas, for in accordance with her "Lesser Germany" policy, she wanted by all means to keep Austria from any share in the administration of the Customs Union. The economic movements of the period before 1866 cannot be understood at all apart from contemporary politics, for they form a part of the latter. We have explained in an earlier chapter how essential Bismarck's founding of the German Empire was for the whole of Central Europe, but that it was not the final settlement of the Central European question. With a like meaning Philippovich remarks of Bruck's plan: "History has decided otherwise, but has not buried Bruck's conceptions." Bismarck's various utterances about the impracticability of a Customs Union date from this period between 1852 and 1866, and, as is almost always the case with his statements, their tone of uncompromising rejection is to be explained by the circumstances of contemporary history. The economist Schäffle, who was afterwards Austrian Minister, judged the matter differently: "I live more than ever in the hope that, even if only very slowly, this idea will attain to full recognition."

. . . . . .

Thus people in Austria are falling back upon this old Austrian scheme, which was at that time fruitless, whilst in the German Empire we are reminded once again of the former Prusso-German Customs Union because it points the way to Central European unity. In those days the German Empire developed out of the Customs Union, and in like manner a newer and greater State association may form itself out of a present-day customs partnership with Austria-Hungary. Truth is mingled with error in this way of looking at things. The error consists in an over-estimation of the political influence of mere customs unions in general. It must not be forgotten that the Prussian Customs Union with Hanover, Bavaria and Württemberg did not prevent these States from taking up arms against each other in 1866. It is true that the Customs Union persisted, and outlasted the war, but it was not in itself strong enough to make war impossible. The same thing was demonstrated in 1870 in the case of France, which had an excellent tariff treaty with Prussia. And the most favoured nation clause of commercial policy which Bismarck inserted in the Franco-German peace terms ripened into no political *rapprochement*. Tariff questions had no such strong influence then, and have even less of it to-day. The German Imperial union became a self-contained political whole only because its unity stretched far, very far beyond questions of tariffs and commerce and was reciprocally military, legal, financial and industrial. It was this alone that made an economic organism out of the constituent States. Therefore if to-day we wish to establish a future Mid-European political unity, the history of this old Prusso-German Customs Union shows that a most favoured nation arrangement will not by itself be sufficient. It seems to be the most convenient step towards the great object, and on account of its comparative facility will be regarded by the Government departments concerned in the question as, for the time being, the best means to a nearer approach. But there is the danger that we shall then believe that something tangible has been attained which is yet not the case. By this method we shall arrive at greater reciprocal adaptation of imports and exports, but also at a permanent atmosphere of continuous tariff rivalries and mutual agitations. So long as the old Customs Union lasted it was, it is true, certainly an aid to compromise, but the feeling of mutually belonging to one another altogether was wanting. Even the Customs Parliament of 1867 to 1870 played only a secondary part. And the general temperature was much more tuned to commercial policy at that time than it is to-day, for it was the period of strengthening belief in free trade. The removal of tariffs served the general cause of progress. These matters are not so simple, however, to our present way of thinking.

· · · · · ·

I may be allowed here to insert a personal confession in respect to the tariff question as a whole, because I have to justify co-operation in the Central European customs union to myself and my own past commercial policy. In the years 1901 to 1903 under the leadership of my dead friend Theodor Barth, of ineffaceable memory, and guided by my honoured friend Professor Brentano, I shared with all my energies in the agitation against the raising of the German customs tariff, and especially in the opposition to higher bread prices, and I have expressed the principles underlying this action more recently still in my *Neudeutsche Wirthschafts-politik* written in 1905. I am not in the least ashamed of my attitude at that time, because it entirely corresponded to my convictions, and I still find pleasure in retrospect over the vigorous fight. As far as pure theory is concerned I have nothing to retract from the views then advocated, for I am still of the opinion that our economic system in the German Empire and our material preparedness for war would have been somewhat different, but no weaker, if the older system had been continued. But in the interval the world has gone on further and the decisive politico-economic victory of the German protectionist party in

December 1902 has brought about conditions in the German economic system which cannot be ignored even by those who previously opposed the new movement. The position here is similar to that in all important political adjustments. Some Liberals and Social Democrats, to take this as an example, were at the time prejudiced for different reasons against Old Age and Sickness Insurance, partly on principle and partly on account of its piecemeal achievement. But when it was once in existence it became a constituent part of our life, and though it might be reformed and improved it could not be cut out again. Obviously it is now very difficult for those who opposed it at the time to say, after the event, how things would have turned out if their proposals had been adopted. The conquered has no evidence, even if much suggests that he was, to say the least, as reasonable and well-disposed as the conqueror. Thus, in brief, I maintain that the increase in German agricultural production has not been essentially affected by the new tariff which came into force on April 1, 1906, but would, on the whole, have gone its own way upwards even if the old Caprivi duties had been retained. The rise in price was very desirable in the individualistic economic interests of those concerned, but it has ushered in no new epoch from the standpoint of national economics. There has been a certain relatively small increase in the area harvested, but the product per hectare has kept on its previous line which was already rising (with variations according to the year's harvest). The same is true of cattle-raising, only here it is allowable to think that our stock of cattle available at the beginning of the war might have been still greater under a system of cheaper fodder imports, without our own production of fodder being any less in consequence than it is at present. Comparison with duty-free agriculture in Switzerland, Belgium, Holland and Denmark shows that the improvement is at least as great in the duty-free countries as in those with protective tariffs. When, therefore, at the present day the agrarians express the opinion that the economic war was won by the customs tariff of 1902–3 and by the treaty tariff which came into force on April 1, 1906, I for my part regard this as mischievous agitation, and oppose it in the interests of actual fact and of truth. Our reasoning in 1912 was just as good as that of our opponents, but the question now is for us whether or no we can turn back to the old starting-point of 1902 or, indeed, to that of 1881. This is what I deny, at least for the period which we are now in a position in some degree to survey. For by reason of the general international economic movement upwards the rise in tariffs and in the prices of necessaries has been compensated for by the rising wages, salaries and prices of all goods to a much greater extent than we and our opponents were able to take for granted beforehand. Things do not turn out either exactly as they hoped nor yet as we feared. They had to find by experience that their financial gain was absorbed by the increase in their private and public expenditure. We, for our part, found or could have found that the prophesied lowering of the standard of life among the working classes did not make its appearance because, with the co-operation of the trade-union organisations, wages adapted themselves more quickly than was expected to the altered conditions of prices. All prices rose: real estate, goods, labour power. This meant a burden on our foreign trade, but no noticeable displacement at home. Moreover, the foreign trade could bear the burden because the amounts demanded on the international market increased extraordinarily, and also because elsewhere a simultaneous depreciation in the value of money set in. Owing to a combination of circumstances and to rapid adaptation the whole proceeding was of much less importance than it should have been according to the predictions of both sides. This explains what I said above: that tariff questions were of more importance fifty years ago than at present. But it also explains my assertion that we cannot simply turn back to the earlier state of things because for a long time it has been no mere question of forcing back certain items in the tariff, but of bending back all prices and with them the value of money within Germany. If officials and workers are asked whether, supposing the corn prices of 1902 were re-established, they would be willing to return also to the salaries and wages of that time seeing that the principal reason for the

TARIFF PROBLEMS

rise in wages would be obviated, they find this notion, to say the least of it, not unquestionable. It is, however, certain that we cannot make such an experiment at the moment, amidst the uncertainty of the whole economic system after the war, when anyhow there is prospect of a further reduction in the value of money. At present we must work on further on the foundation laid against our will. And in addition there is a constant parliamentary majority in favour of the existing tariff system, and we have too much else to do in German politics during these next years to begin afresh after the war, with no prospect of securing a majority, a theoretical tariff dispute between the existing and the new regulation of trade.

* * * * * * *

But now for the matter itself! What comes to us from Austria-Hungary, and vice versa? Of course we shall mention only the big items and refer to the statistical section of our book.

The idea still frequently subsists that Austria-Hungary, the "agrarian country," supplies the German Empire with much corn and other agricultural products. The reader who has followed our previous exposition knows already that this is not the case, especially during recent years. Rye is sent, according to the yearly harvest, by us to them, and wheat-flour, of rather higher value, by them to us, but this is no great matter whilst the product per hectare in Hungary stands at its present level. Of much greater importance are malt-barley, malt and hops for our beer breweries. Potatoes are only exchanged in certain districts. Fruit of all kinds comes to us from over there in not inconsiderable quantities. The importation of wood from Austria-Hungary is of very much more importance, because wood, generally speaking, is a vital factor in the Danubian Monarchy: timber, planks, wood pulp, mine timber, wood alcohol. The imports of cattle and cattle products are exceedingly numerous: eggs, oxen, horses, cows, geese, chickens, goats, milk, butter, bed-feathers, calves' skins, sheepskins. Other hides, skins and furs are exchanged so that certain qualities go in one direction and others in the other. The mutual relations in regard to wool are fairly complex, for a part of the overseas wool reaches Austria-Hungary through German hands. Manufactured woollens go as half-finished goods more from Germany to Austria-Hungary than vice versa. Linen yarn comes from Austria-Hungary to us. Cotton waste is exchanged, cotton yarn has recently been imported in larger quantities to Germany (perhaps temporarily). In coal and coal products the German importation into Austria-Hungary is very great, whereas in lignite Austria surpasses us. Books are exported more from Germany than vice versa. Purely industrial goods pass quite preponderatingly from Germany to Austria-Hungary: tubes, stoves, machines of all kinds, motors, ships, electrical appliances, chemicals, leather goods, clothing materials, etc. The springs gush out from both sides, flow hither and thither and are worked up a thousandfold in opposition to one another and on behalf of one another. All this is a daily changing, revolving life and cannot be expressed at all in a few general formulæ. It must be followed bit by bit with the help of the statistical tables. But then we find that all relations anyhow possible in our mutual economic relationship are actually to be met with somewhere or other. Austria-Hungary is a raw material country to us, but yet not so much so as to be for us a raw material country as such. It is the exchange country for specialities which exist either here or there in great quantities or excellent qualities. It is the receiving country for our industries, but not in the sense that it has not similar industries of its own, or tries to promote them. As a whole the position is more like the relation between two brothers than that between man and wife; competition between brothers, which is best settled by their both taking a share in the business.

・　　　・　　　・　　　・　　　・　　　・

Geh. Finanzrat Losch of Stuttgart, in his work, *Der Mittel-Europäische Wirtschaftsblock,* attempted to mark out three principal groups from the multitude of cases: partnership in demand, supplementary partnership and pure competition. We wish to follow this classification, not as though it included everything, but because it helps towards insight into the reality to be mastered, and actual perception is here more important than a formal discussion of tariff classifications.

To the class of goods for which there is partnership in demand belong all those goods which the two great States either do not produce at all or only in small quantities (such as perhaps tobacco). These are primarily the products of subtropical and tropical climates. Cotton is imported by both parties in large quantities. Here there is no question of any necessity for protection, but a commercial union can, as has been remarked before, make use of the joint annual purchase of almost 900 million marks as a means of securing better terms from foreign nations. Coffee is in the same position, and in this case the taxation of a luxury comes into view. The joint purchase is nearly 350 million marks. The same applies with sundry differences to wool, copper, silk, tobacco, rice and many southern fruits, food-stuffs, other metals, caoutchouc, foreign woods, petroleum (except the Galician production), tea, furs, etc. When the new joint classification is being prepared, it will be best to place by itself this group of goods for which there is a partnership in demand, because from the outset it forms a common objective.

The matter is not so clearly defined for the group of goods for which supplementary partnership exists. For in this case both customs areas generally produce a considerable amount for their own use and only supply one another with the surplus, so that as a rule other sources of supply come into account. The example for Germany is wood. Here Germany has a demand of 350 million marks, Austria-Hungary a surplus of over 200 million, which is capable of further increase. The easier the export of wood for Austria-Hungary to Germany is made, the more will Austrian wood be able to force all other woods off the German market, which will benefit Austria-Hungary and do no direct injury to Germany, since the readjustment will work mainly to the disadvantage of the Russians. The only question is how this favour to Austria will affect the Russo-German commercial treaty. Here the one advantage must be weighed against the other. The case is the same in regard to the big demand in Germany for eggs. Varying with the annual production it is almost entirely met by Austria and Russia, and it is possible by our commercial policy greatly to increase Austria's share to the disadvantage of Russia. In 1913 Russia supplied us with eggs to the value of 80 million marks and Austria to the value of 76 million. These figures might be transposed so soon as Galicia is again in order and the hens there have recovered from the Russian invasion. The position is reversed in the case of coal, an article which has not hitherto been touched by the tariff system, but which by joint syndicates with tariff barriers under State control may be helped forward into partnership. Germany exports pit-coal of the value of 450 million marks (along with an importation, mostly from England, of 200 million). But Austria-Hungary has a demand of over 150 million in excess of its own coal. Of course differences of quality must be taken into account, but there is no doubt that a better adjustment is possible. Austria is already in possession of the attainable German market for lignite. Things are very much the same in the case of maize, barley, malt, fruit, in short, for all the home products of our zone which are produced in surplus in one or another place in Central Europe. This group too must be put into the classification by itself, since it stands out with a character of its own.

The third group, which we have called the purely competitive group, includes all those products and manufactures which from the outset are produced in both customs areas with a view to foreign trade, and in respect to which Germans, Austrians and Hungarians come forward as sellers to the foreigner, but in respect to which, according to the degree of their ability, Germans will prevail in the Austro-Hungarian market and vice versa. Many of the raw materials and some of the half-manufactured goods required for this group belong to the first group mentioned above. The mutual competition in cotton-spinning and machine-making affords an example. The German manufacturers supply cycles to Austria, but the Austrian cycle makers wish, with equal justice, to supply them to Germany. Both dispute together over the market for cycles in the Balkan States. The same applies to arms, locomotives, agricultural machines, stoves, cooking utensils, clothing materials, ready-made underlinen and a hundred other things. In this connection it must be taken into consideration that an industry which wishes to succeed in foreign markets needs, for its own safety, to have firm possession of the home market. Thus, for instance, a Bohemian textile manufacturer cannot succeed in Roumania if meanwhile the Viennese market is taken from him by competitors from the German Empire. Herein lie the most characteristic difficulties of a customs partnership. The more Austria-Hungary becomes an industrial State the more anxiously will her export industries regard an event whose results cannot be estimated in advance. It may be that everything will go much more easily than people think beforehand, but no one can give any guarantee for this. Hence the closest attention must be directed towards this group in the case of a customs union, just as in the case of preferential treatment. Things are simpler even now with regard to the vigorous mutual export trade in sugar, for which already agreements have been arrived at.

. . . . . .

A special group is formed by the temporary duty-free importation of articles to be re-exported after being worked up (*Veredelung*). I confess that it is not easy to get a good grasp of this greatly varied class. Some examples must serve to throw light on the matter: the Austrian chocolate factories get their cocoa from abroad, work it up with home-grown sugar and other ingredients and sell the finished product abroad, of course generally elsewhere than in the place of origin of the raw material. But in this way the original raw material is only, so to speak, on a visit in Austria, and is treated by the customs administration as only temporarily present, the duty being refunded, or cancelled if it has merely been entered. But sugar is exported combined with the original product, cocoa, so that the country outside the tariff barrier is confronted with a new dutiable article. Or half-finished furniture in the rough is imported into Austria, there polished, veneered, upholstered and then again disposed of in foreign countries. In this case practically no new material is added, but only the value of labour. It may so happen that a sale is effected when the customs frontier is crossed, but very often the object remains, during its detention in Austria, in the possession of perhaps some German of the Empire, who has the work in question done in Austria because it is done there specially well or cheaply. In the branches of the textile trade it frequently happens that dressing or dyeing is carried out across the customs barrier since the land frontier often accidentally cuts through an industrial province. The most extensive business procedure of this kind in Germany is in the case of rice polishing: to the value of 85 million marks. Then there is benzine refining, wood and iron finishing, the fitting up of machinery, etc. Here the closer approach of the two customs areas ought to be received from the outset in as conciliatory a spirit as is in any way possible, for nothing promotes the joint economic system so much as this kind of partnership in work. As concerns foreign countries the customs and financial boundaries will remain in existence, but in the common home country they ought in principle to disappear in regard to all working-up processes.

. . . . . .

All duties are from their nature somewhat arbitrary, for they are an additional factor introduced deliberately into the formation of prices. In the case of the most important duties, the frontier imposts on corn, an attempt has indeed been made to establish a sort of theory of the proper height of the duty out of the difference between home and foreign cost of production, and to say perhaps: the farmer in the Argentine can supply wheat at so many marks per ton cheaper than can the farmer in Germany, hence the difference in cost of production must be expressed in the duty. We shall not indeed deny that there is actually some justice about this conception of the matter, but yet it involves serious omission. For what is taken as the home cost of production is already influenced by increases of price due to tariffs, both past and to be expected, and hence is not purely natural, and above all costs of production even in the home country differ widely among them-

TARIFF PROBLEMS 233

selves and are dependent upon the prices of land, whether actual or aspired to. No duty can in itself be fixed on any calculable basis, it is essentially an act of volition. This does not exclude the fact that the duties may be so interconnected, that if A has been decided on, B must follow it. So long as there are duties on articles used for fodder, there must also be duties on cattle, since otherwise evidently cattle imports from abroad will be artificially impelled in this direction to the injury of the home cattle-breeder. So long as there are corn duties there must be corresponding duties on flour. A superstructure of duties on worked-up products builds itself upon every duty on raw material. In this sense there are duties of the first grade and duties of later stages. Thus, in order to establish a customs association, it is necessary to go down to the primary duties and from thence work the equality upwards. This is not difficult, as things are, in the case of the corn tariff, for the treaty duties since 1906 are almost equal, viz. for rye in Germany 5.00 M., in Austria-Hungary 6.00 Kr., for wheat 5.50 M. and 6.50 Kr. for the 100 kilograms. This could easily (with a uniform standard) be brought to a common denominator, so that from this starting-point the whole department of corn, flour, bread and fodder would reach uniformity. The case of iron presents rather more difficulties, for pig-iron pays in Germany 1.00 M., in Austria-Hungary 1.5 Kr. = 1.27 M. And the superstructure dependent on this base figure shows greater differences still. Bar-iron pays, expressed in marks, 2.5 M. in Germany, 5.20 M. in Austria-Hungary. Tin in Germany varies from 3.00 M. to 4.50 M., but in Austria-Hungary it pays 7.65 M.! The differences in the case of tools, screws and cutlery are quite enormous; here in some cases the Austrian duty is five times that of the German Empire. These duties on finished iron goods are directed against the imports from Germany. Thus here it would not suffice to make the primary figure the same, but in addition the whole superstructure must be agreed upon. The department of textiles does not show quite such extensive differences, but yet contains very notable distinctions; here, however, the number of items is so great that the existing conditions can hardly be expressed in any understandable form by a few figures. The duty on worsted begins in Germany at 8 M. and increases according to the qualities up to 24 M., in Austria-Hungary it begins at 10.20 and increases up to 40.80 M.! Any one who has not a copy of the tariff duties himself will find further data of this kind in the work by Professor Philippovich which we have already referred to, *Ein Wirtschafts-und Zollverband zwischen Deutschland und Österreich-Ungarn.* There are also goods which are duty-free in Germany because we have no competition to fear in regard to them, but which are protected by a tariff in Austria-Hungary, as for example many chemicals. These differences are mostly the result of forcible pressure by the interests affected, and will be insisted on so much the more because in the first instance they were secured laboriously, with difficulty and entreaties. Consequently, any one who wants to make alterations here will meet with opposition at every turn from those most nearly concerned. And in such questions where it is a matter of money figures, those interested are generally obstinate and are often actually fighting for the lucrativeness of their capital and machinery. Thus no one need suppose that a customs unity can be produced, so to speak, by a stroke of the pen from above. But above all it follows from this that the persons interested cannot be made the only judges in their own affairs, because in this case the great national economic object will hardly be attained.

. . . . . .

If we suppose for a moment that the war had not happened just now, we should be faced by the question of the renewal of the present commercial treaty system. Then both sides would propose the alterations they desired, but Austria-Hungary in particular would try to improve the position of their customs policy in regard to Germany. For there exists a widespread conviction in Austria-Hungary that in 1903 the special interests of the country were falsely represented. At that time the Austro-Hungarian negotiators still proceeded on the assumption that a reduction in the German corn duties was of vital importance for them. But this was a mistake, for the moment was at hand when Austria-Hungary herself would need corn from abroad. Austria-Hungary increased in amount of population and consuming ability, but her agricultural production did not increase to the same extent. And the Austrian corn duties had no noticeable effect on the latter. The consequence was that a part of the Austro-Hungarian energies were wrongly directed. And hence for the more important export items, namely, cattle, cattle products, wood and also fruit, according to the Austrian understanding of the matter, that relief was not obtained which a different procedure would have secured. Whether this latter is true or not (and it is hard to say after the event), it may anyhow be taken for granted that, but for the war, a serious effort would have been made by Austria-Hungary to obtain further concessions for the articles of export mentioned by a further screwing up of the industrial duties. It would certainly not have been carried to the length of a tariff war, but the negotiations would have taken no very smooth course. Temper in respect to customs policy was not quite harmonious since there was an obvious decline in the export trade to Germany in various directions. This temper is now restrained by the overpowering importance of the war partnership, but it will not be entirely under the surface during the negotiations. We must count on it, and may be prepared for a regular trench-making war round each individual item during the conferences over the tariff. If, then, economic unity is to be attained Austria-Hungary must at the same time be assured that it will not be thrust into a corner. But this means that intermediate customs duties or something similar must be set up between the two countries as a protective measure.

. . . . . .

We have already mentioned incidentally that German and Austrian textile firms may encounter one another on the Roumanian market. This was no example chosen at haphazard, for rivalries in the sphere of the Balkan markets form one of the special difficulties in the commercial policy of the two Great Powers. It is not what is bought there that makes the matter difficult, but what is to be sold there. The Austrian manufacturers cannot equal the manufacturers of the German Empire in distant and overseas countries, and go thither gladly under the protection of German export firms and consulates, but in the Balkan States they think they possess a kind of unwritten prerogative, and take it amiss that in recent years before the war the Germans of the Empire offered their goods with visibly increasing success in Roumania, Bulgaria and even in Serbia. How this is connected with the Austro-Hungarian Balkan policy may here be left undecided: the actual fact is that in three years (1910–1913) the exports from the German Empire to Roumania increased in value from 66 to 140 million marks, and to Bulgaria from 19 to 30 million marks, not indeed for the most part directly at the expense of Austria, but yet in such a way that Germany stands for 140 as a seller in Roumania, but Austria only for 114. The corresponding figures for Bulgaria are in reverse order, 30:40; for Serbia 19:37. Similar feelings and experiences also characterise the Austro-Hungarian export trade to Turkey. If we attempt to obtain a more exact picture in this case from the customs records, we shall find that the German advance does not proceed with equal weight in all departments of industry. It is greater in iron than in woollen goods, but this must be admitted: Austria-Hungary has no country except Bulgaria and Serbia where it is of more importance industrially than Germany. Without colonies, and almost without special economic spheres of interest, it is yet obliged to export goods in order not to force its population to emigrate to an even greater extent than at present. We Germans of the Empire ought first really to get a grasp of this confined and isolated position, before we object to the suspicion with which the Austrians and Hungarians frequently watch our successful economic policy. To speak frankly: the Austrian has for us on many occasions the same feeling that we have for the English world-group economic system, a mixture of respect, envy and defiance. It is unusual to speak of such intangibilities: the literature relating to the customs partnership avoids these less palpable matters, but I am firmly persuaded that without a perfectly frank exposure of all the depths the Mid-European lifelong union will never come about. We need for it not only a bargaining spirit, but a sympathetic creative conviction. But this means when translated into practice: the tariff and commercial treaty between Germany and Austria-Hungary will only have a constructive significance if it reaches out beyond the mutual barter of advantages and disadvantages to the joint regulation of the foreign markets to be kept or to be won. If this is not arrived at, the treaty will in all probability be a treaty of estrangement.

. . . .

The above, in our opinion, describes the Central European commercial problem in general, but we have not yet entered upon the question at the root of the present discussions: what must be the character of the new treaty. So far we have insisted on uniformity in the classification of goods, and have spoken of the necessity for a considerate adjustment of the transition; two demands which must be made whatever be the nature of the solution. But the technical question at the root of the matter is whether the two, or three, commercial States desire to have and are able to have a joint commercial policy with intermediate frontiers between the countries, or two commercial policies in whose adjustment they co-operate. It is the old question of a federal State or a State confederation transferred to commercial policy. But the remembrance of this same old political dispute shows us how vague and transitory all concepts are in this connection, because in practice the federal State may have its bonds so weakened by numerous exceptions that it means less than a confederation of States with developing organs for common activities. Hence it is useless to swear by one of these formulæ from the outset, in any doctrinaire spirit. What is needed is to create the will to bring out further developments from well-conceived beginnings. The existing technical possibilities are ably analysed in a pamphlet by Professor Julius Wolf: *Ein deutsch-österreichish-ungarischer Zollverband* (published at Leipzig by Deichert). There the question is stated thus: Customs union or preferential treatment?

A customs union means that round the frontier of the joint territory (that is round the trench-made frontier of Central Europe) there will be established the customs administration of the union, with frontier stations and officials, all controlled from some central place in Mid-Europe. This administration will levy the same duties and imports in accordance with like principles and reckoned in a unified standard of value, and so strict will this equality be that it will be just the same whether the wheat-ship or the barley-steamer came to port in Hamburg, Bremen, Mannheim or Trieste, or whether the coffee or caoutchouc is used in Antwerp, Fiume or Cattaro. A head of cattle will be treated no differently in Flensburg than in Semlin provided that no further agreements are made with these countries. This idea supposes a joint machinery and that the people managing it will be interchangeable over the whole line, since only in this way can equality of application be ensured.

Preferential treatment, on the other hand, means that the two (or three?) commercial States will remain in existence afterwards as before, and will have their own separate machinery for the collection of customs, as Austria and Hungary have at present, but that they will agree with one another to apply a joint classification of goods with as far as possible equal customs rates at the outer frontiers bordering on foreign countries; whilst on their mutual joint frontier either special mitigations or deductions of duty will be accorded, so that perhaps 20 per cent. less duty is collected from friend than from foreigner. Of course the percentage rate of the deduction may be variously arranged.

Intermediate forms may indeed be conceived of between these two fundamental forms, and the future discussions will probably centre round these intermediate forms. But before speaking of them it will be useful to consider the fundamental forms themselves.

. . . . . .

Preferential treatment offers one very evident advantage, that with it all State rights remain as they were before and that each section can do what it likes in the future within the conditions of the treaty. On this account it is liked at the present time, especially by the Austrians and Hungarians, and appears the easier solution. This notion must, however, be somewhat disturbed when the matter is examined more closely, for preferential treatment involves serious grounds for hesitation for Austria-Hungary, which will be understood in virtue of our previous exposition. In the first place it must be taken into account that export from Austria-Hungary to Germany (according to the German statistics 827 million marks in value) is substantially less than the export from Germany to Austria-Hungary (1105 million in value). So that if an equal preferential quota is chosen it will certainly work out more to the advantage of Germany than to that of Austria-Hungary. But besides this the German exports belong far more to the group called competitive than do the Austro-Hungarian. All the articles in the group which we have called above that of supplementary partnership, disturb our home production only a little or not at all. For example, if mine timber comes to us from Austria and not from Russia, this is pleasant for Austria without endangering our own production of wood. But if German small-iron is brought into Austria more cheaply it will be noticed in the iron trade over there as a direct pressure on the home market. This is exactly what Austria-Hungary wishes to avoid, viz. pressure on an industrial system which is only just beginning to be conscious of advance. In order to avoid these results an attempt might indeed be made to facilitate supplementary importation to Germany by the Austrians and Hungarians, whilst encouraging the German competitive imports as little as possible. But this will result in an agreement which does not differ in essentials from the existing situation and which can only be of minor interest to the German Empire since it offers no closer political union, sensibly disturbs the treaties with Russia and other States, and does not create a Central European world-group. The more accurately the preference idea is thought out the more dangerous it appears for Austria-Hungary, and especially because it includes no security for the Austrian foreign trade to the Balkan States or to other foreign countries. If Austria-Hungary as a whole were still an agricultural State in the old style, preferential treatment would be a sensible arrangement for both sides. But since this condition is past, and since the Dual Monarchy has little more to offer us in respect to the most important food-stuffs, every settlement which is based on simple give and take must narrow down Austria's position still further. By this procedure it gains too little on the German market, nothing on foreign markets, and must endanger its home production. I should not have thought it necessary, merely from the standpoint of German industry, to make these statements with such deliberate clearness but that I am of opinion that Mid-European modes of thought should show themselves from the beginning in this matter, and that the interests of our companion in the union should be regarded equally with our own. And so I consider it a duty to make my understanding of the position of affairs as intelligible as possible.

. . . . . .

We have already emphasised the fact that a customs partnership will involve much greater introductory difficulties and more serious problems connected with individual State rights. But it alone will render it feasible for the German Empire to make provision for the Austro-Hungarian economic future as well as for its own. It involves for Austria certain sacrifice, not to be regarded lightly, of economic independence and of its rights as a free State. But in the first place the bond is mutual, in the second place the Austro-Hungarian economic benefit will be great, and in the third place the transaction is necessary, according to the teaching of history, to the further continuance of the Austro-Hungarian Dual Monarchy. An Austria-Hungary isolated in the world's economic system cannot put forth sufficient financial strength to raise up its own industries from under the burden of war debts. Let us grant that Austria-Hungary must first re-examine thoroughly all other possibilities before taking the irrevocable step of forming the customs partnership. Irrevocable it will be even if provision is made in the treaty of union for notice of withdrawal, which I for my part advocate because the possibility of withdrawal is a certain safety-valve against dissension, and affords a handle for necessary alterations. But the fusion, even in a single economic period, will be so powerful that it will no longer be possible to

TARIFF PROBLEMS 241

talk seriously of complete separation, so long as the mutual economic resources, with the joint increase per cent., correspond roughly with present conditions. As soon as Austria-Hungary has convinced herself, after careful examination of all other possibilities, of the necessity of the future economic partnership, it will be able to approach Germany with quite different demands than in the case of a mere preferential treaty. For from thenceforward it will be not merely economic advantage set against economic advantage, but both parties will unite to establish a world-group economic area. And the extent of the area thus united will be such that no resources need be wasted in any part whatever of the whole. When once this foundation is laid Austria-Hungary will not only have the right, but it will be her sacred duty to demand our agreement and co-operation in all the measures which may facilitate the transition and render easy the further working out of all Austro-Hungarian possibilities of development. In this way the customs partnership will, of itself, become more than a customs partnership. For when once the two sections have come to an understanding over the desire for unity, they are technically on the way not only to find means for the customs treaties, but also to solve with other and better methods some portion of the joint economic problem, such as a State system of storage and association in syndicates.

. . . .

In various parts of our book we have already alluded to the effects which the experiences of war economics will continue to have in the future after the war. In particular the storage of food-stuffs and of endangered raw materials and the regulation of syndicates for the purposes of taxation will come under consideration. If we assume that both will be taken in hand in an assured partnership, then what has hitherto appeared as a commercial treaty will divide itself into three interconnected groups of treaties: storage treaties, syndicate treaties, and a commercial treaty in the narrower sense of the word. This aspect of the matter has been much too little considered by previous authors.

The central point of the storage treaties will be the State

granaries. How far these must be extended to fodderstuffs, we shall leave for later consideration. Here it is essential from the outset to place the Hungarian system of farming, which supplies the only agricultural surplus in the whole area, and whose surplus can become much larger, in an assured position. The Hungarian farmer must be placed completely on a level with the corn-growers in Germany and Austria in the unified economic system, and be differentiated once for all from all foreign competitors. There would be no absolute necessity for this under a bare system of commercial treaties, but from the outset it forms one of the principles of a complete union. In this case the Hungarian corn-growers are the same to us as are our own great landed proprietors and small farmers: they form the basis of an economic system of food-supply in the Mid-European union. After our previous statements there is no need to explain further what this signifies for Hungary.

The central point of the syndicate treaties will be the Central European iron syndicate, through which, with the co-operation of the State Governments concerned, the position of the Austrian and Hungarian iron industrials, hitherto assured to them through tariffs and State protection, will be guaranteed in the form of zones determined by cartels. What is thought of as the intermediate customs duty between the two countries will become the tax paid to the cartel, and the cartel as a whole will pay the State Government, a point to which we shall allude again later. In this way too a definite partition of the foreign export market can be arrived at, and in this way alone. The proved organising powers of the syndicates on both sides will be placed at the service of the joint economic area. This, if it succeeds, will be much better and more effective for the Austrian and Hungarian iron industry, with all its ramifications and superstructures, than any mere protection of the home market by tariff. But when once the model of a joint syndicate has been discovered in the important department of iron, this plan can be applied, with needful alterations, to all industries where syndicates are feasible. In this way the group of products for which intermediate duties are needed

TARIFF PROBLEMS 243

will decrease with every new fusion into a syndicate. Combined syndicates with well-calculated quotas and with a preferential limitation of the home market under politically guaranteed penalties for their agreements, need nothing more than the common customs line against the foreigner. This is conceived in a very strongly syndicalistic spirit and may on this account seem distasteful at first to many of those engaged in industry. But the fact itself that we are face to face with the formation of syndicates in all main departments of the manufacture of half-finished goods and of wholesale goods is already in evidence, and it is only a question of laying hold of the existing bias of the age and placing it in relation to the Central European problem.

It is much to be desired that the foundation lines of the future systems of storage and of the regulation of syndicates should be laid down before the erection of the new Central European tariff system is entered upon. For this will present quite a different appearance as soon as the most difficult main items of the intermediate customs problem are removed. To guide public discussions in this direction is one essential purpose of our book.

· · · · · · ·

But what will then be the position of the intermediate duties so often referred to? They will still be necessary as a means of adjustment for all those productions which cannot be better regulated in any different way. The following cases may be distinguished:

(*a*) One of the two economic areas needs no duty at all on certain goods because it stands of itself above all competitors, as for example in many sections of the German chemical industry. In this case the other area may be in the position of having a small but yet not worthless industry to protect. Then, supposing that regulation by syndicate is inapplicable, the second area must be entitled to add an additional duty to the joint tariff on its outer frontiers, and to levy this additional sum as an intermediate duty on the boundary between Germany and Austria.

(*b*) In both areas industries of the same kind exist which demand a like protection with regard to the foreigner, but which are of such different strengths compared with one another that the one desires protection against the other in home trade, as for instance certain sections of the German glass industry or of the Austrian clothing manufacture. In this case a duty will be levied on the inner boundary in favour of the weaker party. This duty will be less than the tariff for foreigners, but high enough to do away with the superiority. This group may be called that of industrial maintenance duties (*Aufrechterhaltungszölle*).

(c) In both areas there exist products which are in a weak position in international trade, but which are saved from extinction by the support of the home population. Examples of this are tobacco as cultivated on certain tracts of land in Germany, grapes grown in the less favourable districts, fruits cultivated in indifferent climates. These cases will need to be examined to see whether here also risks do not arise from the union which may be warded off by preservative duties (*Bewahrungszölle*).

The difference between the second and third groups is this, that the industrial maintenance duties may, in the abstract, be of a temporary character, either serving as educational duties (*Erziehungszölle*) for infant industries or making possible a peaceful remoulding of the industries affected. On the other hand the preservative duties are essentially of a more permanent character. It is clear from this distinction that the demand to do away with the intermediate duties cannot be urged in like manner for all such duties, at any rate not within a measurable space of time.

What intermediate duties and how many of them will be necessary can only be investigated in a most laborious manner by going through all the separate items. In this matter the first preliminary is to establish the joint classification. A possible average of the existing duties will next be entered in this classification as against foreign countries, and submitted for discussion. Whether or no in individual cases not only duties against the foreigner, except for articles in group (a), but also intermediate duties calculated to correspond with them will be needed, the attempt to draw up the tariff must show. In every case where a superstructure is added on to the common tariff, it will appear automatically on the inner frontier as an intermediate duty.

By this arrangement a customs service will still be needed on the inner boundary for a very long time. But this is hardly avoidable and has its advantages, for by its means the economic position on both sides can still be distinguished for statistical purposes, so that people can tell what each party has gained or lost through the new joint system. This is particularly necessary for the weaker section concerned, so that it can protect itself if the arrangements do not have the effect that they ought to have.

. . . . . .

To provide for the development of the Austrian foreign export trade is one of the most essential and also one of the most difficult problems of the joint commercial policy. Things are much simpler so far as Hungary comes into question, since in this case the exports are of raw materials, and of worked-up products of wood and corn, and will remain predominantly so in the future. But Austria, as we have repeatedly said, is in such a position that she thrusts her finished manufactures, which from their nature cannot be sold in industrial Germany, across the frontiers in any direction where they will not be so fatally pressed by competition from the German Empire and elsewhere. We have previously remarked that should the economic partnership not come into existence there will be no possibility or inducement for Germany to make over to the Austrians and (so far as they wish it) to the Hungarians, the Balkan market or any other eligible section of the international market, as a special zone. Now we must touch upon the same question again on the hypothesis of an economic partnership, and declare in principle that the Austro-Hungarian industries will need not only intermediate duties for internal trade, but in the case of certain neighbouring localities will need also preferential conditions for their export trade. According to tariff technicalities this is not easy, for it must either be done through commercial treaties with the neighbouring States affected, in which case these must agree, or through export premiums for assignable

Austro-Hungarian products, which must be paid from the joint customs receipts. The ministries of commerce and chief customs administrations will probably only enter upon this kind of regulation with reluctance, but provisionally we know of nothing better.

In connection, too, with the important matter of the Turkish treaties, care must be taken from the outset that Austria-Hungary is not passed over. The difference between mere preferential tariffs in the sense of commercial treaties and complete economic partnership is in practice hardly so great anywhere as here. But we do not intend to write about future Turkish economic problems so long as fighting troops are occupying the trenches in Gallipoli.

A customs and economic partnership which removes or reduces intermediate duties, involves, as a matter of course, financial consequences for the State treasuries, since the customs receipts will be regarded as a part of the Imperial and State revenues. We shall speak at first of the matter not as it affects State rights but only as it affects State economics. Even this subject is so complex that here only its most general characteristics can be indicated.

The German Empire receives about 700 million marks a year from customs duties, in which administrative repayments are not included, since these would make the matter still more complicated. The Austro-Hungarian joint administration receives about 240 million kronen. But the question arises whether this is properly to be understood as revenue from the standpoint of national economics, since each duty simultaneously brings receipts into the State treasury and increases expenditure. For the State itself is the greatest purchaser. All Government offices erect buildings, use iron, buy leather, pay for uniforms, employ workpeople. And above all, the army of officials rightly demands higher salaries with every increase in the price of necessaries. Consequently the usual process is that every increase in the customs receipts is followed by a screwing up of Government expenditure, and my friend Gothein is probably correct in saying that the State treasury itself has never yet made any real, permanent gain through tariffs. But

TARIFF PROBLEMS 247

to infer from this that a decrease in the duties will have the effect of reducing the expenditure of the State treasury is, to say the least, unwise. And it is even more unwise to prophesy beforehand whether and how far the decrease in the internal duties of the Central European economic union will show itself in a decline in State expenditure. In order to avoid disappointment the whole amount of the decrease in receipts must be written off. What this will be depends on the height of and the proceeds from the intermediate duties. A complete economic partnership without any intermediate duties might mean for Germany a loss of perhaps 60 million marks a year, and for Austria-Hungary one of 90 or 100 million kronen. It is clear at once that the loss would be greater both in itself and relatively, in Austria-Hungary, a fact which would have to be taken into account in dividing the joint customs revenue. But no one thinks seriously of an unchecked transit of all goods free from intermediate duties, so that the amounts to be deducted in the State budgets will be appreciably smaller, perhaps only a third of the sums quoted. But all this must be explained from the outset so that objections may not subsequently be brought forward on account of it.

In regard to the division of the joint customs revenue probably the State treasuries concerned must be assured of their existing amount of revenue — so far, indeed, as this amount can be obtained under the changed economic system after the war — in order that existing conditions may be disturbed as little as possible by the new arrangement. Whatever surplus there may be over and above the guaranteed sums will then belong to joint objects. But this takes us well into the subject of the following chapter.

CHAPTER VIII

CONSTITUTIONAL PROBLEMS

AS we look forward into a future which we ourselves shall never see, but which will be the "present day" of our grandsons and granddaughters who are born in these days of war, the super-State of Mid-Europe appears before our mind's eye as a constitutional body whose existence will then rest on its own stable footing and which will need no special creation since it is actually there. Is any one still engaged to-day in founding the German Empire? It exists! But before Mid-Europe reaches this position of obviousness there must unfortunately be an endless number of debates and discussions over State rights; so many that I am almost afraid lest people should lose all enthusiasm for the business owing to the interminable formal discussions. But what is the good? The next generation must go through this confusion and noise of State rights. In old days an affair of this sort passed comparatively painlessly since it was accomplished over the heads of the mass of little people. But now, in this age of democracy and newspapers, now every sentence will be turned over a hundred times. This is a part of the very character and essence of our time and also of the essence of the Mid-European question, for Mid-Europe will assuredly be no gift of princes but the desire of the nations. The princes will take part in what is necessary, as they nearly always do, with more or less pleasure and inward sympathy, but they do not of themselves readily cross the laboriously established boundaries of sovereign territories, unless the passing to and fro of the peoples is already becoming a mighty flood. And the existing Government officials especially are generally conservative in the sense of maintaining their previous mode of life, and they defend themselves

CONSTITUTIONAL PROBLEMS

partly against an increase in their duties, partly against the enforced understanding with foreign officials, partly against the disarrangement of spheres of competence and business customs in general. Almost all the great things in the world have to be wrung from those most nearly concerned in carrying on affairs, for these are the greatest experts indeed, but at the same time they are the most affected by any alteration. Of course a creative spirit may always arise in their midst, as Bismarck revealed himself in the Frankfurt Federal Diet, but such a development is no historical necessity. And the more difficult and insuperable a transaction appears at the outset, the less is a complicated heavily worked system inclined to burden itself with preliminary labours whose results lie in the distance and whose success cannot be foreseen with certainty. Thus even the most important of present-day problems cannot be left with simple confidence only to those Government officials most nearly concerned. Naturally they will ultimately have the last word to say in this matter and will undertake the technical formulation, but before they speak the air must be permeated by Mid-European ideas. In this great present-day affair the will of the people will have to show itself less in the fact that the representatives in Parliament finally give their assent to the treaties of union than in the fact that the temper of the populations demands the new creation as a preliminary to all treaties and proposals. Mid-Europe must be talked about, Mid-Europe the coming, necessary, indispensable State association and union of nations. Every journalist up to the very frontier places ought to help in this. Every one who has oratorical power ought to do his share of public speaking. Now is the time for this, even now before the Peace Congress and before the decisive moment for humanity. Rise, Mid-Europe, in poetry and prose be exalted!

The greatest danger in such thoughts and proposals is, however, that the opposition of the existing forces, arrangements and departments may be underestimated. It is so easy to draft upon paper an ideal Mid-European construction! It is merely necessary to borrow a few quite general ideas out of the treasure of existing conceptions of State rights, and to apply them to the subject to be dealt with. In so doing it is always supposed that there is an invisible dictatorial power over the existing Governments, which can make these ideas into binding precepts. But this is not the case. The carrying out of all our ideas rests in reality in those same hands which have guided our States so far. Certain changes of personnel may indeed be made, but in the main the new, as old Liebknecht once expressed it, must always be " the legitimate child of the present." We are no Utopia, but an area occupied by ancient State formations of the longest standing which have grown up promiscuously together. Whether we conclude treaties or make adjustments they must all, in order to be valid, bear the signature of the German Emperor, of the Austrian Emperor and of the King of Hungary, and must be resolved upon by the Bundesrat, the Delegations, the Reichsrat and the Reichstag. We enter upon the work with earnest and serious remembrance of all these essential factors and co-operators, none of whom must fail if the enterprise is to succeed.

It is very important at this stage that the content of the problem should not be increased, but on the contrary decreased as far as possible, since an overladen boat cannot be pushed off from the bank at all. The final aims should be great, but the immediate demands should be attainable. We cannot venture to ask that the super-State of Mid-Europe shall be in existence after a short delay, but only that its beginnings shall be so well conceived that the first steps will thereupon of themselves lead further forward. Moreover it is essential that the first settlements should be planned only between Germany, Austria and Hungary. The nucleus must be there before further crystallisation can take place. The discussion of many European States at once destroys businesslike progress from the outset. What is wanted here is restrained and disciplined political imagination, no universal, boldly arbitrary spirit of prophecy, leaping over whole decades.

· · · · ·

Looked at as technical politics, the creation of Mid-Europe is the centralisation of certain political activities, that is to say the establishment of fresh central points for the joint working of the

CONSTITUTIONAL PROBLEMS 251

whole of the enlarged territory. But before we speak of such a centralisation it will be advisable to dwell upon what we cannot venture to influence or to gain by centralisation. For many objections to the new ideas arise on all sides from anxiety lest a foreign and unfamiliar co-operative Government might interfere with matters that we have hitherto desired under all circumstances to keep in our own hands. No State becoming a partner in the new super-State will consent to sacrifice thereby its political dignity, its own sovereignty which it has won with difficulty and defended with its blood. To begin with the Hungarians, without whom we cannot complete Mid-Europe; they will grasp at once the immense advantages of the Mid-European plan from the point of view of economics and of historical development, for they have an intelligent knowledge of the world and are clever calculators. But for them the struggle waged by their fathers for the independence of a special Hungarian State ranks higher than advantage and than the philosophy of history. And they would join in nothing which might at the same time lead to any reduction of political rights even in the most distant future. On this point they are obdurate, and we recognise that they are so. But the same thing applies to the sphere of Austrian authority. The Austrian State knows its limitations and its historical subjections, it has emerged from the schooling of continual negotiations with the Hungarians over the Ausgleich and of ceaseless concessions to its individual refactory members. But in spite of all it retains a vitality of its own, and that indeed both deep-seated and vigorous, which will at no price be cut short or injured. And again the same thing applies to the German Empire. It discovered, through Bismarck, the form suited to it, and has worked with it successfully for a period. Shall the German Empire allow itself to be lectured about its own concerns by companions who have newly joined themselves with it? People are ready on all sides to make certain necessary concessions for Mid-Europe, but the dignity of the State itself must not be touched. That may not please the purely theoretical thinker, but it is the actual situation: Mid-Europe is no new country. Hence it is in the interests of all concerned that ambitious schemes for fusion should not be brought forward. In other words: under the superscription Mid-Europe no new State will be created, but a union of existing States will be formed. In using the word "super-State" for this union we have intended no decrease in political dignity for the separate portions; it ought not, will not and cannot mean this. Those who determine on the development are responsible for it and carry it on, will be and will remain the present sovereign States concluding the treaty. These will make mutual concessions to one another, but it is they who do this, and they will not cease to be the subjects of future joint activities. If people like to call the new creation a confederation of States, this hits its character, but it cannot become a federal State. The second would indeed be essentially more than the first, but it is not feasible.

. . . . . .

If it comes into existence the Mid-European State union will decide what matters shall be jointly regulated and administered. Here we must exclude from the outset all those matters wherein old and sacred rights are inherent in local and provincial peculiarities. When we were discussing creeds and nationalities we pointed out that these deeply intricate questions must not be subjected to any centralised regulation, unless insupportable opposition is to be aroused from the outset. We shall discover the proper limitation in this matter most easily if we take a general survey of the historical changes in the character of the State. The older State was based much more on national and Church convictions, and much less on economic organisation than the modern great State. The older State embodied the concept of unity of religious belief amongst its subjects or citizens, and later, when religious unity became defective, the concept of unity of language. It had very few economic questions to regulate since the old type of economic system was almost entirely natural, local and purely individualist. The commune sufficed for the management of the former common lands, the district or the town generally sufficed to regulate the old crafts. There were only a few meagre State provisions for far-distant trade routes and for

CONSTITUTIONAL PROBLEMS 253

extra-provincial trade rights, and the local police were generally sufficient for social duties. But in the place of all this the old State busied itself much more forcibly with the questions whether and after what manner each of its subjects worshipped God and what was the prevailing form of religious ceremony. This was characteristic of the old days when the individual, though able to look after the cultivation of his fields or his business in primitive fashion, was not capable of providing for his spiritual needs. The ancient duty of spiritual guidance and the care of souls which pertained to the State terminated, however, in some measure as the system of State religion became permeated by a certain increasing independence of the individual and by the developing self-government, apart from the State, of the Church corporations. To-day the State is no longer the creator of conviction and the ruler of belief, but at the most a controlling influence to prevent any infringement of their mutual boundaries on the part of religious sects and a protector of the system of public rights and of administration as such, from any Church interference. These functions, so far as they are still necessary, belong exclusively to the older types of State, and even in them are handed over as much as possible to provincial and specific authorities. The world-group economic super-State will have nothing whatever to do with provincial churches, church law, ecclesiastical legislation and representation before the papal throne, even though cases may be thought of in which the last-named matter is not without far-reaching political influence.

Nor will the super-State have anything to do with school affairs. It is true that practically everywhere in Central Europe, so far as primary education is concerned, the school is a State foundation, and was mostly the work of an enlightened State bureaucracy before it was able later to become an object of parliamentary care. The private and sectarian school did not suffice for the average standard of education needed by the developing modern capitalist State. But when once the necessity for universal popular education is recognised everywhere in principle, this department will be made over more and more as time goes on to be worked by the local communal administration. It ought to be much more decentralised and flexible than it generally is at present. It appertains to the legislation, the initiative and the control of the individual State, but is never a matter for higher State or super-State regulation. Even if it be admitted that the training of political opinion in the schools greatly affects the world-group super-State, yet a sharp limitation must be imposed on sovereign rights lest a door should be opened for the effects of majority votes and pressure in a sphere where those most nearly concerned ought to have the responsibility. Voluntary congresses relating to school affairs may, and certainly will, be arranged for the whole of Central Europe, but no legislation which goes beyond existing frontiers will be passed on the subject.

In this it is partially implied that the much disputed language question must be left to the decision of the individual States. Although these language disputes may manifest themselves in school or law court or army, and must there be settled as required, yet in principle they are no subject for Central European deliberations. This may indeed appear a somewhat bold statement, because the general arrangements for the army and for intercommunication in Central Europe will undoubtedly require a certain unity of language, as the war has shown us most effectively in regard to the railways in Galicia. But it will be quite impossible for the small, non-German nations to join themselves to Mid-Europe with feelings of complete freedom and contentment, if they run any risk of their language question, to which they attach such importance, being decided piece-meal by an unapproachable central authority high above them. This shows how little scope there is for a purely academic building plan for Mid-Europe if it is to succeed. In spite of our sympathy for the language rights of the Germans in Hungary we Germans yet cannot dream of depriving the Hungarians of any of their self-governing powers, in the Magyar sense, by means of any sort of superior Mid-European decrees, because this would mean the total impossibility of Mid-Europe. We anticipate that the union of the Central European States will soften

CONSTITUTIONAL PROBLEMS 255

all language disputes and will thrust them into the background by means of new work, new aims and new successes shared in common. We hope that no Pole in Prussia and no German in the Banat will in future have unnecessary language difficulties, but in our present situation, where it is a question of definiteness in regard to State rights, it must be asserted firmly that this matter, however important it is, yet cannot be of a Mid-European character.

. . . .

The whole sphere of internal administration, the constitutions of commune and State in the narrower sense of the word, will also remain, without further discussion, undisturbed by the Central European State union. The question of the State constitution demands some further explanation, for it is likely that the democratic parties in all the connected countries will attempt to direct the great process of transformation which is clearly at hand everywhere after the war, in such a way as to secure a standard law for universal, equal and direct suffrage in Mid-Europe. The returning warriors will say with justice that every humble and insignificant man has been obliged to stake his life for the Fatherland, and that citizen rights, complete and without reserve, are therefore his due. I share this view entirely and shall advocate it in Prussia with all my power, but I contest the idea that this suffrage fight which will probably set in after the war can be a Mid-European concern. Mid-Europe includes countries of different composition and at different stages of development, hence the existing differences in the internal constitutions of the States must be tolerated in themselves on principle. No doubt internal political movements of like tendencies will try to get into touch with one another, and will learn from each other, but the State Parliaments are a law to themselves and must so remain. Neither the Hungarian nor the Austrian constitution altogether suits us Germans of the Empire and vice versa. Here also the situation is this: that the consequences of the parliamentary rights of individual States are at the same time Mid-European in character, since the economic and commercial policy of the State union depends on the composition of the governments and representative assemblies of the individual States. But — he who tries to grasp too much loses everything. Neither Prussia nor Hungary will ever commit themselves to a sacrifice of their special historical constitutional forms on the Mid-European altar. Struggles of this sort must be fought out separately in the different territories in future as in the past, until in this way, as we hope, a Mid-European standard of citizen rights will grow up at last in reality everywhere.

The same is true of all the laws and ordinances which regulate the position of the representative assembly and of the Crown. Under no circumstances must Crown rights be touched upon through the creation of Mid-Europe, because that would be the most certain way to ruin the whole affair in its beginnings. This is so obvious that it requires no further explanation. Moreover, the different types of parliamentary and non-parliamentary government are and will remain the business of the countries concerned. Hungary is strongly parliamentary in virtue of its franchise law and its electoral practice, Austria is unparliamentary in principle with varying concessions in practice to majorities. The German Empire as a whole is theoretically unparliamentary with increasing account taken of the position of the parliamentary majority. The individual States within the German Empire vary from Mecklenburg to Baden. All this in the future, too, will grow according to its own law of development, and everywhere parliamentary influence will surely increase during the great financial negotiations after the war, but this can be no concern of the Mid-European union.

But from this it follows already that the administrative bodies and the representative assemblies of the Mid-European union, so far as these are needed, will not be elected or summoned on an equal system. This is a genuine and serious defect, for the system by which the managers and inspectors of a business are selected is never without influence on the business itself. But I repeat what has been already often said: Mid-Europe is a superstructure and not a new building! The existing buildings must remain standing!

The attentive reader may be surprised that I, who am at such pains to urge the foundation of Mid-Europe, am so diligent in reckoning up what must not be Mid-European. But whenever I picture to myself in private all the necessary partners in the union, I feel myself strongly impelled to assure them first of their own long-accustomed ground under their feet, before I venture to discuss with them the free movements and fresh constructions of universal history. Even to-day there are all kinds of anxieties at the thought of Mid-Europe, and these anxieties may be the grave of all our hopes if we cannot understand how to deal with them humanely. The new ought never to come like a landslip, it must appear like healthy and gentle growth, like a natural increase, not like disorganisation. Hence we shall try to build up the plans for unity in what follows only on the basis of treaties between sovereign States with equal rights, leaving it at first an open question how far such treaties should be terminable or not.

Numerous treaties already exist to-day between nearly all the States, and in particular between Germany and Austria-Hungary, through which standards of equality are formed for the subordinate groups in single departments of the life of the State. And such treaties will also be beneficial and possible in considerable abundance in realising the goal Mid-Europe. To refer to existing precedents we call to mind the post and telegraph treaties, extradition treaties, navigation treaties, the agreements about intercourse on the frontiers, the Austro-German treaty for the avoidance of double taxation, the settlement about the law of guardianship, sanitary conventions, the agreement for the suppression of the white slave trade, the international marriage law, the Geneva Red Cross Convention, the international copyright law, the Sugar Convention, and other similar examples. The majority of these treaties are not Central European in the narrower sense, but through them an available method has been discovered in the past to prepare the way for legal and administrative conditions which transcend the separate States, without infringing upon sovereignty. Treaties of this kind must now be established in an increasing number within the Central European territory. They may be divided into two principal groups: treaties which are carried out by each State through its own officials in its own way and without joint control, and treaties which owing to their nature require a mixed Joint Commission to carry them out. The latter group thus paves the way for joint administration in limited spheres. It will be much more readily and frequently possible between two States with a permanent alliance and a joint trench system than between two States which still have to reckon with the possibility of mutual war. Of it, therefore, we must speak more precisely.

After the war general international treaties will be again renewed or established in great numbers. We do not refer here to the peace treaty proper or to future political agreements between States about foreign policy; we are thinking rather of treaties like those mentioned above. Their scope extends over the whole politically organised world. Within them throbs the evolving world organisation. The special State treaty of the united world-group area has, however, its special character as compared with them. For here an exchange may take place, not only of principles and rules, but also of the persons to carry them out. Here the laws and orders for enforcement will, whilst preserving complete independence, yet conform as far as possible to one another even in the wording, and the unity of the whole world-group organism will be aimed at, as far as conceivable, by all legislative means. In this connection the words "as far as possible," "as far as conceivable" are unavoidable, for in them lies the independence of the individual sections. The final examination into the practicability of any fresh modification and adjustment will be effected in the usual way in the existing political capitals, just as we have already in the past dealt with transport treaties, legal agreements or other similar matters in Berlin, Vienna and Budapest.

Let us suppose as an example that the joint-stock company legislation, the insurance company legislation and the practice of State inspection of the Exchanges in Mid-Europe are to be approximated to one another. Then for this purpose there must be an expert Mid-European preparatory Commission sent from the proper departments in the States concerned. This Commission will do the

CONSTITUTIONAL PROBLEMS 259

preliminary work with the assistance of representatives of those interested, until the material is taken over by the Foreign Offices. If the Foreign Offices have serious hesitations they may refer the business back again to the Mid-European Commission in question, until a form is arrived at which (as in the present procedure in the case of political treaties) is submitted as the draft treaty in both the States, subject to the assent of the legislative factors. Whether this draft treaty may still be referred back again or now must simply be accepted or rejected, may be doubtful since either procedure has its advantages and disadvantages. The content of the treaty will now either be such that each State, as already said, carries it out under its own control and with its own administration and jurisdiction, or such that through the treaty a Joint Committee will be set up to make regulations for carrying it out, for administrative decisions, the training of officials and, in the future, also for current control and for managing direction, such as, for example, a joint Office for granting Permits for Capital Issues. These joint managing Commissions or Committees can then be freely appointed by the different Governments in virtue of the treaty, and paid according to an agreed schedule. They are subject to the criticism of all the Parliaments concerned, but are independent within their sphere of activity for the duration of the treaty. They are Mid-European organs, without there being, properly speaking, a Mid-European State.

. . . . . .

It is obvious that these arrangements have their serious defects and do not appear very inviting, for they require homogeneous work from a Board (*Kollegium*) which obtains its authority from various sources, and they entrust that legislative preparatory work, which otherwise would naturally fall to a parliamentary commission, to an officially summoned Committee. If goodwill is lacking it will be an easy matter for each of the federated Governments and every strong parliamentary majority to bring this machinery to a standstill because its own power of motion is too small. This must be readily granted, but it is a part of the complicated Mid-European problem that we should be obliged to follow such adventurous paths. Yet here we have complete confidence that, given favourable results from the first and second of such Mid-European Commissions, the work of the third and fourth will be much easier because by that time a tradition will have grown up. All political activity in the absence of a tradition is like some one trying to ride a bicycle before he has learnt how. But when once he has learnt grasp and balance, he goes on afterwards almost as though it were his nature. And besides, preliminary stages of this kind must be gone through in any case, even if the business procedure in Mid-Europe were to be very different and much more centralised than we have proposed.

Even the customs partnership in the sense in which we have discussed it in the previous chapter will certainly not be possible without some permanent joint mechanism for carrying out decisions and settling accounts. The same applies to a joint storage system involving the State purchase of corn, and to a joint regulation of syndicates. It also applies to a joint fund for war debts and indemnities, should such a fund be resolved on. Whether or no a joint Patent Office will subsequently be added or a joint Railway Department or a joint Navigation Department, these and many other similar points are for later consideration. Some offices of this kind must first be in existence and at work before new ones are added. It was for this reason that we declined, in our first chapter, to give a complete programme of future Mid-European State activities. It is to be hoped that this may and will be the business of the following generation.

But when once we picture to ourselves a certain number of such Mid-European Commissions or higher administrative departments, they form together something like a Mid-European Central Administration. For this reason the Commissions ought to be housed, so far as is feasible, in the same place. This place will become for Mid-Europe in a modernised and better fashion what once, though with a mistaken constitution, Frankfurt-on-Main was or should have been in the old German Confederation. But probably some of the higher departments must be located where the special professional knowledge concerned is available at the closest

CONSTITUTIONAL PROBLEMS 261

quarters. To show how I conceive of the division I should propose Prague as the Mid-European centre for all business connected with treaties that is not obliged to be done locally, but at the same time I should locate the centre for overseas trade at Hamburg, the central money-market at Berlin, and the legal centre at Vienna. But this is only of value as a provisional suggestion for the sake of clearness.

. . . . . .

Whilst discussing the treaty system as the basis of Mid-European unity we have hitherto tacitly done so as though the German Empire on the one hand and the Austro-Hungarian Monarchy on the other were in themselves two simply constituted States. But this they are not. They are themselves the laborious constructions of treaties, and upon their remarkable, historical lower stratum this further upper story of treaties must be erected. And, moreover, the two Empires are different, very different, in their theoretical and actual structure. Hence it will be necessary to consider the Mid-European treaty system first from the standpoint of the German Empire, and then from that of Austria-Hungary. In so doing we shall start in both cases from the question how State treaties come into existence.

In the German Empire the right to conclude State treaties is definitely and undoubtedly an Imperial right. The Emperor, as representative of the Empire in international law, has to enter into alliances with foreign States. But in matters which fall within the scope of imperial legislation he is bound, in regard to the conclusion of the treaty, to have the assent of the Bundesrat, and in regard to its validity to have the ratification of the Reichstag. Here, in theory, there is at once ground for dispute, for it is not always clear whether these conditions were satisfied in the particular case or not. Still the existing practice has led to no special difficulties. So far as we can see, it is necessary that all treaties of an economic or legal character or relating to means of communication on their technical side, and all agreements which involve financial obligations, should take their course through the Bundesrat and Reichstag. The matter is questionable in regard to purely political treaties about foreign policy and military agreements on the one hand, and to mere arrangements about ordinances for carrying out measures on the other. We shall speak later on more particularly of the first group, the political and military State treaties, and it is not worth while to go into details here about the ordinances. But there exists already, in the text of Article II of the Constitution of the German Empire, an important distinction between the co-operation of the Bundesrat and of the Reichstag. The Bundesrat is required to conclude (*Abschlusz*), the Reichstag to ratify (*Gültigkeit*). This means in actual fact that the negotiations for the drawing up of treaties are carried on under the direction of the Bundesrat without the direct co-operation of the Reichstag, whilst only the final draft is presented to the Reichstag for acceptance or rejection. But since in the case of tariff treaties, and in most other cases, the negotiations can only be carried on by the Bundesrat on the basis of existing Imperial laws, the Reichstag has generally a voice in the matter at the very beginning of these negotiations, as for example, through the introduction of minimum and maximum rates in the customs tariff. This process of conducting the business of treaty-making in the German Empire would be very involved if the method had not long since been smoothed out and cut short by custom. Thus the work of the Bundesrat is accomplished through the Imperial Departments and these have in practice become much more independent than appears from the text of the constitution. Consequently the whole preliminary work is carried on by them in constant touch with the Prussian Ministry and the representatives of the federated States, and in many cases the consent of the Bundesrat is only the last and formal acceptance of a document which is already in fact complete. That tradition already exists of which we have previously said that for Mid-Europe it needs first to be formed. Any one who looks at the Government machinery of the German Empire merely as a student of constitutional forms would think it much more complicated than do those who have the opportunity of observing it at work. Not that no friction occurs! But it is only the necessary friction which is un-

CONSTITUTIONAL PROBLEMS 263

avoidable in all forms of collegial action. The Office of the German Imperial Chancellor forms a central point for adjustments such as unfortunately does not exist in Austria-Hungary with the same efficiency and coherence. A real check can scarcely occur so long and in so far as there is a fundamental understanding between the Imperial Chancellor's Office and the majority in the Reichstag. This means — and this is significant for the Mid-European problem — that the state of affairs is itself sufficiently definite in spite of the obscurity of the clauses. The security for the continuance of the treaty system when begun lies in the permanence of the Imperial Chancellor's Office and in the comparative stability of the parliamentary relations in the German Empire. It cannot be doubted that the determination to establish Mid-Europe, when once formed, will not subsequently be subject to any great variations. The first debates will abound in objections and attempts at alteration, but then the machinery, as far as the German Empire is concerned, will soon work quite quietly, and the addition of new treaties to the system when it has once started will in all human probability go on without any fresh disturbances of importance.

. . . .

We are not so sure about a quiet progress of events in Austria-Hungary since there the constitutional bases and, above all, the traditions of government are different. Austria and Hungary are two States which are as it is dependent on mutual treaties, and which have accomplished between themselves almost exactly what should now be repeated for them and for us in the upper story of the world-group area. Consequently the Austrians and Hungarians have incomparably more experience in this matter than we Germans of the Empire, but an experience that is not without its scars and bruises. In spite of the unity of the throne at the head, the department of adjustment is lacking which the Imperial Chancellor's Office supplies for us. The Sovereign acts, so to speak, by himself in his two capacities as Austrian Emperor and as King of Hungary. The unity ultimately rests with him, with him but not with an Imperial Department, for the joint Ministry is not a supreme authority for both States, but a Central Administration based on treaties such as we have outlined above for Mid-Europe. Expressed otherwise: the Imperial unity of the Austro-Hungarian Monarchy covers many fewer objects than does that of the German Empire. In virtue of the law of 1867 it comprises the unity of the Foreign Office, of the management of the army and the expenses arising out of it, and in addition the joint administration of Bosnia and Herzegovina. The Delegations, that rudimentary Imperial Parliament, have only to determine points connected with these matters. Everything else appertains to the special Governments of the two States. To these appertain, for example, the sanctioning of international treaties and the recruiting for the army, two points of the very greatest importance for our investigation. Thus when we conclude treaties with Austria-Hungary, as we have already done and as we wish to do very much more in the future, we conclude them formally with the homogeneous body representing the Foreign Office but actually with two States and two Parliaments. From our point of view it would be simpler if each of these two States could do business with us independently, since then the number of factors concerned would be smaller. But this remark has a merely academic value because we, as well as the Austrians and Hungarians, have to reckon with the existing position of the State as an actual fact. All this would give just as little ground for hesitation as the complicated system of political law in the German Empire, if the tradition in Austria-Hungary were as firmly established as it is with us. But this is unfortunately not the case as is shown by the course of events hitherto. The unity of the State, it is true, is firmly maintained upon the whole and will be more secure after the war than before, but all treaty ties between Austria and Hungary are only concluded for definite periods of time, and their renewal is invariably accompanied by difficult negotiations concerning treaty and Ausgleich. According to our political experience it will be very unfamiliar and very undesirable for us Germans of the Empire to have to share in these convulsions, and many critics on our side, notwithstanding a most sympathetic grasp of the principle involved, hesitate at the establishment of a Mid-European system of treaties, because they do not wish to be drawn into recurrent conflicts of this kind about the Ausgleich. On this account it may be allowable to enter somewhat more deeply — so far as an outsider can — into the historical bases of this constitutional position which for us is difficult to grasp.

. . . . . .

The German Imperial constitution is, as was explained in the second chapter, the outcome of a national movement towards unity, and its aim is consolidation. The Austro-Hungarian constitution of 1867, on the other hand, is the outcome of a national process of partition. Moreover, the German Imperial constitution was essentially a result of the pressure of economic forces, whilst the Austro-Hungarian constitution still shows practically no trace of the economic character of this age of intercommunication.

In order to inquire into the origins of the German Imperial constitution we must take up the draft constitution of the German national assembly of March 28, 1849, and learn from it the aims of the national movement of that date. In this old draft the idea of economic partnership prevails along with the conception of partnership in military and naval power. The following matters were transferred to the Imperial authority: the regulation of ocean navigation, river navigation, railway affairs, inspection of high-roads, the formation of a customs and commercial area, joint taxes on production and consumption, industrial legislation, the postal system, coinage, weights and measures, the banking system, the rights of citizens, sanitation, civil law, commercial law, law of exchange, criminal law. The German national movement was quite saturated with economic tendencies. And afterwards the Imperial constitution drawn up by Bismarck on the basis of the Frankfurt draft was in accordance with it. Article 4 of the German Imperial Constitution is a more precise remodelling of the Frankfurt aims, and adds the following to the subjects mentioned: patents for invention, protection of literary property, protection of German trade abroad, law of contracts. It is very remarkable that in this Article military affairs and the navy only occupy the fourteenth place. So great was the importance attached to economic claims in drawing up the constitution. The German Empire, which is generally regarded abroad as a purely military State, is at least equally an economic State, and has been from the very first. The two characteristics mutually permeate it and give to the whole its firm stability.

In contrast to this, even in 1867, the Austro-Hungarian Ausgleich gave no sign of any feeling of the necessity for a closer economic unity, and was entirely dictated by the aspirations of the Hungarians to separate themselves as much as possible from the existing unity of the State owing to their feeling for their own nationalist and political State rights. All economic questions are disposed of in Section 2 of the fundamental law under matters "which will not indeed be jointly managed but which will be treated according to similar principles to be agreed upon from time to time." The list of matters under this head contains only: commercial affairs, especially tariff legislation, legislation about indirect taxes which are in close connection with industrial production, the establishment of the coinage system and the gold standard, arrangements with respect to lines of railway which affect the interests of both halves of the Empire; the establishment of a military organisation. That is all! This was the basis on which treaties were concluded, not laws enacted or ordinances issued.

Thus there is the customs and commercial treaty of December 30, 1907, between Austria and Hungary, which remains valid until December 31, 1917. It covers: uniform customs frontiers without intermediate duties, partnership in foreign commercial treaties until notice of withdrawal is given, regulation of the relations of courts of justice, mutual inspection of the customs administration, equality of maritime regulations, agreement concerning river navigation, closer connection of railway administration, partnership in the consular system, closer connection in statistical work, like management of salt and tobacco, equal taxation of beer, brandy, petroleum and sugar, maintenance of the system of weights

CONSTITUTIONAL PROBLEMS 267

and measures, equal treatment of commercial travellers, reciprocal recognition of patents and trade marks, regulation of the traffic between the separate postal administrations, recognition of joint-stock companies, insurance companies and so on, joint procedure for the protection of the vine, establishment of a court of arbitration for all these questions.

It is evident how much more is included in the actual treaty than was assumed in the few lines in the fundamental law. The economic State has won for itself certain opportunities, but with what effort, and the whole is terminable on notice of withdrawal! These economic arrangements, terminable at will, lend an element of insecurity to the whole industrial economic system of the Danubian Monarchy. Since the treaty embodying them is only of short duration it renders impossible the conclusion of any treaty of long duration.

Now it is easy enough to say, from the point of view of the German Empire, that the Austrians and Hungarians must put their treaties on a permanent footing by authorising their Delegations to enact economic legislation for the whole kingdom. But the Hungarians are unwilling to take even this step, because it seems to them like a return to the old position of inferiority in respect to Austria. They are well aware that the relation here described has serious defects, but what can they do in order to arrive at a complete Austro-Hungarian economic State without violating the nationalism of their fathers and their heroes, a nationalism which extends also into economic matters?

We for our part can merely state these things, for it would not facilitate the attainment of our object in Mid-Europe to try to come in from outside with proposals about matters which are essentially of a purely Austro-Hungarian character. But there are men among the Hungarians and Austrians who are able to understand the world's economic movement, and who possess that inherited knowledge about treaty and Ausgleich negotiations which is inherent on the Danube. These men will seek some way, in spite of opposing clauses, to pave the way for a tradition which will make an advantageous and much-needed Central European economic system possible for all parties. Where there is a will there is a way.

. . . . . .

These last explanations have brought us quite near to the inmost kernel of the Mid-European constitutional problem, that is to the progressive separation of the national State from the economic State and from the military State. In order to grasp this fundamental problem our explanation of the world-group economic areas must be kept in mind. The world-group area of Mid-Europe must become greater than the existing dimensions of the States of Germany, Austria and Hungary. We have refrained, by reason of the circumstances of the war, from naming definite neighbouring States, and have only worked out in general the conception that further accessions are necessary. And to what shall these neighbouring States join themselves? To a military union and an economic union! Everything else is superfluous and hence harmful. They ought to and must retain their own political independence in all other matters. Thus it is important so to cut out the military union and the economic union from the remaining multitude of political activities as to make it possible to join with them separately. Here we shall discuss first the economic union, or if people prefer to call it so, the economic State. This State is bound up with the language of no country and can tolerate the most diverse nationalities and religious creeds within its borders. No Central European nationality, not even the German, is in itself big enough for a world-group economic State. That is the result of the capitalist system of interchange. This economic State has its customs frontiers just as the military State has its trench defences. Within these frontiers it tries to establish a sphere of continually active exchange. An economic Government is required for this which is directly competent for one part of the economic laws and for the remaining part advises the national Governments. Customs, the regulation of syndicates, export organisations, patent law, trade marks, the control of material and similar matters are under the direct control of the economic State. Commercial law, traffic policy, social policy and many other things belong to its indirect sphere of activities. But this economic State, which is independent of nationality, cannot be decided in a day, it must go on growing from one event to another. The more it completes itself the more will it create its own organs and its economic parliamentary system.

When we use the expression economic parliamentary system we are referring to a development far ahead. But we do this in order to come to an understanding in regard to scruples about the Mid-European plan which are at present making themselves heard in strongly Liberal and democratic circles. It is said there: owing to the position of affairs the partnership between Germany and Austria-Hungary cannot come into existence as a federal State provided with a parliament, hence this otherwise very desirable event means a real loss to practical parliamentary work and thus to active citizenship. Theoretically considered this is certainly true. For if such important departments of life as customs, a system of storage, the administration of war debts, the regulation of syndicates, maritime regulations, etc., are made the subjects of investigations by a Central European Commission and of arrangements by treaty, the final assent would still, it is true, rest with parliament, but it is indisputable that these matters will be put outside the field of practical collaboration even more than hitherto. I attach importance to this "even more than hitherto," and it was on account of these words that I previously termed the whole objection theoretical. For any one who follows carefully the progress of important economic legislation will already have come to the conclusion that often parliament as a whole has but little share in the preliminary work. This is only assigned to individual members who are specially interested or expert, and who on account of these qualifications would be and will be consulted whatever the method of preparation. The work of the parliamentary majority — over and above a few changes in detail — lies in the final vote of acceptance or rejection. This results from the nature of the case, for no representative of the people can be acquainted with all the individual questions of economic life. When the parliamentary system was formed the economic duties of parliament were immeasurably simpler, and could generally be grasped by that normal understanding which may be presumed in every deputy. In the interval economic policy has become a technical matter, much more so than foreign policy. If somewhat more of it than hitherto is assigned to Commissions and Boards of experts this will be by no means merely a loss to the parliamentary system, but will be at the same time a certain relief in that it takes from the people's representative something of the technical side of national economics with which he, strictly speaking, can no longer cope.

· · · · · ·

Yet after all, this only touches upon one side of the matter. It is the professional duty of the deputy to see that the electoral district or class of people represented by him does not come off the loser. How can he do this if he does not get a sight of a treaty except in its final stage? The answer to which is that the officials whose business it is to choose and to send up the Mid-European Commission members and experts, must be attentive, whenever they are considering plans of expenditure, to the criticism of the popular assembly. That this is no mere figure of speech every one will aver who is in a position to know about the negotiations of the budget committee of the German Reichstag. Moreover the proposed new system will be submitted to the judgment of the popular assembly. But more cannot in reality be attained. Only ask indeed what influence the individual member of the English Parliament has upon the economic policy of Greater Britain! The answer may reveal strange things about the model country of the parliamentary system. The development in the important relations of communications, commerce and labour swallow up the unorganised private motion in parliament. But organised motions always find their way to an effective position.

This, in truth, is the further answer which must be given to the democratic-parliamentary scruples that we have mentioned: the Mid-European economic Commissions must be bound, in con-

CONSTITUTIONAL PROBLEMS 271

formity with regulation and treaty, to hear and record the representations of the parties interested in all the countries and branches of industry involved. This is less than an Act of Parliament in one way and more in another; less because it at most only deals with hearing, more because it is a question of professional experts. In this connection it must be established from the outset that employees and workpeople must be regarded in all matters involving their trade as parties interested. Something similar may be established for the consumer in regard to articles of consumption. Thus in a natural way may begin the economic parliament of the future which we need more and more alongside of the political national assembly. We need it for economic mobilisation, for the system of storage, for the customs tariff and for much besides.

It would be an essential mistake to set to work now to construct, out of the existing popular assemblies, such a Mid-European parliament, with powers of final decision in economic and tariff matters, even apart from the Austro-Hungarian constitutional obstacles. For the material for deliberation and administration must first be in existence before a deliberative body has meaning; and above all, Mid-Europe, the new economic State, needs its own future economic constitution. It would be a serious blunder to burden it with a Delegations Parliament in which all the contentions of all the separate parliaments are assembled in a mass. Even if the new creation makes its appearance at first as formless, shapeless and democratically inadequate, yet the main thing truly is that the new production should not be accompanied from the outset by a smell of the past. It must be something creative, and three and more nations will be on the lookout to see that it is so.

. . . . . .

It is permissible to express what has hitherto been stated formally in a somewhat more palpable form. Let us suppose that in ten years' time, or it may be even longer, I go to Prague and visit the Chairman or Deputy Chairman (they interchange!) of the Mid-European Economic Commission. He will show me his fine new building, and say: "When we came we thought we should have nothing to do, and now it is growing up on all sides! For so long as no one considers Mid-Europe in an official capacity, Mid-Europe is only an idea. But from the day when an office is provided the first cell of a new brain exists, the first machine of a new factory. So long as treaties are only concluded, without the provision of any location for the administration, there is nobody in evidence who advocates from his heart the cause on account of which the treaties were made, but each contracting party to the treaty is only the agent of his State or of the party in which his interests are concerned. "That," as the shrewd old gentleman remarked, "we have gone through here quite sufficiently. People come to us from all sides, from Hungary, from Graz, from Mannheim, from Altona, also from . . . and from . . . Each one wants something for himself, makes complaints on his own account, wants a special raisin out of the big cake, but we, in contrast to him, look after the general interests in a hundred ways. Even the great amount of detail we have to concern ourselves with obliges us to think over the general nature of Mid-Europe carefully, even to the last hole and corner. Thus our conception of it grows with and out of our work. That in itself forms the unity between us and our colleagues from over there. Little clouds and sun-spots appear, but in the main they signify but little, for our life's ideal is greater than us all. Things here are not as they were formerly in the Eschersheimer Gasse at Frankfurt-on-Main, for we have ten times more to do than those gentlemen, and the world economic system is daily throwing fresh material at our feet." Thus he spoke, and we went along the edge of the hill and saw the town and the bridge. I asked: "How do things go with the Tzechs and the other non-German Mid-Europeans?" "Oh," said he, "at first intercourse did not come to much, for we speak German in the office; but in the end it became much too serious for the Tzech farmers and business people not to be in touch with us. And I can put in a few Tzech words here and there; that often goes a long way to make the German easier to understand. We purposely make no ques-

CONSTITUTIONAL PROBLEMS 273

tion of principle out of these things and don't allow ourselves to be forced into taking sides within Mid-Europe. The Germans at first thought rather ill of us on this account, but they too see well enough that a world-group area can only be managed with a certain measure of common humanity. It is the tone that makes the music. And besides, what the people who come to us do outside in politics does not concern us, for we represent here nothing but economic ideas. But it seems to me that this in itself has a soothing effect politically." "And how is it with the new members of the union and their special rights?" He knew whom I meant, I cannot say at present. His answer was: "It always takes a little time to get accustomed to things, but since we ask nothing beyond what is actually necessary, and since the advantages of inclusion within our great market area are obvious, all that remains is only discussions about putting things into effect. Come, I will show you the hall with the statistics on the walls! Here I always gladly leave strange visitors to wait awhile. They see there the pictures of all the allied sovereigns and then wall blackboards full of imports, exports, production, consumption, so much that the size of Mid-Europe is impressed upon them once more really effectively, before they enter the room to see me or my colleague. . . ." Thus should I gladly hear him speaking if I dreamt of the future of our scheme.

. . . .

But how will it be with the military State? It too must go beyond the frontiers of the national States, and must include the trench-protected community. People have coined for it the term "military convention" without any one having so far stated exactly all that can and must be agreed upon. I myself, as a civilian, am not in a position to do this, and if I could make such a statement I should perhaps think it more useful to communicate it only to those most concerned. We Central European citizens only ask to be secure in the military sense for a further period of the world's history, and in spite of great financial burdens we shall be ready to sanction in our State Parliaments what is absolutely necessary for this. Probably this will no longer be a party question after the war, but a general concern of the nation. But all the experiences of this immense war must here be used to the full in order to complete and simplify the machinery. In this connection it will be impossible to avoid introducing afresh the question of the constitution of the army. We intend only to bring up here the chief points of the two constitutions.

In the German Empire the whole of Prussian military legislation was placed in the sphere of the federal union by Article 61 of the Constitution, and then in 1874 the so-called great military law was issued, to which later numerous additions and accessory laws have been added. The uniformity is complete with the exception of special provisions for Bavaria and Württemberg.

As far as Bavaria is concerned the treaty of November 23, 1870, determined, in consideration of the sovereign dignity of Bavaria, that Bavaria should bear exclusively and alone the expenses and burdens of its military affairs (including the maintenance of fortresses within its territory and other fortifications). And moreover Bavaria engaged to expend the same amount of money upon its contingent as was decided upon, in proportion to the numerical strength, for the remaining parts of the union. The Bavarian army forms a part of the German federal army, which is complete in itself and has an independent administration under the military sovereignty of the King of Bavaria; but which in war time, and indeed from the beginning of mobilisation, is under the command of the federal commander-in-chief. Complete uniformity prevails in respect to organisation, formation, instruction, pay and instructions for mobilisation. The federal commander-in-chief has the duty and the right of assuring himself by inspection as to the uniformity and the completeness of the army. Since that time growing tradition has modified the statement relating to the financial independence of the Bavarian army so that the expenses of Bavarian military affairs are in fact defrayed by the Empire and all that remains is a process of mutual liquidation of accounts.

The military convention with Württemberg secures to the Württemberg division of troops its own colours and designation.

CONSTITUTIONAL PROBLEMS

The military oath includes king and federal commander-in-chief alike. Promotions are accorded by the king with the consent of the federal commander-in-chief. The Württemberg army corps remains in its own territory. Interchange of officers is provided for and inspections.

These German Imperial military agreements do not destroy the uniformity of the army, but the conditions in Austria-Hungary are more complicated in this department too, for there are three army organisations which possess their own military machinery, viz.: the joint army, the Austrian Landwehr and the Hungarian Landwehr. To understand this we must refer again to the fundamental law of 1867. There the joint business is explained as: "Military affairs, including the navy, but excluding the actual sanction by voting of the contingent of recruits, legislation relating to the manner and method of discharging the obligation to serve in the army, regulations in regard to the removal and maintenance of the army, and further regulation of the civil relations and of those rights and obligations of members of the army which do not refer to military service." This somewhat difficult sentence signifies roughly that the formation of the army is the business of the single States whilst the leadership of the army is a joint affair. In regard to the formation of the army the "establishment of the military organisation" is placed in the fundamental law among the objects about which from time to time settlements shall be made. Thus, here too, in respect to the army we find that feature of terminability already known to us! The levying and division of the expenses of the joint army is subject to the same condition.

Hungary, notwithstanding its share in the joint army, is not willing to dispense with a special, purely Hungarian army system. Hence in the agreement of 1867 it preserved for itself the right to supplement the Hungarian army proper from time to time, and formed or maintained with its special system of recruiting and administration its Hungarian Landwehr (Honved). The result of this was to bring into existence a special Austrian Landwehr, on grounds of equality. Before the outbreak of war the position of the forces in peace time was numerically that the joint army amounted to 339,000 men, the Austrian Landwehr, 49,000, the Hungarian Landwehr, 36,000. A memorial which we have before us estimates the extra expense of this triple system at 75 million kronen a year. Each of the two States has two separate organisations for recruitment, whence it follows that two different systems of recruiting are carried on in the same territory.

If we look forward, in this case too, beyond the present to a somewhat distant future we see that a Mid-European army statute will be necessary, which will distinguish precisely between the general military obligations of the allied States, which must be the same for all who share in the trench-protected partnership, and the special rights and sovereignty of the single States. The same applies to the navy. The navy is a joint business in both Empires and will be paid for out of the common treasury.

.   .   .   .   .   .

The military partnership results from the conception of the world-group economic area. If such an area is to be established it must be a self-contained body for purposes of defence. This must find constitutional expression after the war just as much in Greater Britain as in Mid-Europe. And this involves for all the States and sections of States concerned a certain limitation of their particular political sphere, for they must renounce the ability to wage a special war for themselves alone. But at the same time the limitation contains a powerful safeguard for their existence, for they can no longer be attacked alone. Any one who belongs to the military union is guaranteed by it in so far as this is within the power of the joint army.

We have previously compared this event, rendered necessary by the course of history, with the formation of industrial syndicates. When a single industrial undertaking joins a syndicate it gives up something of its independence, but it strengthens its power of existence in so doing. The weighing of the advantages and disadvantages of this system has given very serious and earnest occupation to many large and small industrial and Government undertakings, but the final result is an almost universal victory for the syndicate idea. Owing to the position of the Central European States between East and West nothing else is left them in the long run but to strengthen themselves mutually through association.

This is conclusive also for the neighbouring small neutral States.

. . . . . .

The effects of the economic union and the military union on the conduct and management of foreign policy are of course far-reaching, and involve many material difficulties, especially in regard to constitutional technicalities. We must say something on this point, but we realise that in this matter little can be done by formulation, but that things will only be cleared up by actual joint work and tradition.

A complete partnership exists between Austria and Hungary in the conduct of foreign policy. The fundamental law says on this point: " Foreign affairs are in common, including diplomatic and commercial representation in foreign countries, as well as arrangements that may be necessary in reference to international treaties, whereby however the ratification of the international treaties, in so far as this is constitutionally necessary, is reserved to the representative bodies of the two halves of the Empire (to the Reichsrat and to the Hungarian Reichstag)." Thus whereas the two halves of the Empire have separate Ministries in other cases, they have a joint Minister for Foreign Affairs, but he is responsible to two independent national representative assemblies. This Minister is selected in course of time both from Austria and Hungary. The present holder of the office is a Hungarian. It is obvious that the system, looked at theoretically, may lead to mischievous disputes, but in practice it has not worked badly, for which the eminent personality of the Austrian Emperor is especially to be thanked.

In the German Empire the conduct of foreign affairs is the business of the Bundesrat and is represented by the Imperial Chancellor. But in order to secure a share in determining foreign policy to the small kingdoms in particular which belong to the German Empire, a committee to deal with foreign affairs has been formed in the Bundesrat, under Bavarian presidency, of plenipotentiaries from Bavaria, Saxony, Württemberg, and the representatives of two other federated States. This committee has actually met only on quite rare occasions, but its existence serves as security against one-sided Prussian action. Here too the reality has worked more simply than the theory in constitutional law. In reality the Foreign Office, dependent on the Imperial Chancellor, manages the foreign relations and submits, in its public acts, to the judgment of the Bundesrat and Reichstag.

In both Empires accordingly the principle of uniform conduct of foreign business has prevailed of itself. The problem of how the will of the people ought to obtain expression in foreign politics is incompletely solved in both cases, but the same applies to all the written and unwritten constitutions of every nation. It is technically impossible to make the representatives of the people accessories to all international relations which are still in an undetermined position. Some things may be communicated in parliamentary committees, which with us is indeed happening to an increasing extent, but the choice of what information to communicate still rests with those who are conducting affairs. Here there is a deficiency in the democratic political system as such which cannot be supplied by conferring on the people's representatives the duty of passing resolutions in regard to war and peace or by demanding the publication of all secret treaties. In August, 1914, we have seen that nothing would have come about differently even if that national right had been recognised in the text of the Constitution. The voting of war credits and of wartime economic laws is in reality the same as a parliamentary vote on the war itself, but all that results at a given moment within the already existing tension of the war is, strictly speaking, an act in the war. What saves the nations from rash declarations of war is the knowledge possessed by all Governments that in our day no war can be carried on without the sincere concurrence of the great majority of the population. Democracy has its say in fact but without formulation. And it is the same with the treaties. Certainly it would be better if yet more treaties were made public, and if thus the nations themselves were made guarantors for them. But there would still be need for some confidential archives, as in the management of every great business. The conduct of foreign policy, that foremost and most difficult and responsible task of statesmen, remains essentially a confidential matter. This is a somewhat painful fact for all citizens, since they must pay for the mistakes of the Foreign Office with their lives and money, but it cannot be altered. All constitutional definitions in this supreme matter are hardly more than attempts at control.

. . . . . .

The significance of this for Mid-Europe is, however, that it will be of but little use for any one to think out a model statute for the joint conduct of foreign policy. The attempt may be made, but the officials of the allied Empires and States will put this paper amongst their many other documents, and will only produce it in individual cases when it suits them. Moreover, foreign policy is too diverse to be managed according to a general scheme worked out beforehand. We see this now in the war: people work together in Vienna and Berlin, dispute, grow irritated, and come to an agreement and try to get over misunderstandings by a sense of duty and by goodwill. The dualism is there but is no absolute hindrance. So far as we can see we shall not get out of this situation in principle within any measurable space of time, but we shall mutually come to work better and better with one another. There will be no change in the Constitution, but here too a tradition will grow up.

Any one who wanted to construct things of this sort out of hand without recognition of realities might well demand a single Foreign Office for Mid-Europe, just as there is a single Minister for Austria and Hungary. But this suggestion overlooks the fact that Austria and Hungary have the same sovereign. Without this personal union the single Minister for Foreign Affairs could hardly exist, for the unity of the source of the orders would be lacking. If Mid-Europe were a republic many other things might perhaps be different, but it suffices to express this proposition to be conscious of its unhistorical character. Moreover the, in itself, natural idea of a single Ministry of Foreign Affairs cannot be thought out at all seriously so long as the mutual relations between the allied Empires are themselves foreign politics. The treaty system with joint treaty organs as we have expounded it, supposes contracting parties on both sides. The new feature is thus not a new Foreign Office for Mid-Europe, but a growing stability in joint work and adjustments between the two Offices already in existence.

In this connection many other matters come into consideration alongside of the joint economic and commercial committees already discussed. Each of the two Empires has its own complete system of embassies and consulates. This must continue so in the main, but here, too, closer approach and joint representation is possible. In the consulate system especially, where even as it is mutual representation is used in the most diverse places, a single representative for small stations should be preferred on principle. Mid-Europeans abroad must have feelings of fellowship. It would be very desirable to organise jointly a place at home for the interchange of consular reports. And as regards the embassies, there can hardly be any discussion of a joint organisation at the present stage of affairs, but it appears conceivable that all general letters and communications might be interchanged without further ceremony.

It would certainly be going too far to say that in future only joint treaties must be concluded; for the subjects of many treaties in fact concern only one or the other State. For example, the agreements about the navigation on the Danube down to the Black Sea are the business of Austria-Hungary, whilst a navigation treaty between Germany and Sweden is the affair of the German Empire. But whenever both Empires are concerned in the same matter, the attempt ought to be made on principle to obtain the same terms. This must be desired by both sides!

. . . . . .

And this brings us to the end of our exposition. We dedicate

CONSTITUTIONAL PROBLEMS 281

it to the statesmen and to the nations. It is not necessary to summarise the contents of the book, for the reader will have them in mind. He will, we hope, have grasped one point as certain, that the Central European Empires cannot let themselves be pushed thoughtlessly into this affair, but must take a fundamental resolution as to whether they desire Mid-Europe or not. If they do not desire it they will go to the Peace Conference in quite a different spirit from that which will inspire them if they do desire it — every question of the war will have a different conclusion so soon as the great preliminary question is answered. Our future German Imperial policy will be quite different in one case from what it will be in the other. And it is the same with Austria-Hungary. Only think of Poland, the position in the Balkans, Turkey, the Mediterranean, the commercial settlements in the treaty of peace; everything depends on the Mid-European decision.

The resolution to desire Mid-Europe is an important step for all the States affected and one with momentous consequences. Hence each State will consider carefully and unreservedly all the relevant possibilities. We acknowledge that this is not easy, and especially for Hungary. Perhaps Hungary has to bear the heaviest burden of responsibility since now for the first time Graf Andrassy's policy of 1879 must be advanced to a national conclusion. Hungary, as a non-German State, has in its hands a portion of the future fate of the German nation. For if Hungary rejects the idea of Mid-Europe decisively it will be hardly possible for this idea to be realised. The Hungarians understand this, and are preparing themselves to make a decision of primary importance in international affairs. If they do not decide in the affirmative then for them and for us a fateful moment has gone by. But the Austrian Emperor too, in consultation with his successors, will weigh the arguments for and against Mid-Europe, and with a wisdom ripened by a wonderfully eventful life, will know how to distinguish what is transitory from what is permanent. He knew the old German Confederation, lived before Bismarck and survives him, and his last will and testament will be sacred to the nations. He will let the teaching of this war make itself heard in his decision. And the Austrian people will ponder over the future with him from the point of view of general international development, and will wish to establish the basis of a new and safer period of evolution for themselves and their children. In like manner the German Emperor and his people will see that they too are faced by a decision which must involve a forgetting of much that is old and an acceptance of much that is new. The Nibelungen faith of the Emperor Wilhelm II shall be raised to the formation of a State. Ancient disputes about development, for us already settled, must begin afresh in this connection. But does not this great war say to us all that we cannot remain where we are? We shall emerge from it other than what we were when we entered upon it. We shall emerge from the war as Mid-Europeans.

· · · · · ·

It was in April that I conceived the plan of this book. At that time fighting was still going on in the Carpathians. Our sons and sons-in-law were defending Hungary and Austria, just as previously Austrians and Hungarians had sustained for us the Russian impact. In the interval many loyal children of Central Europe have been carried off by death, or wounded, many good and noble men who had their life before them. But they did not die in vain, for our joint army pressed back the enemy before it, freed Galicia, and released Poland from a Russian jurisdiction of a hundred years' duration. The advance has lasted from May onwards. This work has grown amidst the news of this, the greatest victorious attack in the world's history. It is not to be regarded as a speculation which might have been framed at any moment; on the contrary it has taken to itself flesh and blood out of the war. Thus will it be understood by those who have become different during the war from what they were previously.

What ought to be our profit from the war? For what ought our dead to have died? To the end that we should part from one another again the day after the war and act as though we had never known one another? That would be to squander the noblest spiritual good.

Mid-Europe is the fruit of war. We have sat together in the war's economic prison, we have fought together, we are determined to live together!

CHAPTER IX

STATISTICAL AND HISTORICAL

IN the text of this book hitherto, we have only used figures and historical data very sparingly, for the benefit of those readers who want to be spared the apparatus of knowledge. But fortunately these are not the only type of reader, and many of the statements and remarks in the text can only be properly illustrated and secure the desired demonstrative force by means of figures and numbers. Hence in the following section we shall gather together information and data, following the course of the previous chapters.

The statistical material is obtained almost entirely from the statistical year books for Germany, Austria and Hungary. To these must be added Hübner's geographical and statistical tables and Hickmann's pocket atlas of Austria-Hungary. Dr. Pistov's book, *Die Österreichisch-ungarische Volkswirthschaft* came out, published by the same publisher, just as this book was being completed, and I was able to make use of it in a few places. For the compiling of the historical tables under Chapter II reference was made to the historical summaries in Perthes' *Geschichts-atlas*. Guttentag's edition was used for the constitution of the German Empire; and for the fundamental law of the Austro-Hungarian State, Giegl's edition (Manz, Vienna). The remaining general literature is given in Section X. We may mention the following later pamphlets referring to the same subject:

Philippovich, Professor, Geh. Hofrat, member of the Austrian Herrenhaus: *Ein Wirtschafts und Zollverband zwischen Deutschland und Österreich-Ungarn,* Leipzig, 1915.

Losch, Geh. Finanzrat: *Der mittel europäische Wirthschaftsblock und das Schicksal Belgiens,* Leipzig, 1914.

Munin: *Österreich nach dem Kriege, Forderungen eines aktiven öfterreichischen Politikers,* Jena, 1915.

Wolf, Professor: *Ein deutsch-österreichisch-ungarischer Zollverband,* Leipzig, 1915.

I. PARTNERSHIP IN THE WAR AND ITS RESULTS

In order to simplify the statistical summaries, round numbers are given throughout. Any one who wishes to know the exact figures must refer to the statistical year books. Germany is indicated by G., Austria by A., Hungary by H., Bosnia by B. We begin with general data concerning area and population:

The area is:

G. ....541,000 qkm.
A.-H. ....676,000 "
_____
1,217,000 "

According to the census of 1910 the population of this area is:

G. ....64.9 million inhabitants
A.-H. ....51.4 " "
_____
116.3 " "

But in the interval up to the war the total population of the Central States in Mid-Europe increased to something over 120 millions. Whether during the homicidal war the total population will have increased or decreased cannot be said at the present moment. Probably there will be an increase of females and a decrease of males.

The effective force of the army in peace time was, for 1913–14:

G. 800,000
A.-H. 424,000
_____
1,224,000

The Austro-Hungarian army consists, under peace conditions, of the following divisions:

Joint army	340,000
Austrian Landwehr	48,000
Hungarian Landwehr	36,000
	424,000

Army horses under peace conditions:

G.	160,000
A.-H.	90,000
	250,000

We can say nothing in respect to the numbers of the two armies during the war.

The navy before the war included:

	G.	A.-H.
Battleships	101	30
Guns	2100	910

The fleets are not completely comparable owing to the difference in types.

The Central European military power is the result of long years of development and is closely connected with the increase in population.

Growth of population (reckoned according to the present extent of the country) in millions of inhabitants:

	G.	A.	H.	B.
1850	35.4	17.5	13.2	—
1870	40.8	20.2	—	—
1890	49.4	23.7	17.5	—
1910	64.9	28.6	20.9	1.9

The earlier information for Hungary is not given in the *Statistical Year Book*. The figures under H. 1850, which come from

Hickmann, are in any case correct. At that time the territory of the later German Empire had a population about 5 millions in excess of that of Austria-Hungary. This was not yet the case in 1800. The change in the respective amounts of population took place in the first half of the previous century.

Alterations in population during the last century:

	G.	A.-H. (without B.)	
1800	21.0	23.1	+ 2.1
1850	35.4	30.7	− 4.7
1900	56.4	45.4	−11.0
1910	64.9	49.5	−15.4

The backwardness of Austria-Hungary is quite obvious, and depends partly on the relation between the births and deaths and partly on emigration.

Excess of Births, 1911–12, per Thousand

	Born	Died	Excess
G.	28.3	15.6	12.7
A.	31.5	22.0	9.5
H.	35.0	25.1	9.9

In spite of its smaller number of births, Germany shows far the better percentage result. In the German Empire there are somewhat too few births, but in Austria, and still more in Hungary, there are far more deaths than necessary.

Emigration Questions. Emigration is at present of little importance for Germany, it is rather a question of immigration. In Austria-Hungary things are different. The over-seas emigration amounted to:

1908	192,000
1909	199,000
1910	277,000
1911	187,000
1912	213,000

These figures are very high! In addition there is a constant seasonal emigration across the land frontiers.

Comparison of the increase in population of the Great Powers (according to Hickmann), in millions:

	1800	1900	Increase
European Russian	38.8	111.3	+72.5
United States	5.3	77.1	+71.8
Germany	21.0	56.4	+35.4
Austria-Hungary without B	23.1	45.4	+22.3
Great Britain	16.2	41.6	+25.4
France	26.9	39.0	+12.1
Italy	18.1	32.5	+14.4
Spain	11.5	18.2	+ 6.7
Belgium	3.0	6.9	+ 3.9
Roumania	2.7	6.0	+ 3.3
Portugal	2.9	5.1	+ 2.2
The Netherlands	2.0	5.1	+ 3.1
Sweden	2.3	5.1	+ 2.8
	173.8	449.7	

Unfortunately I cannot continue these tables up to the present with the information at my disposal, since the censuses take place at different times and must therefore be converted, and because the exact area of country to which Hickmann's tables refer is not known to me in every case. But even thus continued only up to 1900 the juxtaposition is of the greatest interest.

The sequence among the European Great Powers according to this manner of reckoning was:

1800. Russia, France, Austria-Hungary, Germany, Italy, Great Britain.

1900. Russia, Germany, Austria-Hungary, Great Britain, France, Italy.

(For a comparison of the great World-States with colonial provinces see Section V.)

From a purely statistical point of view European policy is fre-

STATISTICAL AND HISTORICAL

quently nothing but a realisation in political law of the above shiftings of population. But the figures alone are not decisive, as is shown by the example of Russia. Amount of population is only one of the important historical properties of nations.

II. OF THE PREVIOUS HISTORY OF CENTRAL EUROPE

The following collection of historical dates is only intended to remind the reader of individual events which are of importance for the previous history of Mid-Europe:

1211. Saint Elizabeth, Germany's most popular saint, comes from Hungary into Thüringia.
1273–1291. Rudolf I. of Hapsburg founds the Austrian Monarchy, defeats Ottokar of Bohemia in 1278 on the Marchfeld.
1314–1330. Struggle between Friedrich of Austria and Ludwig of Bavaria for the Imperial Crown.
1348. King Karl IV. founds the first German University in Prague.
1409. Emigration of the German and Polish students from Prague. Foundation of the University of Leipzig.
1410. Battle of Tannenberg. Jagello of Lithuania and Poland.
1415. Friedrich I. of Hohenzollern, Burggraf of Nürnberg, takes over the Mark Brandenburg.
1419–36. Hussite wars.
1438. Albrecht II., Duke of Austria, as Sigmund's son-in-law, becomes also King of Bohemia and Hungary.
1440–70. Friedrich II. of Brandenburg makes his royal residence at Berlin.
1457. Mathias Corvinus is elected King of Hungary, Georg Podiebrad is elected King of Bohemia.
1466. West Prussia becomes Polish, East Prussia a Polish fief.
1519–56. Emperor Karl V., world-embracing empire on an Austro-Spanish basis.
1525. The Duchy of Prussia.
1526. Battle of Mohacs against the Turks. Ferdinand of Aus-

tria, the brother of Karl V., becomes King of Bohemia, Moravia, Silesia and Hungary. From henceforward the Austro-Hungarian Monarchy exists.

1521–38. Karl V.'s Italian wars.
1529. Vienna besieged by the Turks.
1539. Protestant Reformation in Brandenburg.
1555. Religious Peace of Augsberg; *cuius regio eius religio.*
1556. Abdication of Karl V. Separation between the Austrian and Spanish sections of the World-Power.
1576–1612. Emperor Rudolf II.; the Hungarian Protestants revolt. Counter-Reformation.
1608–9. Formation of the Protestant Union and the Catholic League.
1609. Disputed succession in Jülich and Cleve. Brandenburg extends itself to West Germany.
1618. Prussia falls to Brandenburg.
1618–48. Thirty Years War.
1620. Battle of the White Hill. Break up of Protestantism in Bohemia.
1630–32. Gustavus Adolphus of Sweden in Germany, attempted Baltic Sea Empire.
1640–88. Friedrich Wilhelm of Brandenburg, the Great Elector, the true founder of the North German power.
1660. Prussia freed from Polish suzerainty at the Peace of Oliva.
1681. Strasburg becomes French; influence of France on the west.
1683. Vienna besieged by the Turks, saved by the Polish King Johann Sobieski.
1697. August the Strong, Elector of Saxony, becomes King of Poland.
1699. Peace of Carlowitz. Prince Eugene, the noble knight. Siebenbürgen secured by Austria.
1701. Prussia becomes a kingdom.
1714. Peace of Rastadt; Emperor Karl VI. receives the Spanish Netherlands, Milan, Sardinia, Naples.

1718. Peace of Passarowitz; Austria receives Croatia and parts of Bosnia and Serbia (lost again in 1739).
1732. Exiled Salzburg Protestants are received in Prussia.
1713–38. Pragmatic sanction; indivisibility of the Austrian States, female succession.
1740–86. King Friedrich II. of Prussia.
1740–80. Queen Maria Theresa of Austria.
1740–42. First Silesian War.
1741–48. War of the Austrian Succession.
1744–5. Second Silesian War.
1745–1806. The House of Lorraine on the Imperial throne.
1756–63. Seven Years War. Prussia becomes the North German Great Power.
1772. First Partition of Poland.
1778–79. War of the Bavarian Succession. Peace of Teschen. Bavaria receives Kurpfalz.
1792–97. First Coalition War against France. Agreement of Pillnitz between Austria and Prussia.
1793. Second Partition of Poland.
1795. Third Partition of Poland. Prussia concludes a separate peace with France at Basle.
1797. Peace of Campo Formio. Austria receives Venice, Istria and Dalmatia.
1798–1802. Second Coalition War against France.
1804. Franz II. as Hereditary Emperor of Austria.
1805. Third Coalition War without Prussia. Vienna occupied by the French. Battle of Austerlitz. Peace of Pressburg. Italian and Tyrolese possessions lost.
1806. Napoleon establishes the Confederation of the Rhine. Franz II. resigns the German Imperial crown.
1806. Prussia defeated at Jena and Auerstadt, Napoleon in Berlin.
1807. Peace of Tilsit. Prussia reduced. Poland re-established.
1809. Austria fights without Prussia against Napoleon. West Galicia to Poland, East Galicia to Russia.

1812. The great army of Napoleon advances against Russia. Prussia and Austria with France against Russia.
1813. Prussia and Austria with Russia against France. Battle of Leipzig.
1815. Vienna Congress; Act of the German Confederation; Austria receives Milan, Venice, Istria, Dalmatia, Tyrol. Prussia receives the province of Saxony. Federal Diet at Frankfurt-on-Main under Austrian presidency. Poland divided again.
1815–26. Holy Alliance; Prussia and Austria under Russian guidance. Metternich.
1818–53. Formation of the German Customs Union under Prussian guidance.
1830–31. Polish rising put down.
1848–49. Revolution in Berlin and Vienna. Hungarian nationalist rising. Emperor Franz Josef. German Parliament in St. Paul's Church at Frankfurt-on-Main. Archduke Johann of Austria as Imperial administrator. Friedrich Wilhelm IV. of Prussia does not accept the Imperial crown. Re-establishment of the German Confederation. Hungary subdued with Russian help.
1850. Prussia humbles herself at Olmütz before Austria.
1853–56. Crimean War; the Western Powers against Russia. Austria takes part as the protecting Power of Roumania. Prussia remains neutral. Nicholas I. dies. Peace of Paris. Russia enters the mouth of the Danube.
1859. The Kingdom of Roumania.
1861–88. King Wilhelm I. of Prussia.
1862–90. Bismarck as Minister-President and Imperial Chancellor.
1864. Danish War carried on by Austria and Prussia together.
1866. Austrian, Prussian and Italian War; Battle of Königgrätz; Venice for Italy, North German Confederation, Customs Parliament, Prussian treaties with South German States.
1867. Ausgleich between Austria and Hungary. Franz Josef has himself crowned King of Hungary.

STATISTICAL AND HISTORICAL

1870–71. Franco-German War. Neutrality of Austria and Russia. Foundation of the German Empire, coronation of the Emperor at Versailles. Alsace-Lorraine as the Reichsland. Imperial constitution.

1872. Meeting of the three Emperors.

1877–78. Russo-Turkish War. Berlin Congress. Serbia, Roumania, Montenegro become independent of Turkey. Bulgaria becomes a suzerainty. Bosnia and Herzegovina come under Austro-Hungarian administration. Russia receives Bessarabia, but resigns part of Dobrudscha to Roumania.

1879. Treaty of alliance between Germany and Austria-Hungary arranged by Bismarck and Count Andrassy.

1887. Italy joins the Dual Alliance (until 1915!).

1888. Emperor Friedrich III.; beginning of the reign of Emperor Wilhelm II.

III. CREEDS AND NATIONALITIES

Central Europe, the battle-ground of violent religious disputes, is very diversified as regards its religious creeds. Austria is the most uniform with over nine-tenths Catholics.

Summary of religious creeds in 1910, in millions:

	G.	A.	H.	
Catholics	23.8	25.9	12.9	= 62.6
Protestants	40.0	0.6	4.0	= 44.6
Other Christians	0.3	0.1	0.1	= 0.5
Jews	0.6	1.3	0.9	= 2.8
Eastern Greek Church	—	0.7	3.0	= 3.7
Others	0.2	—	—	= 0.2
	64.9	28.6	20.9	114.4

Bosnia and Herzegovina are not included in this summary. There are there 0.4 Catholics, 0.8 Orthodox Serbs, 0.6 Mohammedans and a quite negligible minority of Protestants and Jews.

Members of the United Church subject to the Pope are counted as Catholics.

Any alteration of the Central European land frontiers that is at all possible or to be expected at the conclusion of peace, except in regard to Kurland or Livland, will lead to an increase in the number of Catholics.

Of the large towns of over 200,000 inhabitants the following are substantially Protestant: Berlin, Hamburg, Dresden, Leipzig, Breslau (very mixed), Frankfurt-on-Main, Hanover, Nürnberg, Chemnitz, Magdeburg, Bremen, Charlottenburg, Kiel, Königsberg, Neukölln, Stettin, Stuttgart; the following are substantially Catholic: Vienna, Budapest, Munich, Cologne, Prague, Düsseldorf, Lemberg.

There are strong Jewish minorities (over 5 per cent.) in Vienna, Budapest, Prague, Lemberg, Frankfurt, Breslau and Berlin.

Nationalities in the German Empire in thousands. Unfortunately we can only give the somewhat out-of-date figures for 1900, since neither the *Statistical Year Book* nor Hübner's Tables give the nationality census for 1910. Apparently it is not yet complete. Owing to this a uniform Central European table for 1910 cannot be made up.

Germans	52,140 = 925	per thousand
Poles	3,090 = 55	"	"
French	210 = 3.7	"	"
Masovians	140 = 2.5	"	"
Danes	140 = 2.5	"	"
Lithuanians	110 = 1.9	"	"
Cassubians	100 = 1.8	"	"
Wends	90 = 1.7	"	"

Those otherwise enumerated are immigrant minorities. The preponderance of Germans is obvious. And a part of the 1,260,000 " aliens to the Empire " are born Germans. The Austrians in Germany number 630,000, the Hungarians in Germany 32,000.

Nationalities in Austria in thousands, according to the census of 1910:

STATISTICAL AND HISTORICAL

Germans . . .	9950 = 356	per thousand
Bohemians, Moravians, Slovaks .	6440 = 230	,, ,,
Poles	4970 = 178	,, ,,
Ruthenians . .	3520 = 126	,, ,,
Slovenians . .	1250 = 45	,, ,,
Serbian Croats .	781 = 28	,, ,,
Italians . . .	770 = 27	,, ,,
Roumanians . .	270 = 10	,, ,,

The Germans amount to rather more than one-third. The political effect of this is that in order to form a majority at any time they need to be supplemented by another language group, even if they are entirely united, which seldom happens. Supposing that in consequence of the war Galicia is separated from the union of countries represented in the Reichsrat, the division of nationalities will be as follows:

Nationalities in Austria without Galicia and Bukowina (the Ruthenian question remains untouched in this case):

Germans	9690	
Tzechs	6430	
Slovenians	1250	
Serbian Croats	780	} 9500
Italians	770	
Poles	260	
Ruthenians	10	

This involves a German majority which is almost as narrow as the Magyar majority in Hungary.

Nationalities in Hungary, in thousands, according to the census of 1910:

Magyars . .	10,050 = 482	per thousand
Roumanians .	2,950 = 141	,, ,,
Germans . .	2,030 = 98	,, ,,
Slovaks . .	2,030 = 94	,, ,,

Croats . . .	1,830 =	88 per thousand
Serbs . . .	1,110 =	53 " "
Ruthenians .	470 =	23 " "
Others . .	460 =	21 " "

The position as regards a majority is evident. The Magyars, without the help of geometrical manipulation of the electoral districts and pressure on the voter, cannot be certain that they will not be outvoted on national questions, although they are united amongst themselves.

In Bosnia and Herzegovina there are 1760 Serbian Croats out of 1930 thousand. The next biggest group is that of the Turks with 150 thousand; they are, however, enumerated as "aliens."

Austria-Hungary with Bosnia and Herzegovina, that is the whole monarchy, contains in millions:

Germans	12.0
Magyars	10.1
Bohemians, Slovaks	8.5
Serbian Croats	5.5
Poles	5.0
Ruthenians	4.0
Roumanians	3.2
Slovenians	1.3
Italians	1.0
Others	0.2
	50.8

If the general conception of the Austro-Hungarian Slavs is considered, a big group of 24.3 millions can be made up of Tzechs, Slovaks, Poles, Serbian Croats, Ruthenians and Slovenians, which would be the greatest numerically in the whole State; but the various Slav groups are not a unity in this sense. Their strength is noticeable enough without this.

Most of these figures may be altered as a result of the conclusion of peace, it is only certain from the outset that any Magyar in-

STATISTICAL AND HISTORICAL 297

crease is out of the question, and that a German increase is only possible to a very limited extent. Further discussions about other possibilities of increase are at present ill-timed. It may be noticed merely that the number of Russian Poles is given in an out-of-date census as about 8 millions.

IV. THE ECONOMIC LIFE OF CENTRAL EUROPE

The number of illiterates cannot be determined either from the recruiting figures or from the population census. Germany does the former and Austria-Hungary the latter, so that the information is not quite comparable. Germany has 0.5 recruits per 1000 who cannot read and write; Austria had 356 per 1000 inhabitants in 1900, a figure which must have decreased considerably in the interval; Hungary had 437 per 1000 inhabitants in 1910, Bosnia as many as 878! The Hungarian figures sank from 502 to 437 between 1900 and 1910, because the generation growing up are almost universally subject to compulsory education. But the underlying and characteristic difference is that we in Germany have already reached perhaps the third generation of a universally enforced compulsory education, in Austria they are on the whole at about the second, in Hungary hardly at the first. At present Austria may be regarded as completely embarked on the normal school system, and Hungary as nearly so embarked. In Prussia 1625 per 10,000 inhabitants are primary scholars, in Austria 1705, in Hungary 1319, but in Bosnia only 222.

For the sake of comparison we will add some data concerning the educational system in other States. Great Britain has 1664 primary scholars per 10,000 inhabitants, France 1435, Belgium 1246, Italy 908, Roumania 831, Russia 370, United States 1924. It must be taken into account here that the length of compulsory schooling or of actual attendance at school is different.

The censuses of industrial activities are almost entirely incomparable, because they are carried out according to different principles. For example, when in Germany 30.4 per cent., in Austria 42.8 per cent., in Hungary 26.7 per cent. of the female population are declared to be engaged in industry this does not mean that the employment of women is more frequent in Austria than in Germany, but only that wives and daughters living at home are counted differently. The number of males employed in trades and professions appear fairly equal in the two cases as something over 60 per cent. of the existing male population. Owing to the different methods of calculation, however, the equality of the occupational groups is very defective, apart from the fact that the occupational census was held in different years, and the last one available for Austria is that of 1900.

The following summary of occupational groups must be taken with all these limitations and provisos. Out of every 100 inhabitants the numbers belonging to the following occupational groups are:

	G.	A.	H.
Agriculture and forestry	35.2	60.9	69.7
Industry and mining	40.0	23.3	13.6
Trade and commerce	12.4	5.4	4.2
Army and navy	2.3	1.7	1.5
Public service and independent professions	3.9	2.9	2.5
Domestic and personal service	4.5	3.5	4.4
Others	1.7	2.3	4.1

In almost every group there are besides still further differences in the methods of enumeration. For example, inns and public houses are classed under industries in Austria-Hungary, but in Germany under trade, which goes a long way to explain the different figures for trade. Hungary too counts under "others" people whom we in Germany do not regard as engaged in industry at all, such as dependents and vagrants.

The degree of organisation in the occupations cannot be compared statistically at all except in the case of the wage-earners, which is a great defect from our point of view. Even here it would be too risky to attempt to calculate percentages.

	G.	A.	H.
Trade-union membership	3,754,000	693,000	119,000

STATISTICAL AND HISTORICAL

	Mill. Mk.	Mill. Mk.	Mill. Mk.
Trade-union property	94	19.7	2.8
Trade-union receipts	90	11.4	2.1

For purposes of comparison we give the trade-union membership for various countries:

Germany	3,754,000
Great Britain	3,281,000
United States	2,526,000
France	1,027,000
Italy	872,000
Austria	693,000
Belgium	232,000
Holland	189,000
Denmark	139,000
Switzerland	131,000
Sweden	122,000
Hungary	119,000

The international significance of a Central European centralised system of trade unions is obvious from these figures without further discussion. Unfortunately we cannot offer a comparison of the degree of organisation amongst agricultural and industrial producers.

The international summaries concerning the average produce per hectare of arable land serve best to measure the productivity of labour.

The hectare produces in 100 kilograms as follows:

	Wheat	Barley	Potatoes
Belgium	26	27	211
Ireland	26	25	161
Holland	25	27	174
Germany	24	22	159
Switzerland	22	19	155
England	21	18	164
Sweden	21	17	100

	Wheat	Barley	Potatoes
Norway	18	20	168
Austria	15	16	100
Roumania	14	11	68
Canada	14	16	112
Japan	14	19	100
Hungary	13	14	75
Italy	12	9	61
Bulgaria	12	11	44
United States	10	13	61
Russia	9	10	74

In order to value this most important and interesting table properly the superiority of the North Sea climate for the production of corn should not be forgotten. But nevertheless there is food for thought in the fact that the North Sea countries (free trade and protectionist without distinction!) boast the highest rate in agricultural output. Industrial capitalism in the first stage, in which it is most strongly developed round the North Sea, indirectly increases agricultural productivity in many ways.

* * * * *

It is regrettable that a comparative estimate of the productivity of industrial labour is not feasible or only yields very doubtful and arbitrary results. Consequently we must attach importance to some indirect data which does not concern productive power itself, but only the technical and capitalist development of the countries.

Postal conditions:

Postal packets in general	7.0	1.9	0.7 milliards
Telephones	2.1	0.3	0.2 "
Telegrams	61	23	13 millions
Staff	233,000	71,000	38,000

It is clear at once that a post office official in the German Empire facilitates more dispatches, telegrams and conversations than one in Austria or Hungary, but it must be remembered that a more thickly populated country is easier to provide for.

STATISTICAL AND HISTORICAL

Railway conditions:

	G.	A.-H.
Length of railways	63,000	46,000 km.
Per 10,000 inhabitants	9.5	9.0 "
Stock per km.	315,000	274,000 mks.

Unfortunately in this case, so far as I can see, the numbers of staff cannot be made comparable with certainty owing to the difference in the railway systems.

Joint-stock companies (1911):

	G.	A.	H.
Number of companies	53,000	740	2900
Nominal capital	16.3	3.3	2.0 milliard mks.

Here it must be remembered that in Hungary banks and savings banks are included. The small number of joint-stock companies in Austria is partly explained by the high joint-stock company tax.

The capital in joint-stock companies in Great Britain is 45.3 milliard mks., in France 10.8, in Russia 5.4, Holland 3.0, Switzerland 2.6, Belgium 2.3.

Average market rate of discount 1913: Paris 3.84, London 4.39, Berlin 4.98, Vienna 5.72.

. . . . . .

Another way in which to compare the position of the population is by means of the statistics of consumption reckoned per head of the population. I quote the following summary (1912–13) from the book by Pistov which has just appeared: *Die österreichisch-ungarische Volkswirtschaft* (published by G. Reimer, Berlin):

	G.		A.-H.		
Wheat	88 }	233	120 }	204	kg.
Rye	145 }		84 }		"

	G.	A.-H	
Meat (1910)	52.6	29.9	kg.
Coffee	2.4	1.1	"
Rice	3.6	2.0	"
Sugar	21.6	13.0	"
Salt	24.6	12.5	"
Beer	101	46	l.
Tobacco	1.7	1.2	kg.
Cotton	7.2	4.3	"

In respect to corn, seed corn and cattle fodder is included, so that a direct inference as to the amount of bread consumed per individual cannot be drawn. In the cases of salt and sugar too, indirect uses are included. The consumption of bread is certainly somewhat lower in Austria-Hungary. But the lower average consumption is especially striking in regard to meat and sugar, of which Austria-Hungary produces so much. The primary attainable aim of the mass of the Austro-Hungarian population must be to arrive at the average consumption of the Germans of the Empire. At this point the national and social advantage involved in the economic stimulation of the whole province shows itself most impressively.

V. Joint Problems in War Economics

The connection with the international economic system before the war is recognisable from the figures for imports and exports. A summary in the appendix to the *Statistical Year Book* for the German Empire gives the following sequence:

Share of the States in international commerce (1912):

	Million mks.	Per cent.
Great Britain	27,400	16.6
Germany	21,300	12.9
United States	16,200	9.9
France	14,800	9.0
Holland	11,400	6.9
Belgium	7,000	4.2

STATISTICAL AND HISTORICAL

	Millions mks.	Per cent.
Russia	5,800	3.5
Austria-Hungary	5,600	3.3
Italy	5,100	3.1

The total amount of goods dealt with in exportation and importation is valued at 164 milliards, but of course the same commodity gets paid for twice, and indeed in case of further removals four and more times over. The amount dealt with actually in international trade may be fixed at 60 to 70 milliards, or approximately twice as much as the calculable annual proceeds of the German national economic system. This immense exchange is in part completely destroyed by the war, in part become unsurveyable.

The English plan of blockade referred originally more to Germany than to Austria-Hungary, still Austria-Hungary too has had to suffer from its effects, but has held out well. The fundamental facts of the blockade scheme were:

German demand from foreign countries (1912, in million marks value):

	Imports	Exports	Mill. kr.
Raw materials	5000	1500	— 3500
Half-finished goods	1200	1100	— 100
Finished goods	1500	6400	+ 4900
Food-stuffs and luxuries	2800	1000	— 1800
Animals	300	—	— 300
Total	10,800	10,000	— 800

Austro-Hungarian demand from foreign countries (1912, in million kronen):

	Imports	Exports	Mill. kr.
Raw materials (including food-stuffs)	2000	960	— 1040
Half-finished goods	570	510	— 60
Finished goods	980	1260	+ 280
Total	3550	2730	— 820

The balance this year (1912) is especially unfavourable owing to the weather conditions, but still it marks the position of affairs in general. Unfortunately I have not yet got the figures for 1913 for Austria.

The English calculations resulted in this: that we could neither of us sell our finished goods abroad and could not buy raw material and food-stuffs from abroad.

The more important items of imports as regards food and cattle fodder in Germany are, after exports or re-exports are deducted, the following (1913) in millions of marks.

	Imports	Exports	Mill. mks.
Wheat	417	88	— 329
Wheaten flour	5	44	+ 39
Rye	42	133	+ 91
Rye flour	—	39	+ 39
Potatoes	25	18	— 7
Beef	36	—	— 36
Pork	24	—	— 24
Eggs	194	2	— 192
Lard	147	—	— 147
Butter	119	1	— 118
Rice	104	43	— 61
Beet sugar	—	265	+ 265
Beer	10	15	+ 5
Coffee	35	—	— 35
Apples	46	—	— 46
Herrings	73	2	— 71
Barley	390	1	— 389
Bran, rice-dust	149	2	— 147
Linseed	130	1	— 129
Oil cakes	119	39	— 80
Palm kernels	104	—	— 104
Oats	60	93	+ 33
Clover seed, lucerne seed	46	17	— 29

This statement includes, of course, the imports from neighbouring countries which have been only slightly disturbed by the war. Still the position was very questionable, for it is evident that the only important positive items were sugar and rye. But rye largely took the place of barley as fodder. Under these circumstances the feeding of humans and cattle could only be continued by the consumption of stores and by systematic economy. We cannot so far prepare statistical data as to the amount of stores. There was more of all the principal stuffs than any one had previously thought.

A collection of the Government regulations for war economics will be found in the *Mitteilungen und Nachrichter der Kriegszentrale des Hansabundes* (Hillger, Berlin).

The best summary of the continually growing materials for the science of war economics will be found in *Weltwirthschaftliches Archiv,* edited by Professor Harms of Kiel (Fischer, Jena). The speech of State Secretary Helfferich, included in the collection *Der deutsche Krieg* (Part No. 41–42), edited by Dr. E. Jäckh, gives information concerning the financial position during the war. General points of view are given in: *Weltwirthschaft und Nationalwirthschaft* by Professor Franz Oppenheimer, and *Vorrathswirthschaft und Volkswirthschaft* by Professor Herm. Levy. Professor Jastrow describes the economic problems at the beginning of the war in *Im Kriegszustand, die Umformung des öffentlichen Lebens in der ersten Kriegswoche* (Georg Reimer, Berlin).

. . . .

With regard to the rise of prices during the war we refer to the *Weltwirthschaftliche Archiv* (memoir by Professor Eulenburg). Here we shall only give retail prices of the Berlin Co-operative Stores.

Retail prices (½ kg. in pfennige):

	July 1914	April 1915	
Butter	136	160	+ 24
Lard	66	160	+ 94
Bacon	80	160	+ 80
Peas	25	58	+ 33

	July 1914	April 1915	
Potatoes	40	95	+ 55
Rye flour	14	24	+ 10
Wheat flour	18	26	+ 8
Rice	26	60	+ 34
Bread	30	44	+ 14

The rise in the price of bread would have been very much greater had it not been for the maximum price regulation. We find a similar rise in prices, in parts even higher, in Austria-Hungary.

It is a number of years since the whole Austria-Hungarian Monarchy was completely self-supporting. The increased importation in the group "corn, pulse, flour" is as follows:

1911	605,000 tons
1912	692,000 tons

In other words: in 1912 Austria-Hungary purchased food-stuffs and luxuries from abroad to the value of about 100 million kronen.

The following table in millions of kronen, for 1912, is, however, important as showing the mutual economic relations of Austria and Hungary, and hence as an aid to understanding the economic tension during the war:

	From Hungary to Austria	From Austria to Hungary
Corn	298 mill. kr.	} 13 mill. kr.
Flour	259 "	
Rice	13 "	3 "
Fruit	8 "	5 "
Potatoes	4 "	—
Beet sugar	6 "	—
Cattle	161 mill. head	} 4 mill. head
Pigs	91 " "	
Milk	12 mill. kr.	—
Eggs	15 "	—
Butter	8 "	—

STATISTICAL AND HISTORICAL

	From Hungary to Austria	From Austria to Hungary
Lard	13 "	—
Bacon	11 "	—
Wine	60 mill. kr.	15 mill. kr.
Meat	17 "	4 "
Sugar	2 "	14 "
Tobacco	17 "	—

The line (—) in the last column does not mean that there is absolutely no importation from Austria to Hungary, but only that it is insignificant. The whole picture is quite clear: Hungary is the agricultural country for Austria! Austria taken by itself is a country importing agricultural produce as much or almost more than Germany.

The Austrian exports to Hungary include the following as chief items (surplus calculated):

	Mill. kr.
Coal	22
Coke	15
Cotton yarn	21
Cotton goods	222
Linen textures	17
Sacks	11
Woollen goods	120
Silk goods	44
Hats	16
Clothes	52
Underlinen	23
Paper and paper goods	30
India-rubber goods	10
Leather, leather goods	80
Wooden wares	25
Glass goods	21
Fancy wares	15
Iron, iron goods	100

	Mill. kr.
Base metal goods	37
Machines, apparatus	64
Electrical apparatus	15
Boats	8
Precious metals, jewels	26
Instruments, clocks	19
Drugs	8

It is only on the basis of these summaries that we can understand the fact that there are two commercial policies and two economic States within the Dual Monarchy. But it would be the same with us in the German Empire if we had a political frontier to cross at the Elbe. Who amongst us would wish to have one?

VI. Our Position in the World's Economic System

Hübner's *Geographisch-statistischen Tabellen* still reckons sixty-one independent States on the earth's surface, amongst which however are included dwarf States such as Andorra, Costa Rica, the Dominican Republic, Honduras, Liechtenstein, San Marino, Monaco, Panama, the Polar regions (!) and Samos, and States whose dependence is well known are still called independent, such as Egypt, Arabia, Nepal, Oman, Morocco. In reality it is impossible to say exactly how many genuinely independent States there are, since the concept of sovereignty is variable. But even on a generous appreciation there are not more than fifty.

If we assume that genuine political sovereignty begins at a million inhabitants we can construct the following groups.

Classification of States according to size (with colonies):

States of over 100 millions:

Great Britain	443	
China	330	1049 mill.
Russia	169	
United States	107	

STATISTICAL AND HISTORICAL

States of from 50 to 100 millions:
- France . . . . . 98 ⎫
- Germany . . . . 77 ⎬ 298 mill.
- Japan . . . . . . 72 ⎪
- Austria-Hungary . . . 51 ⎭

States of from 20 to 50 millions:
- Netherlands . . . . 44 ⎫
- Italy . . . . . . 36 ⎪
- Brazil . . . . . 25 ⎬ 170 mill.
- Turkey . . . . . 22 ⎪
- Belgium . . . . . 22 ⎪
- Spain . . . . . . 21 ⎭

States of from 10 to 20 millions:
- Mexico . . . . . 15 ⎫
- Portugal . . . . . 15 ⎬ 40 mill.
- Persia . . . . . . 10 ⎭

States of from 5 to 10 millions:
- Roumania . . . . 8 ⎫
- Abyssinia . . . . 8 ⎪
- Siam . . . . . . 8 ⎪
- Argentina . . . . 7 ⎬ 48 mill.
- Sweden . . . . . 6 ⎪
- Peru . . . . . . 6 ⎪
- Colombia . . . . 5 ⎭

States of from 1 to 5 millions:
- Afghanistan . . . . 4 ⎫
- Bulgaria . . . . . 4 ⎪
- Greece . . . . . 4 ⎪
- Switzerland . . . 4 ⎬ 29 mill.
- Serbia . . . . . . 4 ⎪
- Chile . . . . . . 3 ⎪
- Denmark . . . . 3 ⎪
- Haiti . . . . . . 3 ⎭

States of from 1 to 5 millions:

Venezuela	3	
Bolivia	2	
Cuba	2	
Ecuador	2	16 mill.
Guatemala	2	
Liberia	2	
Norway	2	
Uruguay	1	

It is unnecessary to say how much States of the same class as to size often differ qualitatively. At the same time this summary shows the complete victory of the political "large scale industry" system. Almost two-thirds of mankind belong to the four world-group economic areas of the first rank. The world's history is in reality a game played by the first eight Powers. In the game a permanent combination between Germany and Austria-Hungary, even without the accession of other neighbouring States, would be a change of the greatest significance. It would then be: Great Britain, China, Russia, Mid-Europe, the United States, France, Japan. But whether China is here a fellow-player or an object remains to be seen.

. . . . . .

The German colonies hitherto existing were or are as follows (area in 1000 sq.km.):

		Population	
	Area	White	Coloured
East Africa	995	5,300	7,660,000
Kamerun	790	1,900	2,650,000
Togo	87	400	1,030,000
South West Africa	835	14,800	84,000
New Guinea	240	1,000	600,000 (?)
Caroline Islands, etc.	2.5	500	
Samoa	2.6	500	38,000
Kiantschou	0.6	4,500	190,000

Thus an area of about 3 mill. sq.km., white inhabitants only

STATISTICAL AND HISTORICAL

perhaps 30,000, coloured inhabitants something over 12 millions. The estimates of population fluctuate greatly.

Austria-Hungary has no colonies.

The colonial possessions of the European neighbouring countries are as follows:

Belgium possesses the Belgian Congo with an area of 2.4 million sq.km. and about 15 million inhabitants.

The Netherlands possess in the East Indies the large and small Sunda Islands with an area of almost 2 million sq.km. and about 38 million inhabitants; in addition smaller territories in the West Indies.

Denmark possesses the Faroe Islands, Greenland, West Indian islands. About 200,000 sq.km. of inhabitable country, 140,000 inhabitants.

Norway and Sweden possess no colonies, nor do Switzerland and the Balkan States.

. . . .

Numbers of populations for all the Central European territories between France and Italy on the one side and Russia on the other side (colonial populations not counted), 1910:

	Mill. inhab.
Germany	64.9
Austria-Hungary	51.4
Roumania	7.6
Belgium	7.5
Netherlands	6.2
Sweden	5.6
Serbia	4.5
Bulgaria	4.3
Greece	4.3
Switzerland	3.8
Denmark	2.8
Norway	2.4
Albania	0.8
Luxemburg	0.3
	166.4

Germany and Austria-Hungary together contain more than two-thirds of the whole number here considered. It lies outside any present consideration that all these States should ever belong to any sort of union, for there is not only their will to be independent, justified as it is by history, to take into account, but also their mutual antagonism.

. . . . . .

The following summaries will serve for the comparison of the four great world-group economic areas amongst which, under Mid-Europe, Germany and Austria-Hungary alone are included. Gr. = Greater Britain, wherein generally the whole wide international province is not considered, but still the greater part of it, that is in addition to the European Home Country also British India, New Zealand, and Australia. Canada and South Africa are wanting for various data. Rs. = Russia, and that unfortunately without the Asiatic portions, and occasionally without North Caucasia and Finland. The inequality of these statistics cannot be remedied even by the Statistical Offices themselves. Us. = the United States; Me. = Mid-Europe.

Uses made of Soil in millions of hectares

	Gr.	Rs.	Us.	Me.
Total area	760	516	770	116
Agriculturally used	146	210	194	67
Forest	50	108	220	33

Here Canada is missing, and its inclusion would noticeably increase the figures for the agricultural area and for forest in the case of Greater Britain.

Crops (1912–13) *in millions of tons*

	Gr.	Rs.	Us.	Me.
Wheat	20	23	21	11
Rye	—	25	1	16
Barley	3	12	4	8

Here Canada is counted in. The quantity of self-produced

STATISTICAL AND HISTORICAL

bread-corn is greater for Mid-Europe than for Greater Britain or for the United States.

Live Stock in millions of heads

	Gr.	Rs.	Us.	Me.
Horses	11	25	21	9
Cattle	149	37	57	36
Pigs	8	12	61	37
Sheep and goats	212	43	54	22

The figures for Greater Britain for cattle are explained by India, those for sheep by Australia.

Sugar Production in millions of tons

	Gr.	Rs.	Us.	Me.
Beet sugar	—	1.2	0.5	4.1
Cane sugar	2.9	—	0.5	—
	2.9	1.2	1.0	4.1

Here Mid-Europe rules the market.

Cotton Crop

Unfortunately data from Russia are lacking. Mid-Europe without colonies has no crop of its own. The world-crop for 1912–13 amounted to 27.2 million bales. Of these the United States yields 14.1 and Greater Britain 5.5.

Cotton Spindles

	Millions
Great Britain with India and Canada	63
United States	32
Mid-Europe	16
Russia	9
World's total	145

Mid-Europe's cotton manufacture ranks thirds in the world.

Coal and Lignite

Greater Britain, including Canada, India, Australia, South Africa and British Borneo, 307 million tons; Russia, including its Asiatic possessions, 31 million tons; the United States, 450 million tons; Mid-Europe, 307 million tons, exactly the same as Greater Britain. In addition the Mid-European coal-supplies are of greater future richness than those of Great Britain; it is true that in Greater Britain the share of pit coal is greater and that of lignite smaller.

Iron Ore and Pig-Iron in millions of tons

	Gr	Rs.	Us.	Me.
Iron ore	15	8	60	38
Pig-iron	10	4	30	20

Here the struggle between the United States and Mid-Europe is a future problem in international economics.

Owing to the dissimilarity in the materials all these summaries are uncertain in details, and are based for the most part on the groupings given in the appendix to the *Statistical Year Book* for the German Empire. We ought to learn from them to think in terms of great national economic quantities. So soon as we do this we arrive inevitably at the conclusion that even the combined quantities of Germany and Austria-Hungary are not, properly speaking, great for international economics, but yet they will form a very excellent basis for the effort and for the future of Mid-Europe.

VII. Tariff Problems

According to the statistics of the German Empire, goods of the following declared values have been imported and exported between Germany and Austria-Hungary during recent years.

German and Austro-Hungarian trade in millions of marks:

	From A.-H. to G.	From G. to A.-H.
1909	750	770
1910	760	820
1911	740	920

STATISTICAL AND HISTORICAL

	From A.-H. to G.	From G. to A.-H.
1912	830	1040
1913	830	1100

The tendency of the development is recognisable at once: Austria-Hungary uses its natural products itself to an increasing extent and cannot increase its industrial imports into Germany as much as the increase in the converse direction. Owing to this development the existing commercial treaty is regarded as unfavourable in Austria (-Hungary).

From the German point of view the increase in our exports to Austria-Hungary is not unusually high, for our exports have increased since 1907 in the following proportions, if the exportation for 1907 is expressed as 100.

Growth of German exports, 1907–1913:

To Great Britain	as 100	: 136
To France	as 100	: 176
To Russia	as 100	: 201
To the United States	as 100	: 109
To Austria-Hungary	as 100	: 154
On the average	as 100	: 155

German exports increased in value from 1909 to 1913 by 3.5 milliard marks. Of this immense increase 330 millions resulted from the exports to Austria-Hungary, or not quite a tenth part of our increase. German exports to Russia rose in the same period by 440 million marks, those to France by 330, likewise those to Great Britain by 420. A quite general emanation of economic vigour in Germany is in question, which is only felt more severely in Austria-Hungary because its own export trade is unable to keep pace.

The Russian imports to Germany during this same period rose and fell according to the results of the harvest, whereas Austria-Hungary, having little surplus crop to dispose of, could share but little in these lucky profits from the German years of scarcity.

German imports from Russia and Austria-Hungary, in million marks:

	From Rs.	From A.-H.
1909	1360	750
1910	1390	760
1911	1630	740
1912	1530	830
1913	1420	830

Since Russia has no more favourable a commercial treaty with Germany than has Austria-Hungary, it is evident that the commercial treaty is not responsible for the difference.

If we examine the individual items, Austrian imports to Germany have increased in the following principal articles: eggs, rough pinewood, calf-skins, hides, linen yarn, bed feathers, petroleum, beer, wood for wood pulp, apples, oil cakes, china, lubricating oil, skins, mine timber, etc. But the imports were decreasing or stationary in the following principal articles: lignite, oxen, sawn pinewood, malt, coal, hops, horses, cows, purple clover seed, hens, French beans, bran, etc. In between there are fluctuating articles. In each individual case the decline may be due to very different causes, to tariff or climate or home demand, but careful reconsideration of the apparently regular occurrence leads back always to the fundamental fact that Austria-Hungary, owing to its too small average crop per acre in relation to its increasing home demand, is, except for forest products, ceasing to be an exporting agricultural country, without so far having the power to secure a corresponding sale on foreign markets by means of its own industries which are closely adapted to native products.

If we attempt to give some meaning to this same process with the help of the Austrian statistics, the impression strengthens that the demand for imports is growing more rapidly than the possibility of exports. The increase in importation swells disquietingly, whilst the exportation makes slower progress. Expressed in money, the adverse balance of trade in 1912 amounted to over 740 million kronen, a sum which is out of all proportion to the relations of Austria-Hungary to foreign countries in respect to capital.

According to the Austrian data the total Austro-Hungarian exportation for 1907 to 1912 has increased in all by 268 million kronen, or about by 100 : 110. The increase consists, if we compare these particular years, in petroleum, sugar, eggs, fats, wood and wooden wares, and also in horses, but not in cattle, scarcely in malt, little in linen and hemp goods, not at all in corn. Most industries gain access to foreign countries slowly and with difficulty.

Considering the state of affairs it is comprehensible if all tariff questions are treated with a certain timidity. It is obvious that a national economic system in the position and under the special pressure of the effects of the war will not embark on experiments which are still incalculable. We Germans of the Empire must understand this if we want to work together at all with the Austrians and Hungarians. But just on account of this position we assert that the change to better things cannot be brought about by a customs union alone. Austria-Hungary needs the increase in intensity and the international-political union with Germany, which has already experienced a development similar to that which Austria-Hungary is now going through, and that about forty years ago, when it was easier to convert oneself from an agricultural exporting country into an industrial exporting country with increased agricultural output at home.

VIII. Constitutional Problems

The German Imperial Constitution has the following preliminary stages:

(1) The Roman Imperial German nation, from the Peace of Westphalia in 1648 to the abdication of the Imperial crown in 1806, was a so-called State of States, that is a union of sovereign reigning princes with an Imperial Diet. This Imperial Diet consisted of the electoral council, the princes' council and the deputies (*Kollegium*) of the Imperial cities. The Emperor, although the Crown in reality devolved by inheritance, was elected after the ancient fashion. He summoned the Diet according to the constitution. But from 1663 onwards the Diet was permanently in

session at Regensburg. For religious affairs there was the *Corpus Catholicorum* and the *Corpus Evangelicorum*. An Imperial decree required the assent of all the corporate bodies summoned for the purpose and the Emperor's decree. The business carried on by deputations. The resolution of a deputation, if confirmed by the Emperor, had the force of an Imperial decree.

The system remained almost inoperative for joint legislation.

(2) The Confederation of the Rhine, 1806–13, arose in virtue of the transformation of the Imperial constitution by the conclusive resolution of the Imperial deputation in 1803 under French management. It included all Germany with the exception of Austria, Prussia on the right bank of the Elbe, the Swedish and Danish possessions and the Hansa towns. The Confederation took over the existing Imperial rights so far as the alterations were not expressly stated. The Diet of the Rhenish Confederation was to be summoned at Frankfurt-on-Main, but it never met.

(3) The German Confederation, 1815–48, was based on the Act of the German Confederation of the Vienna Congress. It included only those territories in Austria and Prussia which had earlier belonged to the Roman Empire of German nations, and in addition all the German moderate-sized and small States, even those which like Hanover and Schleswig-Holstein were united with sovereign States with extra-German rulers. The Confederation was, as Arndt expresses it in *Staatsrecht des Deutschen Reiches,* a "union according to international law of German sovereign princes and free towns." Its inner constitution was based on treaties, and it wished to appear as a politically united Power in its outward relations. Every extension of the Confederation's sphere of activity required the unanimity of the Diet meeting in Frankfurt-on-Main, owing to the adherence to the treaty system. This Diet was under the presidency of Austria, and consisted of representatives of the princes and States concerned. There was no special army of the Confederation, but only an obligation to keep contingents in readiness.

(4) The Revolution Parliament, 1848–50. The National Assembly met in Frankfurt-on-Main as a meeting to prepare the way

for a German Imperial Constitution, and passed a draft constitution, the principal parts of which were later adopted by Bismarck. This draft constitution altered nothing in the previous extent of the Empire, and thus included Austria and Prussia only to the extent of the old German constituent parts. In regard to polyglot State provinces it was resolved: " If a German province and a non-German province have the same sovereign, the German province shall have a separate constitution, Government and administration." Military power was declared to be completely an Imperial matter. Legal regulations, and legislation on economic or commercial matters may only be taken in hand by the Imperial authority in so far as the organs of the Empire determine on it. In this condition lies the essence of the federal State as opposed to the State confederation. Imperial laws take precedence of provincial laws. The Diet consists of a federal Chamber (*Staatenhaus*) and a popular Chamber (*Volkshaus*), of which the former corresponded, say, to the Diet of the German Confederation at Frankfurt-on-Main, the second was conceived somewhat like the later German Reichstag. The Imperial Crown was offered to the Prussian King by 290 votes to 248 abstentions. The whole scheme collapsed when this offer was refused.

(5) The German Confederation, 1850–66, is not distinguished in public law from the Confederation as hitherto existing, but, at its side, grows up the Customs Union founded by Prussia which, since about 1852, comprehended the territory of the later German Empire. In virtue of the Peace of Prague the Austrian Emperor acknowledges the dissolution of the existing confederation, and gives his consent to a German formation without the inclusion of the Austrian Imperial State.

(6) The North German Confederation, 1866–71, embraces North Germany up to the boundary of the Main. The constitution is the same as the present Imperial constitution in all essential parts. The King of Prussia is hereditary President, and has executive power. Legislative power rests with the Bundesrat and Reichstag. The Bundesrat is formed in Berlin on the plan of the Frankfurt example. Alongside of the North German Reichstag

there is the Customs Parliament in which representatives of South Germany take part. The North German Confederation is a federal State, for it has its own legislative powers.

(7) The German Empire from 1871 onwards is an extension of the North German Confederation by the accession of the South German States and by the inclusion of the Customs Union in the confederate organisation. The Prussian King bears the title of German Emperor. Special agreements are in force with Bavaria and Württemberg, of the military part of which we have already spoken in the text of our book. The Imperial organs of government are the Emperor, the Bundesrat and the Reichstag.

The Emperor is General and President of the Confederation, as King of Prussia he instructs the Prussian delegation in the Bundesrat, and appoints and removes from office the Imperial Chancellor. Since the foundation of the Empire his position has on the whole gained in importance as the Imperial activities have increased.

There are sixty-one votes in the Bundesrat, of which Prussia has only seventeen. But in addition Prussia has the right in respect to military, customs and taxation questions to prevent any alteration by her adverse vote alone. Decisions by a majority vote very seldom occur. The Bundesrat has in fact become a permanent representative body which issues proposals for laws as well as regulations for their enforcement. Constitutionally the Bundesrat gives instructions to the Imperial Departments subordinate to the Imperial Chancellor, but in reality the actual initiative often rests with these Departments. The Imperial Departments are: the Foreign Office, the Imperial Home Office, the Admiralty, the Imperial Department of Justice, the Imperial Treasury Department, the Imperial Railway Bureau, the Imperial Colonial Office, etc. There is no Imperial War Office since there still exist Prussian, Bavarian and Württembergish armies. In reality the Prussian Minister of War is almost the same as an Imperial Minister of War.

The Reichstag results from direct election and has nothing to do with delegations from other representative bodies. It is the surest evidence of the existence of Imperial citizenship rights. It contains 397 deputies. The consent of the Reichstag is necessary in order to suspend or alter any Imperial law, and schemes for home finance and loans are counted as laws for this purpose.

This superstructure formed of Emperor, Bundesrat and Reichstag has produced a thoroughly individual and satisfactory political life for the German Empire. Demands for alterations refer rather to the often very antiquated constitutions of the separate States than to the Imperial constitution.

. . . . . .

The Austro-Hungarian Constitution is not a uniform State constitution in the same sense as the German Imperial Constitution. Its older stages are, in respect to the German Austrian Crown lands, the same as those of the German Empire. But the homogeneity of Austria-Hungary is expressed in principle in the Pragmatic Sanction of the Emperor Karl V. in 1713, wherein all the sectional possessions of the whole monarchy bound themselves to the same order of succession and thus to permanent association. The unity of the State is from the outset monarchical. The title of Emperor of Austria dates from 1804.

The constitution of the centralised State was legally formed by the Imperial Diploma of 1860 and the Patent of 1861, depending on it. This constitution comprises a Landtag and Reichsrat with almost the same principle of division as in the German Imperial draft constitution of 1848, except that there is only the one sovereign in question throughout. A distinction is also made in this Act of the Constitution between the countries belonging to the Hungarian Crown and those of the Austrian section, but the preponderating intention is centralisation.

The decisive year for the constitution of the Austro-Hungarian Monarchy is that of 1867, the year of the political separation and peaceable union between Austria and Hungary.

The legal independence and territorial integrity of Hungary and its neighbouring countries is solemnly declared by the oath of the sovereign. In this the older Hungarian constitutions are recurred to, and especially the revolutionary legislation of 1848.

By this act of separation two States, themselves divided several times, arose with foundation and superstructure, each of which already has an imperial constitution superior to its provincial constitutions, but which have the same monarch, and hence carry on certain joint institutions either naturally or by means of a treaty. The principal concerns of the united State are: the joint Ministry for Foreign Affairs, the Imperial Ministry for War for all matters relating to the joint army and the navy (the Landwehr on both sides being still maintained), the joint Ministry for Finance for joint expenses, whilst the financial systems are separate, a joint administration for Bosnia and Herzegovina. The preliminary estimate for joint expenses is presented to a meeting of the Delegations for deliberation (and to be passed), which meeting consists of deputations from the parliaments of both sides.

Germans of the Empire frequently compare the sessions of the Delegations with the German Reichstag, but this is a mistake. Each half of the Empire sends sixty representatives, one-third of whom are chosen from the House of Lords (*Herrenhaus*) or Table of Magnates respectively. The sessions are public and not joint, since each Delegation discusses in its native language. The intercourse between the Delegations is in writing. Differences of opinion, if written communications have been exchanged three times without agreement resulting, are settled in a joint full session by voting without debate. The speech from the throne is given twice, in German and Magyar. It is obvious that this machinery is not formed to produce joint political feelings, but that, on the contrary, it is arranged to settle the necessary joint business with the least conceivable mutual contact.

The agreements at present valid between Austria and Hungary date from December, 1907, and last till December 31, 1917. They include the determination of the contribution obligatory on both sides (*Beitragspflicht*) and the customs and commercial treaty. The collection and administration of the customs is still left, within the frontiers of the States in question, to the Governments of the two parties concluding the treaty. Inspectors are appointed by both sides for the mutual supervision of the customs administration, and they have the right to examine the business routine in the said administration in the other State. There is a Court of Arbitration for disputed questions.

Bosnia and Herzegovina were taken into the joint customs union in 1879. In this respect nothing was altered by the declaration of the hereditary sovereignty of the Imperial house in 1908. The administration there is inspected by Austria and by Hungary.

Central European treaties are prepared by the joint Foreign Office, but must be passed by the separate national representative bodies. Hence it is true to say: we do not know exactly whether we have to deal with one or with two States.

CHAPTER X

BIBLIOGRAPHY

IN the following pages books and pamphlets are mentioned from which Austrians and Hungarians can learn to know the policy of the German Empire, and the Germans of the Empire can learn to know that of Austria-Hungary. The list of Austro-Hungarian literature is borrowed from Richard Charmatz, the author of the *Wegweiser durch die Literatur der österreichischen Geschichte* (Stuttgart, Cotta, 1912), and is published in the *Hilfe* (No. 23, 1915). The list for the German Empire has been compiled for the purpose by a group of competent men and women as an aid to a Central European *rapprochement*. In both cases many books have of course been omitted which might equally well have been included. The choice made in particular cases may always be called in question, since the value of a book always differs according to the reader's taste and type of education, and since in various places writings of lesser merit must be mentioned because no better ones existed or were known. The few notes interspersed are borrowed from Herr R. Charmatz in the case of the Austro-Hungarian list, and are by me in the case of the German list. They are only intended to give hints as to the use of the books.

Austro-Hungarian Literature

For those who cannot devote too much time to the study of Austria-Hungary we must first mention the most important books and those writings which give a survey. The following, especially, will facilitate a knowledge of the events in the nineteenth century:

BIBLIOGRAPHY

Anton Springer, *Geschichte Österreichs seit dem Weiner Frieden,* 1809, 2 vols., Leipzig, 1863 and 1865. (Goes down to 1849.)

Heinrich Friedjung, *Der Kampf um die Vorherrschaft in Deutschland,* 1859–1866, 2 vols., 9th edition. Cotta, Stuttgart. (A monumental Austrian work.)

Heinrich Friedjung, *Österreich von* 1848–1860. Hitherto 2 vols., several editions. Cotta, Stuttgart. (Very arresting and informative.)

Two books published in the collection *Aus Natur und Geisteswelt* supply a brief survey:

Richard Charmatz, *Geschichte der auswärtigen Politik Österreichs im* 19. *Jahrhundert,* 2 vols. Leipzig.

Richard Charmatz, *Österreichs innere Geschichte von* 1848 *bis* 1907, 2 vols., 2nd edition. Leipzig.

The following are mentioned for an explanation of foreign policy:

Heinrich Friedjung, *Der Krimkreig und die österreichische Politik,* 2nd edition. Cotta, Stuttgart.

Eduard von Wertheimer, *Graf Julius Andrassy, Sein Leben und seine Zeit,* 3 vols. Stuttgart, 1913. (Also of importance for Hungarian home policy.)

Theodor von Sosnosky, *Die Balkanpolitik Österreich-Ungarns seit* 1866, 2 vols. Stuttgart, 1913 and 1914.

For an understanding of the political tendencies and national theories the following books are useful:

Rudolf Springer, *Grundlagen und Entwicklungziele der österreichisch-ungarischen Monarchie.* Vienna, 1906. (An excellent book.)

Rudolf Springer, *Der Kampf der österreichischen Nationen um den Staat,* Part I. Vienna, 1902.

Otto Bauer, *Die Nationalitätenfrage und die Sozialdemocratie.*
Vienna, 1907. (Later a popular edition also. Much historical material.)
Aurel C. Popovici, *Die Vereinigten Staaten von Grosz-Österreich.*
Leipzig, 1906.
Paul Samassa, *Die Völkerstreit im Habsburger Staat.* Leipzig, 1910.

In addition these older books:

Paul Dehn, *Deutschland nach Osten,* vols. 2 and 3; *Österreich-Ungarn in reichsdeutschem Licht,* 2 parts. Munich, 1888 and 1890.
Adolf Fischhof, *Österreich und die Bürgschaften seines Bestandes.*
Vienna, 1869.
Joseph Freiherr von Cötvös, *Die Nationalitätenfrage.* Budapest, 1865.

Finally:

Richard Charmatz, *Deutsch-österreichische Politik. Studien über den Liberalismus und über die auswärtige Politik.* Leipzig, 1907.

On the constitution and constitutional history:

Alfons Huber, *Österreichische Reichsgeschichte.* Vienna, 1895.
Ludwig Gumplowicz, *Das österreichische Staatsrecht,* 3rd edition. Vienna, 1907.
Heinrich Rauchberg, *Österreichische Bürgerkunde.* Vienna, published by Tempsky.

Statistical:

A. L. Hickman, *Geographisch-statistischer Taschenatlas von Österreich-Ungarn.* Vienna, publisher, Freytag.

BIBLIOGRAPHY

Österreichisches statistisches Handbuch. Issued by the Central Imperial Statistical Commission (1 vol. annually). Vienna, published by Gerold.

. . . .

Some works are now mentioned which treat of longer periods of time or of individual persons, and which will serve to deepen preliminary knowledge. Among general accounts of Austrian history the following may be noticed:

Franz Martin Mayer, *Geschichte Österreichs mit besonderer Rücksicht auf das Kulturleben,* 2 vols., 3rd edition. Vienna, 1909. (Good comprehensive account.)

Richard Kralik, *Österreichische Geschichte,* 3rd edition. Vienna, 1914. (Clerical conservative view of events.)

In addition:

Franz Krones, *Geschichte der Neuzeit Österreichs vom 18. Jahrhundert bis auf die Gegenwart.* Berlin 1879. (Also vol. iv. of the same author's *Handbuch der Geschichte Österreichs.*)

H. von Zwiedineck-Südenhorst, *Deutsche Geschichte von der Auflösung des alten bis zur Errichtung des neuen Kaiserreiches* (1806-1871), 3 vols. Cotta, Stuttgart, 1897, 1903, 1905.

For Hungary:

Michael Horvath, *Kurzgefaszte Geschichte Ungarns,* 2 vols. Budapest, 1863. (Goes down to 1848.)

Eugen Csuday, *Die Geschichte der Ungarn,* 2 vols. Vienna, 1898.

Further:

Michael Horvath, *Geschichte des Unabhängigkeitskrieges im Ungarn,* 1848-1849, 3 vols., 2nd edition. Budapest, 1872.

Michael Horvath, 25 *Jahre aus der Geschichte Ungarns,* 1825-1848, 2 vols. Leipzig, 1867.

Heinrich Marczali, *Ungarische Verfassungsgeschichte*. Tübingen, 1910.
Joseph von Jekelfalussy, *Der tausendjährige ungarische Staat und sein Volk*. Issued by order of the Hungarian Ministry of Commerce. Budapest, 1896.

Detached periods of time:
Adam Wolf and Hans von Zwiedineck-Südenhorst, *Österreich unter Maria Theresa, Josef II. und Leopold II.* (From Oucken, *Augemeine Geschichte in Einszeldarstellungen.* Berlin, 1884.)
H. von Zwiedineck-Südenhorst, *Maria Theresa (Monographien zur Weltgeschichte)*. Velhagen and Klasing.
Johann Wendrinsky, *Kaiser Josef II*. Vienna, 1880.
A. Dove, *Ausgewählte Schriften*. Leipzig, 1898. (Contains memoirs on Maria Theresa and Kaunitz.)
August Fournier, *Historische Studien und Skizzen*, 3 vols. Prague, 1885; Vienna, 1908 and 1912. (Many contributions relating to the times of Maria Theresa, Josef II., Napoleon and Metternich.)
Eduard Wertheimer, *Geschichte Österreichs und Ungarns im ersten Jahrzehnt des 19. Jahrhunderts*, 2 vols. Leipzig, 1884 and 1890.
Ernst Viktor Zenker, *Die Wiener Revolution 1848 im ihren sozialen Voraussetzungen und Beziehungen*. Vienna, 1897.
Maximilian Bach, *Geschichte der Weiner Revolution im Jahre 1848*. Vienna, 1898. (Social Democratic point of view.)
Joseph Alexander Freiherr von Helfert, *Geschichte der österreichischen Revolution im Zusammenhange mit der mitteleuropäischen Bewegung*, 2 vols. Freiburg in Breisgau, 1907 and 1908. (Goes down to June, 1848. Conservative point of view.)
Friedrich Schütz, *Werden und Wirken des Bürgerministeriums.* Leipzig, 1909. (Feuilletons.)
Walter Rogge, *Österreich von Vilagos bis zur Gegenwart*, 3 vols. Leipzig, 1872, 1873.

BIBLIOGRAPHY

Walter Rogge, *Österreich seit der Katastrophe Hohenwart-Beust*, 2 vols. Leipzig, 1879. (Rogge's books are badly arranged and full of prejudice.)
Gustav Kolmer, *Parlament und Verfassung in Österreich*, 8 vols. Vienna, 1902–14. (Covers the years 1861–1904.)

The following give information about civilisation and social life:

Gustav Strakosch-Grassmann, *Geschichte des österreichischen Unterrichtswesens*. Vienna, 1905.
Ludwig Hevesi, *Österreichische Kunst im 19. Jahrhundert*, 2 parts. Leipzig, 1903. (From *Geschichte der modernen Kunst*.)
J. W. Nagl and J. Zeidler, *Deutsch-österreichische Literaturgeschichte*, 2 vols. Vienna, 1896–1915.
K. Grünberg, *Die Bauernbefreiung und die Auflösung des Gutsherrlich-bäuerlichen Verhältnisses in Böhmen, Mähren und Schlesien*, 2 parts. Leipzig, 1894.
Heinrich Waentig, *Gewerbliche Mittelstandspolitik*. Leipzig, 1898. (Based on Austrian sources.)
Julius Deutsch, *Geschichte der österreichischen Gewerkschaftsbewegung*. Vienna, 1908.
Georg Loesche, *Geschichte des Protestantismus in Österreich*. Tubingen, 1902. (This excellent little booklet gives a bibliography at the end for the important period of the Reformation and Counter-Reformation.)
Georg Loesche, *Von der Toleranz zur Parität in Österreich, 1781–1861*. Leipzig, 1911.

For commercial policy the following must be mentioned:

Adolf Beer, *Die österreichische Handelspolitik im 19. Jahrhundert*. Vienna, 1891.
Ludwig Lang, *Hundert Jahre Zollpolitik 1805–1905*. Translated from the Magyar. Vienna, 1906.

. . . .

Biographies or memoirs of the most important personalities are given in alphabetic order; some knowledge of the history will make it possible to understand the volumes which come under consideration for special departments of interest.

Friedrich Ferdinand Graf von Beust, *Aus drei Viertel-Jahr-hunterten.* 1866 bis 1885, vol. ii. Stuttgart, 1887.

Oskar Criste, *Das Buch vom Erzherzog Carl.* Vienna, 1914 (Popular abridgment of the big three-volume biography.)

Gustav Steinbach, *Franz Deak, Eine Biographie.* Published by Manz, Vienna, 1888.

Karl Ritter von Landmann, *Prinz Eugen von Savoyen.* (From *Weltgeschichte in Characterbildern*). Munich, 1905.

Heinrich von Sybel, *Prince Eugen.* Munich, 1861.

Richard Charmatz, *Adolf Fischof.* Cotta, Stuttgart, 1910.

Arthur Görgei, *Mein Leben und Wirken in Ungarn in dem Jahren 1848 und 1849*, 2 vols. Leipzig, 1852.

F. von Krones, *Moritz von Kaiserfeld.* Leipzig, 1888.

Ludwig Kossuth, *Meine Schriften aus der Emigration,* 3 vols. Pressburg, 1880 and 1882.

K. Th. Heigel, *Essays aus neuerer Geschichte.* Bamberg, 1892. (Essays about Metternich.)

Aus Metternichs nachgelassenen Papieren. Edited by Prince Richard Metternich-Winneburg. Vienna, 1880. (Vol i. of this four-volumed work contains the autobiographical notes of the Chancellor of State.)

Feldmarschall Graf Radetzky, Eine biographische Skizze nach den eigenen Dikaten. By an Austrian Veteran. Cotta, Stuttgart, 1858.

C. Wolfsgruber, *Joseph Othmar Kardinal Rauscher.* Freiburg in Breisgau, 1888.

Albert Eberhard Friedrich Schäffle, *Aus meinem Leben,* 2 vols. Berlin, 1905.

Hugo Kerchnawe and Alois Veltzé, *Feldmarschall Karl Fürst zu Schwarzenberg.* Vienna, 1913.

A. F. Berger, *Felix Fürst zu Schwarzenberg, k.k. Ministerpräsident.* Leipzig, 1853.

BIBLIOGRAPHY

Adolf Beer, *Aus Wilhelm von Tegetthoffs Nachlasz.* Vienna, 1882.

L. von Ranke, *Geschichte Wallensteins.* Leipzig, several editions.

. . . . . .

The relations of individual nations to each other and to the State are of the greatest importance. Although the pamphlet literature is so extensive there is yet a lack of comprehensive single presentations giving full information.

First of all we may perhaps refer to the compilation:
Die Völker Österreich-Ungarns, Ethnographische und kulturhistorische Schilderungen, 12 vols. Vienna, 1881, etc. (Special portions of it are quite applicable even to-day.)

Further may be mentioned:

Ludwig Schlesinger, *Geschichte Böhmens,* 2nd edition. Prague, 1870. (A detailed account only up to the end of the eighteenth century.)

Teutsch, G. D., *Geschichte der Siebenbürger Sachsen,* 2 vols., 3rd edition. Kronstadt, 1899. (The third volume is a continuation by Fr. Teutsch up to 1815. Kronstadt, 1910.)

Raimund Fr. Kaindl, *Geschichte der Deutschen in Ungarn.* Gotha, 1912.

Alfred von Skene, *Entstehen und Entwickelung der slawisch-nationalen Bewegung in Böhmen und Mähren in 19. Jahrhundert.* Vienna, 1893.

Wilhelm Kosch, *Die Deutschen in Österreich und ihr Ausgleich mit den Tschen.* Leipzig, 1909.

Max Menger, *Der böhmische Ausgleich.* Stuttgart, 1891.

Karl Türk, *Böhmen, Mähren und Schlesien.* (From the collection: *Der Kamf um das Deutschtum.*) Munich, 1898.

Heinrich Rauchberg, *Die Bedeutung der Deutschen in Österreich.* (From *Neue Zeit-und Streitfragen.*) Dresden, 1908.

R. W. Seton-Watson (Scotus Viator), *Die südslavische Frage im Habsburger Reiche.* Berlin, 1913.

Herm. Jg. Bidermann, *Die Italiener im Tiroler Provinzialverbande*. Innsbruck, 1874.
Gregor Kupzanko, *Das Schicksal der Ruthenen*. Leipzig, 1887.
Roman Sembratowycz, *Polonia inedenta*. Frankfurt-on-Main, 1907.

In addition the collection of material:
Alfred Fischer, *Das österreichische Sprachenrecht*, 2nd edition. Brünn. Published by Irrgang.

LITERATURE FOR THE GERMAN EMPIRE

We leave aside intentionally the older German histories and hence pass over the great works of Ranke, Raumer, Giesebrecht, Ritsch, Häusser, Schlosser, Lamprecht and others. Similarly we pass over also the political dictionaries and almost all properly specialist literature.

The previous history and the history of the German Empire is not to be found complete in any single book, since the greatest historical works of modern times are those that deal only with sections of the subject. We may consider the following as complete accounts:

Heinrich v. Treitschke, *Deutsche Geschichte im 19. Jahrhundert*, 5 vols. Leipzig, 1908–13, S. Hirzel. (The chief work on the preparatory period; goes down to 1848.)
Br. Gebhardt, *Handbuch der deutschen Geschichte*, 2 vols., 5th edition. Stuttgart, 1913, Union, Deutsche Verlagsgesellschaft.
D. Schäfer, *Deutsche Geschichte*, 2 vols., 4th edition. Jena, 1914, S. Fischer. (International politics.)
G. Egelhaaf, *Geschichte der neuesten Zeit vom Frankfurter Frieden bis zur Gegenwart*, 5th edition. Stuttgart, 1915, C. Krabbe. (Much intelligible detailed material.)
G. Kaufmann, *Politische Geschichte Deutschlands im 19. Jahrhundert*. Berlin, 1912, G. Bondi. (National and liberal.)

BIBLIOGRAPHY

R. Schwemer, *Vom Bund zum Reich*, 2nd edition. Leipzig, 1912. B. G. Teubner. (*Aus Natur und Geisteswelt*, vol. 102.)

Schulthess, *Europäischer Geschichtskalender*. Munich, C. H. Beck.

Wippermann, *Deutscher Geschichtskalender*. Leipzig, Felix Meiner.

Dahlmann-Waitz, *Quellenkunde der deutschen Geschichte*, 8th edition. Leipzig, 1912, F. K. Koehler.

Statistiches Jahrbuch für das Deutsche Reich. Issued by the Imperial Department of Statistics. Berlin, Puttkammer and Mühlbrecht. (The most interesting book about Germany.)

The following relate to the previous history of the foundation of the Empire:

Die Befreiung 1813, 1814, 1815. *Urkunden, Berichte und Briefe.* Düsseldorf-Ebenhausen, W. Langewiesche. (Clear, popular.)

1848, *Der Vorkampf deutscher Einheit und Freiheit. Urkunden, Berichte und Briefe.* Düsseldorf-Ebenhausen, W. Langewiesche. (The same.)

G. Mollat, *Reden und Redner des ersten Deutschen Parlaments.* Osterwieck, 1895, A. W. Zickfeld. (Good introduction into the spirit of 1848.)

Fr. Meinecke, *Weltbürgertum und Nationalstaat,* 2nd edition. Munich, 1911. R. Oldenbourg. (Very valuable for the distinction between the "Greater Germany" and the "Lesser Germany" parties.)

W. Maurenbrecher, *Gründung des Deutschen Reiches* 1859–1871, 4th edition. Leipzig, 1910, C. C. M. Pfeffer.

H. v. Sybel, *Begründing des Deutschen Reiches durch Wilhelm I.* Popular edition, 7 vols., 3rd edition. Munich, 1913. R. Oldenbourg. (The chief book for the Bismarckian period. Rather lengthy.)

The literature relating to Bismarck is very extensive. We mention only the principal works:

CENTRAL EUROPE

Gedanken und Erinnerungen, edited by H. Kohl, popular edition, 2 vols. Stuttgart, 1915, Cotta Nachf. New large octavo edition, 2 vols. (The vital book for German politics.)

Bismarck's Gesammelte Reden mit verbindlich Geschichtlichen Darstellungen, by Ph. Stein, 13 *vols.* Leipzig, 1895–99, Ph. Reclam.

Heinr. v. Poschinger, *Preussen im Bundestag* 1851–1859. Documents of the Royal Prussian Bundestag-Gesandschaft, edited by H. Poschinger, 4 parts, 2nd edition. Leipzig, 1882–84, S. Hirzel. (Poschinger's other collections also come under consideration.)

Heinr. Friedjung, *Der Kampf um die Vorherrschaft in Deutschland,* 1859–1866, 2 vols., 9th edition. Stuttgart, 1912 and 1913, Cotta Nachf. (This brilliant Austrian work relates also to the history of the German Empire.)

For the post-Bismarckian period the following may be mentioned:

Karl Lamprecht, *Deutsche Geschichte der jungsten Vergangenheit und Gegenwart,* vols. i. and ii. *Geschichte der wirthschaftlichen und sozialen Entwicklung in den 70er–90er jahren des 19. Jahrhunderts, Geschichte der inneren und äusseren Politik in den 70–90 Jahren des 19. Jahrhunderts,* 5th edition. Berlin, 1912 and 1915, Weidmann.

Fürst Hohenlohe-Schillingsfürst, *Denkwürdigkeiten,* edited by Fr. Curtius under the direction of Prince Al. zu Hohenlohe-Schillingsfürst, 2 vols. Stuttgart, 1906. Deutsche Verlagsanstalt, 2 vols., cheap edition, 1914. (Recollections of the third Imperial Chancellor.)

Fürst Bülow, *Reden,* 4 vols. Leipzig, 1914, Ph. Reclam. (Quite interesting as supplementary reading.)

Deutschland unter Kaiser Wilhelm II., 3 vols. Berlin, 1914, Reimar Hobbing. (A many-sided compilation.)

BIBLIOGRAPHY

Imperial constitution and administration, statistical:

Graf Hue de Grais, *Handbuch der Verfassung und Verwaltung in Preussen und des Deutschen Reiches,* 22nd edition. Berlin, 1914, Springer. (Practical, a much used hand-book.)

P. Laband, *Deutsches Reichstaatsrecht,* 6th edition. (Collection: *Das öffentl. Recht der Gegenwart.*) Tübingen, 1912, J. C. B. Mohr.

C. Loening, *Reichsverfassung,* 4th edition. (Collection: *Aus Natur und Geisteswelt,* vol. 34.) Leipzig, 1913, B. G. Teubner.

Der deutsche Staatsbürger, 2nd edition. Leipzig, 1912, C. E. Poeschel. (Easily understood civic information.)

. . . .

Only a scanty selection can be offered in regard to the federated States of the German Empire. For Prussia:

W. Pierson, *Preussiche Geschichte,* 2 vols., 10th edition. Berlin, 1910, Gebr. Paetel.

O. Hintze, *Die Hohenzollern und ihr Werk, 500 Jahre vaterländischer Geschichte.* Berlin, 1915, P. Parey.

Gerh. Anschütz, *Die Verfassungsurkunde für den Preuss. Staat,* 2 vols. Berlin, 1912, O. Häring. (Detailed commentary.)

A. Arndt, *Die Verfassungs-Urkunde für den Preussischen Staat,* 7th edition. Berlin, 1911, J. Guttentag. (With short explanations.)

C. Bornhak, *Grundriss des Verwaltungsrechts in Preussen,* 4th edition. Leipzig, 1912, Deichert Nachf.

Statisches Jahrbuch des Preussischen Staates, issued by the Prussian Royal Statistical Department, Berlin.

To the Prussian books we add some German Imperial Polish literature:

Ludwig Bernhard, *Die Polenfrage, Das polnische Gemeinwesen im Preuss. Staat.* 2nd edition. Munich, Leipzig, 1910. Duncker and Humblot. (Impressive essays.)

Gg. Cleinow, *Die Zukunft Polens,* vol. i. *Wirthschaft,* vol. ii. *Politik.* Leipzig, 1908 and 1914, Fr. W. Grunow. (Much material, poorly arranged.)

Die Deutsche Ostmark, issued by the Deutschen Ostmarkenverein. Lissa, 1913, O. Eulitz. (Polemical writing against Poland.)

C. Brandenburger, *Polnische Geschichte.* Leipzig, Göschen. (Göschen Collection, 338.)

For the constitution and situation in the larger federated States the following are instructive:

F. Stoerk and F. W. Rauchhaupt, *Handbuch der deutschen Verfassungen,* 2nd edition. Leipzig, 1913, Duncker and Humblot. (Gives the constitutions of all the individual States.)

Karl Braun, *Aus der deutschen Kleinstaaterei, Randglossen zu den politischen Wandlungen der letzten Jahre. Aus den Papieren eines deutschen Abgeordneten.* Bromberg, 1878. (Cheerful, interesting reminiscences.)

C. Brandenburger, *Der Eintritt der süddeutschen Staaten in den Norddeutschen Bund.* Berlin, 1910, Gebr. Paetel.

H. Ockel, *Bayerische Geschichte.* Leipzig, Göschen. (Göschen Collection, 160.)

Th. Flathe, *Geschichte des Kurstaates und Königreichs Sachsen,* 3 vols., 2nd edition. Gotha, 1867–1873, Fr. A. Perthes.

O. Kämmel, *Sachsens Geschichte.* Leipzig, Göschen. (Göschen Collection, 100.)

K. Weller, *Württembergs Geschichte.* Leipzig, Göschen. (Göschen Collection, 462.)

A. Dove, *Grossherzog Friedrich von Baden als Landesherr und deutscher Fürst.* Heidelberg, 1902, C. Winter.

. . . .

In passing to domestic politics we shall first notice the handbooks of the parties and political groups.

Konservatives Handbuch. Berlin, 1911, R. Hobbing.
Politisch-soziales A.B.C. Handbuch für die Mitglieder der Zentrumspartei. Stuttgart, 1900, Süddeutsche Verlagsbuchhandlung.
Agarisches Handbuch. Berlin, 1911, Farmers' Union. (Chief source of information for the agrarian movement.)
Politisches Handbuch der Nationalliberalen Partei. Berlin, 1914. Published by the National Liberal Party. (Comprehensive.)
Eugen Richter, *Politisches A.B.C.* (Out of print. The best of the older handbooks.)
Martin Wenck, *Handbuch für liberale Politik.* Berlin-Schöneberg, 1911, *Fortschritt* (publishers of the *Hilfe*).
G. Gothein, *Agrarpolitisches Handbuch.* Berlin, 1910, Liebheit and Thiessen. (Free Trade liberal, full of significance.)
Handbuch für sozialdem. Landtagswähler. Berlin, 1913. Publishers, *Vorwärts*.
Handbuch des alldeutschen Verbandes, 18th edition. Munich, 1915, Lehmann.

For the history of parties:

Friedrich Naumann, *Die politischen Parteien in Deutschland.* Berlin, 1911, Georg Reimer. (Figures out of date.)
F. Salomon, *Deutsche Parteiprogramme,* 2nd edition, vol. i. from 1844–1871, vol. ii. from 1871–1890. Leipzig, B. G. Teubner.
Oskar Klein-Hattingen, *Geschichte des deutschen Liberalismus,* cheap edition, 2 vols. Berlin-Schöneberg, 1912. Publishers of the *Hilfe*. (Abundant historical material.)
Oskar Stillich, *Die politischen Parteien in Deutschland,* 2 vols. Vol i., *Die Konservativen;* vol. ii., *Der Liberalismus.* Leipzig, 1908 and 1911, Klinkhardt.
F. Mehring, *Geschichte der deutschen Sozialdemokratie,* 4 vols., 4th edition. Stuttgart, 1909, Dietz Nachf. (Partisan, but clever.)
Werner Sombart, *Sozialismus und soziale Bewegung in* 19. Jahr-

hundert. Jena, 1908, G. Fischer. (Excellent introduction.)

Hugo Preusz, *Das deutsche Volk und die Politik.* Jena, 1915, C. Diederichs. (Polit. Bibl.) Valuable contemporary book of liberal politics.)

For special departments:

August Pfannkuche, *Staat und Kirche.* Leipzig, 1915, B. G. Teubner.
W. v. Lexis, *Das Unterrichtswesen im Deutschen Reich,* 4 vols. Berlin, 1904, Behrend and Co.
Gertrud Bäumer, *Die Frau im Volkswirthschaft und Staatsleben der Gegenwart.* Stuttgart, 1914, Deutsche Verlagsanstalt. (Complete summary of the German femininist movement.)

Important books giving summaries on foreign politics, the army and the navy:

Count von Reventlow, *Deutschlands auswärtige Politik 1888–1913,* 2nd edition. Berlin, 1914, C. S. Mittler and Son. (An important book of the chronicle type.)
Paul Rohrbach, *Deutschland unter den Weltvölkern,* 4th edition. Stuttgart, 1912. J. Engelhorns Nachf. (Thoughtful introduction to foreign politics.)
E. Zimmermann, *Unsere Kolonien.* Berlin, 1914, Ullstein and Co.
A. v. Löbell, *Das deutsche Heer.* Stuttgart, Greiner and Pfeiffer. (*Bücher des Wissens,* vol. 92.)
Nauticus, *Jahrbuch für Deutschlands Seeinteressen.* Berlin, E. S. Mittler and Son.

General economic policy is dealt with to suit the needs of political readers in:

Friedrich Naumann, *Neudeutsche Wirthschaftspolitik,* 3rd edition. Berlin, 1911, Georg Reimer.
Werner Sombart, *Die deutsche Volkswirthschaft des 19. Jahr-*

BIBLIOGRAPHY

hunderts, 2nd edition. Berlin, 1909, Georg Bondi. Popular edition, 1913.

Commercial policy:

W. Lotz, *Ideen der deutschen Handelspolitik 1860–1891*. Leipzig, 1892, Verein für Sozialpolitik.
Richard Calwer, *Jahrbuch der Weltwirtschaft*. Jena, G. Fischer.
Lusensky, *Einführung in die deutsche Zoll-und Handels-politik*. Hanover, 1913, Helwing. (Important for the preliminary work for commercial treaties.)

Agrarian policy:

A. Buchenberger, *Grundzüge der deutschen Agrarpolitik*, 2nd edition. Berlin, 1899, P. Parey.
Th. von der Goltz, *Geschichte der deutschen Landwirtschaft*, vol. ii., *Das. 19. Jahrhundert*. Stuttgart, 1903, Cotta Nachf.
Die Deutsche Landwirtschaft, bearbeite v. Kaiserl. Statistischen Amt. Berlin, 1913, Pultkammer and Mühlbrecht. (The best contemporary summary.)

Industrial policy:

Hübener, *Die deutsche Eisenindustrie*. Leipzig, 1913, G. A. Glöckner. (*Handelschochschulbibl.*, vol. 14.)
Die Schwereisenindustrie im deutschen Zollgebiet, ihre Entwicklung und ihre Arbeiten. Stuttgart, 1912, A. Schlicke and Co.
A. Oppel, *Die deutsche Textilindustrie*. Leipzig, 1912, Duncker and Humblot.
F. Baumgarten and A. Meszlény, *Kartelle und Trusts*. Berlin, 1906, O. Liebmann.
Tschierschky, *Kartell und Trust*. Leipzig, B. G. Teubner. (*Aus Natur und Geisteswelt*, 522.)
P. Krusch, *Die Versorgung Deutschlands mit metallischen Rohstoffen*. Leipzig, 1913, Beit and Co.

C. Christiansen, *Chemische und Farbenindustrie*. Tübingen, 1914, J. C. B. Mohr.
M. Levy, *Die Organisation und Bedeutung der deutschen Elektrizitätsindustrie*. (Contained in special industrial reports, series 8.) Berlin, 1914, Georg Reimer.

Financial policy:

R. Helfferich, *Studien über Geld-und Bankwesen*. Berlin, 1900, J. Guttentag. (Out of print.)
R. Helfferich, *Deutschlands Volkswohlstand, 1888–1913*, 4th edition. Berlin, 1914, G. Stilke.
J. Riesser, *Von 1848 bis heute, Bank-und Wirthsch-Studie*. Popular edition of *Die deutschen Grossbanken und ihre Konzentration*. Jena, 1912, G. Fischer.

Social policy:

Leopold von Wiese, *Einführung in die Sozialpolitik*. Leipzig, 1910, G. Glöckner. (*Handelshochschulbibl.*, vol. 8.)
H. Jastrow, *Sozialpolitik und Verwaltungs-Wissenschaft*. Berlin, 1902, Georg Reimer. (Fundamental.)
Heinr. Herkner, *Die Arbeiterfrage*, 5th edition. Berlin, 1908, J. Guttentag. (Gives the history.)
A. Manes, *Sozialversicherung*. Berlin, G. J. Göschen. (Göschen Collection, 267.)

Of course this is only a very small selection from the abundance of national economic and socio-political literature.

· · · · · ·

We shall conclude, like our Austrian colleague, with a brief enumeration of biographies and memoirs, which are of importance for the political history:

R. Koser, *Geschichte Friedrichs des Grossen*, 3 vols., 4th and 5th edition. Stuttgart, 1912–13, Cotta Nachf. Popular edition, 6th and 8th edition, 1913. (Reputable standard work.)

BIBLIOGRAPHY 341

M. Lehmann, *Freiherr von Stein,* 3 vols. Leipzig, 1902–5, S. Hirzel (vol. i. out of print.)   (Inner history of the wars of liberation.)

H. Delbrück, *Das Leben des Feldmarschalls Grafen R. Gneisenau,* 2 vols. in one book. Berlin, 1908, G. Stilke.   (Military and contemporary history.)

J. R. Sepp, Görres. Berlin, 1896, E. Hofmann and Co. (*Geisteshelden,* vol. 23.)   (Catholic romanticist.)

Friedrich Meineike, *Radowitz und die deutsche Revolution.* Berlin, 1913, Mittler and Son.   (Important for 1848.)

L. Parisius, *Freiherr Leopold von Hoverbeck,* 2 vols. Berlin, 1900, J. Guttentag.   (About the older Prussian liberalism.)

Leopold von Gerlach, *Denkwürdigkeiten aus dem Leben,* 2 vols. Berlin, 1892.   (The older Conservative Berlin.)

Karl Jentsch, *Friedrich List.* Berlin, 1901, E. Hofmann and Co.   (The prophet of the eastward extension.)

A. Bergengrün, *David Hausemann.* Berlin, 1901.   (The rise of modern capitalism.)

H. Oncken, Lassalle. Stuttgart, 1904, Fr. Frommann.   (Beginnings of Social Democracy.)

R. Haym, *Das Leben Max Dunckers.* Berlin, 1891, R. Gaertner.   (Liberal developments.)

Briefe von und an Freiherr W. E. Ketteler, edited by J. M. Reich. Mainz, 1879, Kirchheim.   (Beginnings of the Centre.)

E. Marcks, *Kaiser Wilhelm I., Eine Biographie* 6–7 editions. Munich, 1910, Duncker and Humblot.   (Political history.)

Oskar Klein-Hattingen, *Bismarck und seine Welt,* 3 vols. Berlin, Dümmler.   (Critical liberal history of Bismarck.)

M. Lenz, *Geschichte Bismarcks,* 4th edition. Munich, 1914, Duncker and Humblot.

Veit Valentin, *Bismarck und seine Zeit.* Leipzig, 1915, B. G. Teubner.   (*Aus Natur und Geisteswelt,* vol. 500.)

von Blume, *Moltke.* Oldenburg, Gerh. Stalling.   (*Erzieher d. preusz. Heeres,* vol. 1.)

Ludwig Bamberger, *Erinnerungen,* edited by P. Nathan. Berlin, 1899, G. Reimer.   (Economic policy before 1866).

H. Oncken, *Bennigsen, Ein liberal nationaler Politiker,* 2 vols. Stuttgart, 1909 Deutsche Verlagsanstalt. (Rise of the National Liberal party.)

Ed. Hüsgen, *Ludwig Windthorst, Sein Leben, seine Zeit.* Illustrated popular edition, 7–16 thousand. Cologne, 1911, J. P. Bachem. (The leader of the Centre.)

D. v. Oertzen, *Stöcker, Lebensbild und Zeitgeschichte.* Popular edition. Schwerin, 1914, Fr. Bahn. (The Christian Socialist leader.)

Eugen Richter, *Im alter Reichstage, Erinnerungen,* 2 vols. Berlin, 1895 (out of print). (The progressive.)

August Bebel, *Aus meinem Leben,* 3 parts, 2nd edition. Stuttgart, 1911–14, Dietz Nachf. (The Social-Democrat.)

. . . . . .

With these memorials of notable men we conclude our work. They have done what they could. Let us do what we can and ought!

INDEX

AGADIR incident, 1911, 36
Agricultural output:
  Austria-Hungary, 134 *et seq.*
  Various States, table 299, 300
Alexander I. of Russia, 56
Alkali monopoly in Germany, 160
Andrassy, Count Julius, 30, 63, 64, 65, 98, 325
Anschütz, Gerhardt, 335
Anti-Semitism, 146
Army in Central Europe, effective force of, 285
Army legislation in Germany and Austria-Hungary, 274
Arndt, A., 47, 318, 335
Austria-Hungary:
  Agricultural output of, 134, 135, 300
  Ausgleich of 1867, 170 *et seq.*, 251, 266
  Balkan and Turkish interests, 197
  Bibliography on, 324
  Business spirit in, 129
  Central Europe, *see* that Title
  Constitution, historical account, 265, 321
  Economic post-war policy, 169
  Economic relations, statistics, 306, 307
  Educational influences, 132
  Emigration question, 131
  Foreign affairs, 277
  Germans in Austria, position of, 106
  Imports and exports, 314
  Labour reforms, 132, 133
  Magyar language, use of, 99
  Nationalities, method of handling, 33, 84
  Parliament not summoned in 1914, 107, 108
  Political pessimism, 35
  Population statistics, 285, 288
  Poverty in, 130, 131
  Public services, reform of, 133

Austria-Hungary (*continued*):
  Religious struggles from 1517, 75
  Social democracy in, 108, 109
  See also Germany and Austria-Hungary

BACH, Maximilian, 328
Bäumer, Gertrud, 338
Ballin, 127
Bamberger, Ludwig, 341
Barth, Theodor, 224
Bauer, Otto, 326
Baumgarten, F., 47, 339
Bavaria:
  Military affairs of, 274
  Union with North Germany, 144
Bebel, August, 127, 342
Beer, Adolf, 329, 331
Belgium:
  Agricultural statistics, 299
  Colonial possessions, 311
  Educational system, 297
  International trade, 303
  Joint-stock capital, 301
  Population statistics, 287, 311
  Trade-union membership, 298
Bergengrün, A., 341
Berger, A. F., 330
Berlin as the central money market for Mid-Europe, 261
Berlin Congress, 1878, 64
Bernhard, Ludwig, 335
Beust, Frederick F., Count von, 98, 330
Bibliography, 324
Bidermann, H. J., 332
Birth-rate in Central Europe, statistics, 287
Bismarck, 9, 17, 19, 28, 42, 43, 45, 48, 58, 59, 123, 127, 222, 265
  Austria-Hungary, Bismarck's policy, 22, 29, 60, 62
  "Thoughts and Recollections," 26, 47

Blockade by England, discussion of 149 et seq.
Blücher, 19
Blume, von, 341
Bornhak, C., 335
Bosnia and Herzegovina, 323
Brandenburger, C., 336
Braun, Karl, 336
Bretano, Luigi, 224
Bülow, Prince, 334
Buchenberger, H., 339
Business spirit in Germany and Austria, 127 et seq.

CALVIN, 75
Calwer, Richard, 339
Canisius, 76
Capitalism in England and Germany, 117
Cartels and federations in Germany, growth of, 120
Cattle and cattle products, German imports from Austria-Hungary, 227, 228
Central Industries Association, 145
Central Europe:
  Area, 200
  Citizen rights in, 255
  Community of life, necessity of, 37 et seq.
  Constitutional problems, 248 et seq.
  Creeds and nationalities, 69 et seq., 293
  Customs union for, 216 et seq., 237, 238, 260
  Economic life, 115 et seq., 146, 297
  Education in, 253, 254
  Food-supply, independence of, 136
  Foreign policy, 277
  Human type — Mid-European, 72
  International economics, place of Central Europe in, 179 et seq.
  Jewish question, 81
  Language of, 112
  Military obligations of the Allied States, 275
  Napoleonic War, effects upon, 54
  Opposition — possible opposition to scheme of, 27
  Past history, 43, 289

Central Europe (continued):
  Population estimated, 202
  Rome, separatist movement from, 74 et seq.
  Storage of supplies, see that Title
  Tariff problems, 216
  Trade unionism, 146, 299
  See also Germany and Austria-Hungary
Central European Economic Association, 146
Charmatz, Richard, 88, 105, 324, 325
China, population of, 202
Christiansen, C., 339
Citizen rights in Central Europe, 255
Cleinow, G., 336
Coal and coal products:
  German trade with Austria-Hungary, 227, 230
  Statistics for various States, 313
Cötvös, Joseph, Freiherr von, 326
Colonial possessions of various States, 311
Combines as a means toward Mid-European unity, 147
Confederation of the Rhine, 1806–13, 318
Congresses, international, fostering Mid-European unity, 147
Constitutional problems in Central Europe, 248 et seq.
Corn storage in Central Europe, 173
Corn trade, Hungarian, 219, 234, 235
  German imports, 227, 230
  "Kanitz" proposal — State monopoly of foreign corn, 164
Cotton goods, German trade with Austria-Hungary, 229
Creeds and nationalities in Mid-Europe, 69 et seq., 293
Criste, Oskar, 330
Crown rights in Central Europe, 256
Csuday, Eugen, 327
Customs and commercial treaty between Austria and Hungary, 1907, 266
Customs Union, 170, 193, 211, 242
  Central European, 193, 216 et seq., 238, 260

INDEX   345

Customs Union (*continued*):
   Duties, German and Austrian, compared, 233
   Small States, inclusion of, 210, 211

DAHLMANN, 47
Dahlmann-Waitz, 333
Defence — Germany and Austria's motive for war, 17
Dehn, Paul, 326
Delbrück, H. von, 49, 158, 341
Democracy in Germany and Austria, 91, 92
Deutsch, Julius, 329
"Deutschland über Alles," 19
"Dictatorship of the Proletariat" in Germany's war purchase policy, 155
Dislike of the Germans, causes of, 117
Dove, A., 328, 336
Droysen, 47
Dual Alliance, 1879, 64
   See also Germany and Austria-Hungary.

ECONOMIC life of Central Europe, 115 *et seq.*, 146, 297
Economics of war, joint problems, 148 *et seq.*, 302
Education in Central Europe, 253, 254
"Educational" tariff duties, 244
Educational influences in Austria-Hungary, 132
Educational systems compared, 297
Egelhaaf, G., 332
Elizabeth, Empress of Austria, 98
Eltzbacher, 204
Emigration from Germany and Austria-Hungary, 131, 287
Engels, D., 124
England, *see* Great Britain
Eulenburg, Professor, 305

FEDERATIONS of employers in Germany, 120
Ferdinand I. of Austria, 76
Fichte, 149
Finances in Germany and Austria-Hungary, condition of, 174–176

Fischer, Alfred, 332
Fischof, Adolf, 326
Flathe, Th., 336
Food-supply:
   Corn trade, Hungarian, 219, 234, 235
   German professors' inquiry, 204
   Storage, *see* that Title
Fournier, Auguste, 328
France:
   German exports to, 315
   Influence of in Germany, before 1870–71, 62
   International trade of, 302
   Joint-stock capital, 301
   Population statistics, 202, 288
   Trade-union membership, 298
Frankfurt Constitution, 1848, 57, 59
Franz Joseph I. of Austria, 45, 63, 91
Frederick Barbarossa, 49–51
Frederick II. of Prussia, 19, 44, 45, 56, 60, 78, 90, 127, 192
Frederick William IV. of Prussia, 58, 66
Free Trade, effects of, 150
Friedjung, H., 49, 325, 334

GEBHARDT, Br., 332
Gerlach, Leopold von, 341
German Commercial Congress, 145
German Industrial Union, 145
German-Turkish policy, 34, 191, 197
German Work Union, 143
Germany:
   Agricultural statistics, 299
   Alliance with England, results of, 26, 67
   Business competition by, 124
   Business spirit in, 128 *et seq.*
   Cartels and federations, growth of, 120
   Characteristics of German nation, 96, 122, 123, 195
   Civil War of 1866, 12
   Colonies of, 310
   Confederation of 1815–48, 318
   Confederation of 1850–66, 319
   Customs Union, 170, 193, 211, 242
   Democracy in 1848, 91

Germany (*continued*):
  Dislike of the German, causes of, 117
  Economic temperament of North and Central Germany, 115
  Educational statistics, 297
  Emperor's constitutional position, 320
  Exports and imports, 315, 316
  Food-supply and unemployment, adjustment of, 153 *et seq.*
  Foreign affairs, conduct of, 277
  Imperial Constitution, history of, 265, 317
  "Militarism" as a necessary discipline, 125, 126
  National ideals, 20, 21
  Nationalities, methods of handling, 84
  North German Confederation, 1866–71, 319
  Population statistics, 202, 288
  Prices during the war, 305
  Revolution Parliament, 1848–50, 328
  "Self-contained commercial State," 149
  Taxation after the war, 159
  Trade unionism in, 121, 299
  War purchase companies, 155
  See also Central Europe
Germany and Austria-Hungary:
  Agricultural output, 299
  Alternative alliances discussed, 25, 26
  Austria's position in the union, 67
  Bismarck's policy, 22, 29, 60, 62
  Central Europe, *see* that Title
  Consumption of food per head, statistics, 301
  Customs duties compared, 233
  Defence as motive of war, 17
  Differences between the two empires, 20 *et seq.*
  Economic union, 146
  Educational statistics, 297
  Emigration from, 131, 287
  Financial conditions in, 174–176
  Frontiers after the war, 15
  Historical retrospect, 42, 289
  Industrial statistics, 297, 298

Germany and Austria-Hungary (*continued*):
  Joint-stock capital in, 301
  Military affairs of, 40, 273–275
  Political unity, reasons for and against, 26 *et seq.*
  Population of, 202
  Postal conditions in, 300
  Railway conditions, 301
  Religious struggles from 1517, 75
  Sentiment, partnership of, 37
  Sovereign's position compared, 261, 263
  Statistical data, 285 *et seq.*
  Tariff problems, 216, 314
  Trading between, 227, 228
  Wages compared, 138
Gervinus, 47
Giegl, 316
Giesebrecht, 332
Görgei, Arthur, 330
Goltz, Th. von der, 339
Gothein, G., 246, 337
Grais, Count Hue de, 335
Great Britain:
  Administrative system of, 184
  Agricultural production, 312
  Austria-Hungary, effect of an alliance with, 30
  Blockade policy, 150 *et seq.*, 303
  Business competition of Germany, 124
  Coal production, 314
  Colonies, economic value of, 204, 310
  Command of the seas, 17, 149
  Germany, effects of alliance with, 25, 67
  Joint-stock capital in, 301
  Peace treaty — possible character of, 190
  Population statistics, 202, 288
  World-State — Great Britain as, 182
"Greater Germany" ideals, 23, 24, 58, 77, 222
Grünberg, K., 329
Gumplowicz, Ludwig, 326
Guttentag, 340

HÄUSER, 47, 332

Hamburg as the overseas trading centre of Mid-Europe, 261
Havenstein, 157
Haym, R., 341
Hegel, 77, 126
Heinrich I., III. and IV. of Germany, 50
Helfert, J. A. von, 328
Helfferich, State Secretary, 305, 340
Helmholtz, 123
Helmolt, 49
Herkner, Heinrich, 340
Hevesi, Ludwig, 329
Hickmann, A. L., 288, 326
Hindenburg, 157
Hintze, O., 335
Hirsch-Duncker Union, 145
Hobbing, Reimar, 334, 336
Hohenlohe-Schillingsfürst, Prince, 334
Horvarth, Michael, 327
Huber, Alfons, 326
Hübener, 339
Hüsgen, Ed., 342
Hungarian Revolution, 1848–49, 92, 96
Hungary:
  Characteristics of the people, 97
  Economic relations with Austria, statistics, 306, 307
  Legal independence and Territorial integrity, 321
  Military affairs of, 275
  Nationalities in, 294, 295
  Roumanians, position of, 103
Hus, Johann, 93

IMPERIAL German Constitution, history of, 317
"Industrial maintenance" duties, 244
Industrial statistics, 297, 298
International trade and exchange before the war, 148, 302
International treaties after the war, 257, 258
Internationalism, beginning and growth of, 185, 186
Italy:
  Agricultural output, 300
  International trade of, 302
  Population statistics, 288

Italy (*continued*):
  Position in the war, 10
  Trade-union membership in, 298

JÄCKH, Dr. Ernst, 88, 305
Jastrow, H., 340
Jekelfalussy, Joseph von, 328
Jentsch, Karl, 341
Jews in Central Europe, position of, 81 *et seq.*, 293
  Anti-Semites in Germany, 146
Joseph II., 56

KAMMEL, O., 336
Kaindl, R. F., 98, 331
"Kanitz proposal"— State monopoly of foreign corn, 164
Kant, Immanuel, 77, 127
Karl the Great, 50
Karl V. of Germany, 50, 52, 321
Kaufmann, 17, 332
Kerchnawe, Hugo, 330
Kirdorf, 127
Klein-Hattingen, Oskar, 337, 341
Kohl, H., 334
Kolmer, Gustav, 329
Kosch, Wilhelm, 331
Koser, R., 340
Kossuth, Ludwig, 330
Kralik, Richard, 327
Krones, Franz von, 327, 330
Krusch, P., 339
Kupsanko, Gregor, 332

LABAND, P., 335
Labour:
  Austria-Hungary, labour reforms, 132
  Intensification — opposition to, 140
  Socialism, *see* that Title
  Trade-union membership in various countries, 298
Lamprecht, Karl, 49, 332, 334
Landmann, Karl von, 330
Lang, Ludwig, 329
Language:
  Central Europe, language question, 254
  Hungarian National Law of 1868, 102
  Magyar, use of, 99 *et seq.*

348 INDEX

Lassalle, Ferdinand, 134
Legien, 127
Lehmann, M., 340
Lenz, M., 341
"Lesser Germany" ideals, 23, 24, 26, 49, 58, 77
Levy, Hermann, 305
Levy, M., 340
Lexis, W. von, 338
Liebknecht, 250
List, Friedrich, 222
Löbell, A. von, 338
Loening, C., 335
Loesche, Georg, 329
Losch, Finanzrat, 222, 228, 316
Lotz, W., 339
Luther, Martin, 75

MACHINERY, German trade with Austria-Hungary, 228, 230, 231
Mackensen, General, 157
Magyar language, 99 *et seq.*
Magyar revolt, 1866, 96
Magyars and the Russian danger, 28
Manes, A., 340
Marcks, E., 341
Marczali, H., 328
Maria Theresa, 32, 44, 56, 78, 89
Marx, Karl, 124, 155
Maurenbrecher, W., 333
Mayer, Franz Martin, 327
Maximilian I. of Germany, 50
Mehring, F., 337
Meineike, Friedrich, 333, 341
Meisel, Hofrat, 176
Menger, Max, 331
Mesopotamia, 202
Meszlény, A., 339
Metternich, Prince, 89, 90, 333
Mid-Europe, *see* Central Europe
"Militarism" in Germany — a necessary discipline, 125
Military forces in Central Europe, 285
Military legislation in Germany and Austria-Hungary, 274
Mollat, G., 333
Moltke, 19
Mommsen, 46

NAGL, J. W., 329

Napoleon, 21, 53, 56
National spirit in Hungary, 93, 94
Nationalities and creeds in Central Europe, 69 *et seq.*, 293
Naumann, Friedrich, 337, 338
Naval War, Anglo-German, 17, 18
Navy, Central European, statistics of, 286
Netherlands:
  Agricultural statistics, 299
  Colonies of, 310
  International trade, 302
  Joint-stock companies, capital in, 301
  Population statistics, 288, 311
  Trade-union membership, 298
Nicholas I. of Russia, 54, 56
North German Confederation, 1866, 79, 319

OCKEL, H., 336
Oertzen, Dr., 342
Oncken, H., 341
Oppel, A., 339
Oppenheimer, Franz, 305
Organising ability of the Germans, 119
Otto I. of Germany, 50

PAN-GERMANISM, 25, 96, 146
Parisius, L., 341
Parliamentary system in Central Europe, 269 *et seq.*
Partnership among the Powers, results of, 9 *et seq.*
Peace of Westphalia, 1648, 75, 317
Perthes, 316
Pfannkuche, August, 338
Philippovich, Professor von, 222, 223, 316
Pierson, W., 335
Pistov, 301, 316
"Planet and satellite" States, 180
Poeschel, C. E., 335
Poland:
  Conditions of settlement after the war, 111
  German policy in, 84, 85
Political administration of Central Europe, 255, 256
Popovici, Aurel C., 105, 326
Portugal, population statistics, 288

INDEX

Poschinger, Heinrich von, 334
Poverty in Austria-Hungary, 130, 131
Prague as the treaty centre of Mid-Europe, 261
"Preservative" duties, 244
Preusz, Hugo, 338
Prices:
  German, during the war, 305
  Rise of, after war, 166
Producers' socialism, 159
Protestants in a minority in Central Europe, 78
Public services in Austria-Hungary, reforms for, 133

RACIAL problems in Hungary, 96 et seq.
Radetzky, Count, 330
Ranke, L. von, 48, 331, 332
Rauchberg, Heinrich, 326, 331
Rauchhaupt, F. W., 336
Raumer, 47, 332
Reformation, 75
Reich, J. M., 341
Religion in Central Europe, 252, 253
Reventlow, Count von, 338
Revolution Parliament, 1848–50, 318
Rhine Confederation, 1806–13, 62, 318
Richter, Eugen, 337, 342
Risser, J., 340
Rogge, Walter, 328, 329
Rohrbach, Paul, 11, 338
Rome and the Separatist movement in Central Europe, 74 et seq.
Roumania:
  Agricultural statistics, 300
  Educational system, 297
  Hungary, position of Roumanians in, 103
  Population statistics, 288
  Textile market, 235
Rudolf von Hapsburg, 50
Russia:
  Agricultural statistics, 300
  Central Powers and the Russian danger, 17, 18
  Coal-supply of, 314
  Economic power, actual and potential, 208, 209
  Educational system, 297
  German alliance with, 26

Russia (*continued*):
  German exports to, 315
  International trade of, 303
  Joint-stock companies, Russian capital in, 301
  Napoleonic war, Russia's rôle, 53 et seq.
  Peace treaty — possible character of, 190, 191
  Population statistics, 27
  World-State, Russia as, 182, 312, 313
  Russo-Turkish War, 1876, 64

SALOMON, F., 337
Samassa, Paul, 326
"Satellite" States, 180
Savigny, 123
Schäfer, D., 49, 332
Schäffle, A. E. F., 223, 330
Scharnhorst, 127
Schlesinger, Ludwig, 331
Schlosser, 332
Schütz, Friedrich, 328
Schulthess, 333
Schwarzenberg, 59
Schwemer, R., 333
Sembratowycz, R., 332
Sepp, J. R., 341
Seton-Watson, R. W., 331
Seven Years' War, 12, 30, 31
Siemen, 127
Size of States, classification, 308
Skene, Alfred von, 331
Small States:
  Insignificance of, 12
  Trench-making policy in regard to, 16
Socialism:
  Austria, social democracy in, 108
  Germany, social democracy in, 121
  International, development of, 186
  Progress of, 160
  State socialism, *see* that Title
Sombart, Werner, 116, 337, 338
Sosnowsky, Theodor von, 325
Southern Germans union with the North — example for Mid-Europe, 144
Spain, population statistics of, 288
Spiethoff, Professor, 176
Springer, Anton, 105, 325

Springer, Rudolf, 325
Starvation of Germany, *see* Storage
State Socialism:
  Definition of, 159
  Syndicates with guarantees for workers, 161, 168, 176, 177
  War policy of Germany regarded as, 153, 156
States, classification according to size, 308
Statistical data, 284 *et seq.*
Stein, Baron von, 55
Stein, Ph., 334
Steinbach, Gustav, 330
Stillich, Oskar, 337
Stoerk, F., 336
Storage of food-supplies, 163 *et seq.*, 212
  Central Europe, 151, 152, 171, 172, 173
  "Kanitz" proposal, 164
  Syndicate treaties, 241, 242
Strakosch-Grassman, Gustav, 329
Sybel, Heinrich von, 330, 333
Syndicate treaties for storage of food-stuffs, 241
Syndicates, State, with workmen's guarantees, 161, 168, 176, 177
Sweden:
  Population statistics, 288
  Trade-union membership, 298
Switzerland:
  Agricultural statistics, 299
  Joint-stock companies, capital in, 301
  Trade-union membership, 298

TARIFF problems in Central Europe, 216 *et seq.*, 314
Taxation, forms of, after the war, 159, 176
Teutsch, G. D., 331
Textiles, Balkan markets, question of, 240
"Thinking in Continents," 13
Thirty Years' War, 12, 21
Timber, German imports from Austria-Hungary, 227
Tisza, Count, 102
Trade:
  Customs union, *see* that Title

Trade (*continued*):
  Economic exchange through overseas trade, 149
  Germany's trade during the war, 155, 156
  Tariff problems in Central Europe, 216, 314
Trade unionism:
  Germany, 121
  Various countries, comparative table, 299
Treaties:
  Customs and commercial treaty between Austria and Hungary, 1907, 266
  International, after the war, 257, 258
  State treaties in Central Europe, 257, 261
Treitschke, Heinrich von, 47, 48, 77, 332
Trench-making policy, 16, 273
Tschierschky, 339
Türk, Karl, 331
Turkey:
  Balkan and Turkish interests in Austria-Hungary, 197
  Central Powers' alliance with, 10
  Economic problem of, 246
  German reorganisation, effect of, 34, 191, 197

UNITED STATES OF AMERICA:
  Administrative system, 184
  Economic power, actual and potential, 208, 209
  Population statistics, 202, 288
  World-State, 182
"United States of the World," 179

VEIT, Valentin, 341
Veltzé, Alois, 330
Vienna as the legal centre of Mid-Europe, 261
Vienna Congress, 318

WAENTIG, Heinrich, 329
Wages in Germany and Austria-Hungary, 137
War economics, joint problems in, 148 *et seq.*

INDEX

War purchase companies in Germany, 155
War storage system, *see* Storage
Weber, Max, 141
Weller, K., 336
Wenck, Martin, 337
Wendrinsky, Johann, 328
Wertheimer, Eduard von, 325, 328
Wheat, increased production in Hungary, 135
Wieser, Leopold von, 340
Wilhelm I., 45
Wilhelm II., 66, 282
Wippermann, 333
Wood — German imports from Austria-Hungary, 227, 229
Woollen goods, German trade with Austria, 228

Wolf, Adam, 328
Wolf, Julius, 237, 285
Wolfsgrube, C., 330
Women in war occupations, position after the war, 166
Workers' socialism, definition of, 159
"World-States," 179, 182, 312
Württemberg, military affairs of, 274

ZEIDLER, J., 329
Zenker, Ernst Viktor, 328
Zwiedineck-Südenhorst, H. von, 327, 328
Zwingli, 76